Date Due

FEB 2 9 1972			

Demco-293

 THE CREDO SERIES

PLANNED AND EDITED BY
RUTH NANDA ANSHEN

MAN, NATURE
AND GOD

A Quest for
Life's Meaning
BY
F. S. C. NORTHROP

 A TRIDENT PRESS BOOK

SIMON AND SCHUSTER

NEW YORK 1962

Prepared under the supervision of
POCKET BOOKS, INC.

To

Robert Kimball Richardson
Charles Montague Bakewell
William Ernest Hocking
Henry M. Sheffer
L. J. Henderson
John McTaggart Ellis McTaggart
Alfred North Whitehead
Albert Einstein
G. H. Hardy
Ludwig Wittgenstein
Junjirō Takakusu
Sir Muhammad Iqbal
Her Highness Princess Poon Diskul
Christine Johnston Northrop

With gratitude and an indebtedness than can never be repaid.

CONTENTS

THE CREDO SERIES

Its Meaning and Function

The Credo Series suggests that an epoch has come to an end, an epoch in which our best knowledge has been dimmed with boredom or darkened by destruction. We have felt for too long that this must be the very nature of life; this is the way life is, and to such a degree that life has consented to shrink from its own terrors, leading us to a deep apostasy of the heart and a crucifixion of our natural aspiration for experience and growth.

The absolute has surrendered to the relative. Our era of relativity, however, whether in science or in morals, does not allow us to assume that relativity implies an absence of ground to stand on, and therefore a relaxation of all effort toward foundations. "There is no firm ground," the dominant malaise of our time, this acceptance of non-finality, summons us to a heightened task. For the failure of formulated absolutes leaves the absolute requirement to evaluate again that uncaptured reality which contains and guides the total meaning of our existence.

The Credo Series hopes to unlock a consciousness that at first sight may seem to be remote but is proved on acquaintance to be surprisingly immediate since it shows the need to reconcile the life of action with the life of contemplation, practice with principle, thought with feeling, knowledge with being, and work, no longer a form of punishment as in the Judaeo-Christian tradition, but accepted as a way toward the growth and realization of the self in all its plenitude. For the whole meaning of self lies within the observer and its shadow is cast naturally on the object observed. The fragmentation of man from his work, the being of man into an eternal and temporal half, results in an estrangement of man from his creative source, from his fellows and from himself.

The symbol of *The Credo Series* is the Eye of Osiris. It is the inner Eye. Man sees in two ways: with his physical eyes, in an empirical sensing or *seeing* by direct observation, and also by an indirect envisaging. He possesses in addition to his two sensing eyes a single, image-making, spiritual and intellectual Eye. And it is the *in-sight* of this inner Eye that purifies and makes sacred our understanding of the nature of things; for that which was shut fast has been opened by the command of the inner Eye. And we become aware that to believe is to see.

Thus, it is suggested, there may be born a sharpened vision, which comes from seeing reality as the incarnation of associations and affinities with something beyond the visible self. For it is our hope to show the human relevance of ideas, the ways in which knowledge can help us to live in the immediate and real world by pointing to the confluence of man and his vocation, of subject and object, by reverencing the curious and mysterious metabolism between man and matter, the sacred nexus between the person and his work, and by asking whether the freedom now released through the creative energies of mankind will bring salvation or destruction, the answer to which will depend upon the aims we cherish.

The Credo Series submits that the universe itself is a vast entity where man will be lost if it does not converge in the person; for material forces or energies, or impersonal ideals, or scientifically objectified learning are meaningless without their relevance for human life and their power to disclose, even in the dark tendencies of man's nature, a law transcending man's arbitrariness.

For the personal is a far higher category than the abstract universal. Personality itself is an emotional, not an intellectual, experience, and the greatest achievement of knowledge is to combine the personal within a larger unity, just as in the higher stages of development the parts that make up the whole acquire greater and greater independence and individuality within the context of the whole. Reality itself is the harmony which gives to the component particulars of a thing the equilibrium of the whole. And while physical observations are ordered with direct reference to the experimental conditions, we have in sensate experience to do with separate observations whose correlation can only be indicated by their belonging to the wholeness of mind.

It is our endeavor to show that man has reached a turning point in consciousness, that his relationship with his creative self demands a clarification that can widen and deepen his understanding of the nature of reality. Work is made for man, not man for work. This Series hopes to demonstrate the sacramental character of work which is more easily achieved when the principal objects of our attention have taken on a symbolic form that is generally recognized and accepted: in other words, when there is an established iconography relating to the meaningful interpretation of man and his vocation. This suggests a "law" in the relationship of a person and his chosen discipline:

that it is valuable only when the spiritual, the creative, life is strong enough to insist on some expression through symbols. For no work can be based on material, technological or physical aspirations alone.

The human race is now entering upon a new phase of evolutionary progress, a phase in which, impelled by the forces of evolution itself, it must converge upon itself and convert itself into one single human organism dominated by a reconciliation of knowing and being in their inner unity and destined to make a qualitative leap into a higher form of consciousness that would transcend and complement individual consciousness as we know it, or otherwise destroy itself. For the entire universe is one vast field, potential for incarnation, and achieving incandescence here and there of reason and spirit. What to some is mystery and inscrutability, to others symbolizes and declares the very nature of the cosmic process. And in the whole world of *quality* with which category by the nature of our minds we necessarily make contact, we here and there apprehend pre-eminent value. This can be achieved only if we recognize that we are unable to focus our attention on the particulars of a whole without diminishing our comprehension of the whole, and of course conversely, we can focus on the whole only by diminishing our comprehension of the particulars which constitute the whole.

This Series is designed to present a kind of intellectual autobiography of each author, to portray the nature and meaning of the creative process for the creator and to show the relevance of his work to the feelings and aspirations of the man of flesh and bone. This Series endeavors to reflect also the influence of the work on the man and on society and to point to the freedom, or lack of freedom, to choose and pursue one profession rather than another.

It attempts to emphasize that the creator in any realm must surrender himself to a passionate pursuit of the hidden meaning of his labors, guided by deep personal intimations of an as yet undiscovered reality.

These volumes endeavor to indicate that it is impossible to know what constitutes a good society unless we know what defines a good individual. The self is determined by the values according to which it subordinates and integrates the rest of its values. If the values be transient, so is the self. If the values be dispersed and incoherent, so is the self. If they are organic and integrated, so is the self. The unity of human personality is its soundness. The unified self cannot be understood in terms of its constituent parts as dissected away from each other. So that finally what we see and what we do are no more and no less than what we are.

It is the effort of *The Credo Series* to define the new reality in which the estrangement of man and his work, resulting in the self-estrangement in man's existence, is overcome. This new reality is born through the reconciliation of what a man *knows* with what a man *is*. Being itself in all its presuppositions and implications can only be understood through the totality, through wholeness. St. Paul, who, like Isaiah before him, went into the market place not to secularize truth but to proclaim it, taught man that the "new creation" could be explained only by conquering the daemonic cleavages, the destructive split, in soul and cosmos. And that fragmentation always destroys a unity, produces a tearing away from the source and thereby creates disunity and isolation. The fruit can never be separated from the tree. The Tree of Life can never be disjoined from the Tree of Knowledge for both have *one and the same* root. And if man allows himself to fall into isolation, if he seeks to maintain a self segregated from the totality of which he is a necessary part, if he chooses to remain asunder, unrelated to the original context of all created things in which he too has his place—including his own labors—then this act of apostasy bears fruit in the demiurgical presumption of *magic*, a form of animism in which man seeks an authority of the self, placing himself above the law of the universe by attempting to separate the inseparable. He thus creates an unreal world of false contexts after having destroyed or deserted the real. And in this way the method of analysis, of scientific objectivity, which is good and necessary in its right place, is endowed with a destructive power when it is allowed to usurp a place for which it is not fitted.

The naturalist principle that man is the measure of all things has been shattered more than ever in our own age by the question, "What is the measure of man?" Postmodern man is more profoundly perplexed about the nature of man than his ancestors were. He is on the verge of spiritual and moral insanity. He does not know who he is. And having lost the sense of who and what he is, he fails to grasp the meaning of his fellow man, of his vocation, and of the nature and purpose of knowledge itself. For what is not understood cannot be known. And it is this cognitive faculty which is frequently abrogated by the "scientific" theory of knowledge, a theory that refuses to recognize the existence of comprehensive entities as distinct from their particulars. The central act of knowing is indeed that form of comprehension which is never absent from any process of knowing and is finally its ultimate sanction.

Science itself acknowledges as real a host of entities that cannot be described completely in materialistic or mechanistic terms, and it is this transcendence out of the domain of science into a region from which science itself can be appraised that *The Credo Series* hopes to expose. For the essence of the ebb and flow of experience, of sensations, the richness of the immediacy of directly apprehended knowledge, the metaphysical substance of what assails our being, is the very act itself of sensation and affection and therefore must escape the net of rational analysis, yet is intimately related to every cognitive act. It is this increasing intellectual climate that is calling into birth once more the compelling Socratic questions, "What is the purpose of life, the meaning of work?" "What is man?" Plato himself could give us only an indirect answer: "Man is declared to be that creature who is constantly in search of himself, a creature who at every moment of his existence must examine and scrutinize the conditions of his existence. He is a being in search of meaning."

Theory and life always go together. An organic conception of man and his work, man and society, man and the universe, is portrayed in First Corinthians 12 when Paul relates the famous story of the strife that once broke out between the parts of the human body. They refused to fulfill their special functions within the organism until they finally learned that they are all parts of one body and can exist and function only as such. For they all breathe together. And by so doing subordinate themselves to the presentation of the whole body. What may be an explanation of organic life in the human body may be transferred to the life in the universe and to the relationship between the interior and the exterior, for all is permeated by the life-giving creative power—by unity.

The authors in this endeavor are aware that man in the twentieth century finds himself in the greatest revolution since the discovery of agriculture. They show, each in his own way, that part of the meaning of our present turmoil may indeed lie in its being the means to reconcile thought and action, to overcome the parochialism of dogmas that only isolate man from man and man from the implicit meaning of his chosen profession. Our effort is to create an image of man intelligible and unitary, a microcosmic mirror of the greater macrocosm of which he is a part and in which he has his legitimate place in relation to the whole. For even the extraordinary successes of scientific predictions, the fruits of man's ingenuity in inventing the scientific method, seem comprehensible only on the basis that the human mind possesses an inherent logic closely parallel with the structure of the external world itself.

The very interdependence of the observer and the participant can no longer be ignored as part of the essential value of things. To take a definitive example from modern cosmology, it is challenging indeed to note that there is a most unusual connection between the existence of stars and the laws that govern the atomic nuclei. Emphasis is placed upon the existence, not the properties, of stars. For everyone expects the properties of stars and atomic nuclei to be related. It is the *connection* with the *existence* of stars that is so reassuring—and indeed surprising.

From this it is evident that there is present in the universe a *law* applicable to all nature including man and his work. Life itself then is seen to be a creative process elaborating and maintaining *order* out of the randomness of matter, endlessly generating new and unexpected structures and properties by building up associations that qualitatively transcend their constituent parts. This is not to diminish the importance of "scientific objectivity." It is, however, to say that the mind possesses a quality that cannot be isolated or known exclusively in the sense of objective knowledge. For it consists in that elusive humanity in us, our self, that knows. It is that inarticulate awareness that includes and *comprehends* all we know. It consists in the irreducible active voice of man and is recognized only in other things, only when the circle of consciousness closes around its universe of events.

The experience of the modern mind has been expressed in terms of conflict produced by false dualisms, disruption, self-destruction, meaninglessness, purposelessness and desperation. This character of our time has found its expression in literature, in art, in existential philosophy, in some forms of natural science, in political demonologies, and is explored in the psychology of the unconscious. Our authors hope to indicate that through a quickening of awareness man can overcome this dualism and can rise to face the meaning of life and work, keeping his mind and energies awake at full stretch. Such knowledge—that form of knowledge which cannot be disjoined from being—will enable man to embrace life with passion and to work with devotion. It will enable him to absorb experience with his whole nature and thereby to fill a want that is satisfied neither by action alone nor by thought alone. This unity of *being* and *doing* has a justifiable claim to be called a form of enchantment since through it men, who might otherwise give in to the malice of circumstances and conditions, find their old powers revived or new powers stirring within them, and through these life is sustained, renewed and fulfilled.

Man is now confronting himself with the compelling need to create an organic identification between what he *is* and what he *does*. For only in this way can the threat of conformism and the treachery of abstraction, the plight of the modern mind, be conquered. This split, inherited from the seventeenth century, between the transitive and the intransitive, between the creator and the process of creativity, has blunted man's appetite for experience. Language itself in our time has failed because man has forgotten that it is the mother of thought, because of its analytical emphasis and thus lacks ready means to convey associations, emotional or imaginative, that cluster around a subject and give to it a distinctive personal significance. In other words, the symbols by which man lives and has his being, that "tacit coefficient" * of articulate knowledge that is unanalyzable, now knocks at the portals of consciousness waiting to be admitted. For human nature loses its most precious quality when it is robbed of its sense of things beyond, unexplored and yet insistent.

The Credo Series belongs to those ideas that are intuitively conceived and that originate in spheres of a spiritual order and surprise thought, as it were, compelling it to transform its inherited notions conformably with its enlarged vision of the nature of things. It is as though the authors of the Series were recovering this reality out of a memory of a lost harmony, a memory latent in the soul and not distilled from the changing things of mere physical observation. In this way the inner unity of the known and the knower may be preserved, and the almost mythic intuition of reality thereby related to its conceptual and rational forms of expression. For man, unlike a machine, is an organism existing as an end in itself. He *is* the system on which causal explanations are based and to which they have to return; he *is* a historically existent whole, a four-dimensional entity, and not merely an abstraction from which statements about phenomena are deducible under the guise of eternity.

* See the classical work, *Personal Knowledge,* by Michael Polanyi for an enlarged meaning of the nature of reality. (Chicago University Press, 1958)

Our hope is to point to a new dimension of morality—not that of constraint and prohibition but a morality that lies as a fountainhead within the human soul, a morality of aspiration to spiritual experience. It suggests that necessity is laid upon us to infer entities that are not observed and are not observable. For an unseen universe is necessary to explain the seen. The flux is seen, but to account for its structure and its nature we infer particles of various kinds to serve as the vertices of the changing patterns, placing less emphasis on the isolated units and more on the structure and nature of relations. The process of knowing involves an immaterial becoming, an immaterial identification, and finally, knowledge itself is seen to be a dependent variable of immateriality. And somewhere along this spiritual pilgrimage man's pure observation is relinquished and gives way to the deeper experience of awe, for there can be no explanation of a phenomenon by searching for its origin but only by discerning its immanent law—this quality of transcendence that abides even in matter itself.

The present situation in the world and the vast accretion of knowledge have produced a serious anxiety, which may be overcome by re-evaluating the character, kinship, logic and operation of man in relation to his work. For work implies goals and intimately affects the person performing the work. Therefore the correlation and relatedness of ideas, facts and values that are in perpetual interplay could emerge from these volumes as they point to the inner synthesis and organic unity of man and his labors. For though no labor alone can enrich the person, no enrichment can be achieved without absorbing and intense labor. We then experience a unity of faith, labor and grace which prepares the mind for receiving a truth from sources over which it has no control. This is especially true since the great challenge of our age arises out of man's inventions in relation to his life.

Thus *The Credo Series* seeks to encourage the perfection not only of man's works but also and above all the fulfillment of himself as a person. And so we now are summoned to consider not only man in the process of development as a human subject but also his influence on the object of his investigation and creation. Observation alone is interference. The naïve view that we can observe any system and predict its behavior without altering it by the very act of observation was an unjustified extrapolation from Newton's *Celestial Mechanics*. We can observe the moon or even a satellite and predict its behavior without appreciably interfering with it, but we cannot do this with an amoeba, far less with a man and still less with a society of men. It is the heart of the question of the nature of work itself. If we regard our labors as a process of shaping or forming, then the fruits of our labors play the part of a mold by which we ourselves are shaped. And this means, in the preservation of the identity of the knower and the known, that cognition and generation, that is, creation, though in different spheres, are nevertheless alike.

It is hoped that the influence of such a Series may help to overcome the serious bifurcation of function and meaning and may show that the extraordinary crisis through which the world is passing can be fruitfully met by recognizing that knowledge has not been completely dehumanized and has not totally degenerated into a mere notebook over-crowded with formulas that few are able to understand or apply.

For mankind is now engaged in composing a new theme. Life refuses to be embalmed alive. Life cannot abjure life;

nothing that lives is born out of nothingness. But nothing, either, can preserve its form against the ceaseless flux of being. Life never manifests itself in negative terms. And our hope lies in drawing from every category of work a conviction that non-material values can be discovered in positive, affirmative, visible things. The estrangement between the temporal and non-temporal man is coming to an end, community is inviting communion and a vision of the human condition more worthy of man is engendered, connecting ever more closely the creative mind with the currents of spiritual energy which breaks for us the bonds of habit and keeps us in touch with the permanence of being in all its plenitude through our work.

And as, long ago, the Bearers of Bread were succeeded by the Bearers of Torches, so now, in the immediacies of life, it is the image of man and his vocation that can rekindle the high passion of humanity in its quest for light. Refusing to divorce work from life or love from knowledge, it is action, it is passion that enhances our being.

We live in an expanding universe and also in the moral infinite of that other universe, the universe of man. And along the whole stretched arc of this universe we may see that extreme limit of complicity where reality seems to shape itself within the work man has chosen for his realization. Work then becomes not only a way of knowledge, it becomes even more a way of life—of life in its totality. For the last end of every maker is himself.

"And the places that have been desolate for ages shall be built in thee: thou shalt raise up the foundations of generation and generation; and thou shalt be called the repairer of the fences, turning the paths into rest." *

—RUTH NANDA ANSHEN

* Isaiah, 58:12

MAN, NATURE AND GOD

A Quest for Life's Meaning

INTRODUCTORY PREFACE

So FAR as its author is concerned, this book is one of those surprising things that sometimes happen. The independent labors of a lifetime, recorded slowly, piece by piece in my previous books and articles, come to a focus here. Whereas the finding and the recording of the pieces was a frustrating and occasionally agonizing task, full of *Sorge* (concern), as Heidegger and his Existentialists would say, the focusing came quickly and even joyfully within a brief few months. I can but hope that after starting at the beginning and plodding faithfully along the middle path, the reader will feel at the end that this is as it should be.

There is one most charming and persuasive First Cause of this quick focusing. She is Ruth Nanda Anshen, the creator of *The Credo Series,* in which this book is privileged to be one of the first terms. It was her ever faithful, divinely patient insistence that finally, after ten years of trying for her World Perspective Series, persuaded me to become a member of the Board of *The Credo Series* and also to agree when she added: "This is where the book you promised must go. When can it be? I hope soon!"

I replied, "Year after next." Time flies. Year after next
was today late in December of yesterday's 1961. There
came again her gracious New Year wish that she might
have in her hands "your manuscript for our *Credo Series*."
With failing voice and shifting eye, I barely managed the
reply: "Please, year after next; that will be fine." Then,
wandering through the looking glass, I saw that it must
be done today. (So here it is.) Else, as in his verse for
"Loveliest of Trees," Housman's mathematics will soon
be mine:

> Now, of my threescore years and ten,
> Twenty will not come again,
> And take from seventy springs a score,
> It only leaves me fifty more.

Even so, this book would not have been done day before
yesterday, at least in its present form, were there not another person who wants things perfect and finished. The
reader will see that with this very mortal male, things
occasionally may be, within reason, fairly soon, but never
will the prose in which they are put be perfect. This other
person is my loyal and faithful assistant Helen Hamilton
Livingston to whom merely punching the time clock and
then leaving "that messy manuscript" for another day,
means nothing. Were she such a craftswoman, even years,
one hundred and fifty more, would not be enough. When
the final product is the imperfect prose, not to mention
the "poetry," that remains, the reader will realize what
my debt is to her and to the Wenner-Gren Foundation for
Anthropological Research whose grant to the Yale Law
School made her help possible.

There are several parts and pieces of this book, including most of the chapters on altruism and Whitehead's
prose, that have been published before in diverse places
at different times. The editor and I are grateful to the
various publishers for permission to include them here.

I have been urged by the editor of *The Credo Series* to

write in the first person. I do so in this introductory preface, and at times also in what follows. My reason for not using the first person uniformly is twofold. First, what I write is not persuasive even for me, unless it is testable by anyone who will take the trouble to do so. This means that what I believe must also be in the second and third person. Second, my Credo, at least in its separate pieces, is not only my Credo but also that of others—many others. Only some of the pieces, bits of the other pieces, and the putting of them all together is wholly mine. Without what these other beloved persons are in me, my "I Believe" would be a shabby thing indeed. This is why this book had to be dedicated to fourteen people. This list should include countless more, but an artificially arbitrary line had to be drawn somewhere. Otherwise there would be a huge tome of names and nothing more.

Even so, I have thrust in the first person all along the way. Continuously, I refer to my previous books and articles. My excuse is that this is an indispensable part of the story. Although the putting together of the various parts came relatively easily and quickly, the discovery and bringing out in labored scientific and philosophical books of each particular part took, in some cases at least, a decade of time. Also, the empirical evidence, and scientific and philosophical analyses by others, as well as myself, that justifies each piece, is too great to be recorded here. This is to be found only in my previous books and scientific, philosophical, legal, political, economic, religious, and literary articles. Hence, my reference to one or another of them all along the way. In them only will be found all the other persons to whom I am indebted, and who do not appear on the present book's dedicatory page.

There are never any scientific, philosophical, or religious beliefs, and there is not one poem or song except as some particular person, or some chorus of particular persons, has sounded or sung it. Also, because the persons to whom this book is dedicated are so much the chorus of my song, it may help the reader to understand and to put himself in the warm personal and realistically factual and concrete standpoint necessary to understand this "I Believe," if I indicate part of what each one of these persons has been and is for me. This entails that I try to convey certain intimately personal, and even occasionally confidential, experiences. I pray those still on earth and those in Heaven will forgive me. I ask the reader also to read what now follows with one caution in mind. It is what I made of, and the way I interpreted what they wrote and said to me. I believe it is what they believed. Nevertheless, what they believed *per se* as interpreted by themselves may have been different. Hence, they are not to be held responsible for any errors in my interpretation of what they wrote as read by me, or what they said to me. I make no apologies for this since, as we shall see, perfect communication even between the most beloved and beloving persons is, for erring humans, not easy.

With one exception each one of the persons to whom this book is dedicated, I have known personally, mostly over lengthy periods of time. Sir Muhammad Iqbal is the exception. He died in 1938, long before I visited his beautiful Lahore in 1951. Before his untimely death, he was the following assemblage of professionally expert persons, all in one: A lawyer, called to the bar by England's Lincoln's Inn; a poet, whom we shall see in a moment to be a remarkable one; a Professor of History and Philosophy at Lahore, in what today is West Pakistan, with a Ph.D. in philosophy from the University of Munich; a member of the Punjab Legislature during the period of British rule; a Rhodes Scholar lecturer at Oxford; the leader of the Muslims of all India in the fight for legal and political freedom from British rule, as Gandhi and Pandit Nehru were for Buddhists and Hindus; the author of two scholarly and notable philosophical books entitled *The Development of Metaphysics in Persia* (Munich and

Lahore) and *The Reconstruction of Religious Thought in Islam* (Oxford); the political delegate, along with Gandhi and Pandit Nehru, to the Round Table Conference of 1931 in London where the British and these Indians sat down together to determine to whom, officially representing what kind of legal and political government, or, unfortunately, as it turned out, governments, the British Raj would turn over British India when His Majesty ceased to be both their *King* and their *Parliament* and became, as he is with Britishers, merely their *King in* (their own Free Indian) *Parliament*.

One certainly would be justified if one concluded at this point that this multitude of professionally expert Iqbals were all that one person could possibly be. Such a conclusion would, nevertheless, be an error. I first learned of Iqbal's existence in Bombay in January of 1951 from a Buddhist-Hindu member of New Delhi's Free Indian Parliament, whose first name is that of the ancient Buddhist King Asoka. The latter remarkable Buddhist Indian statesman of the third century B.C. is the only one in India's long history, even to the present moment, who ever succeeded in uniting all Indians in one nation.

His (1951) Buddhist-Hindu namesake told me, as we sat alone in the Bombay headquarters of the liberal democratic Socialist Party, of which he was then and still is one of the two national leaders, that I must read all of Iqbal's poetry, philosophical books, and political addresses if I wanted to understand the following three things: (1) the similarities and differences between recent India's greatest Buddhist-Hindu poet, Tagore, and her topmost Muslim poet, Iqbal; (2) the domestically and internationally dangerous Kashmir problem, and the only likely way (Iqbal's way) it can be justly and peacefully solved; (3) The Muslim-Hindu communal problem that is still unsolved even in the piece of India that is New Delhi's Free India. Asoka Mehta then suggested that if his fellow Indians and the British had accepted the kind of single legal and political system which Iqbal tried to get for all the independent Indian people, there would be no present Kashmir impasse but one over-all, truly free, and peaceful India.

With respect to Asoka Mehta's poetic prescription (1), I already knew Tagore's poetry. I then secured and devoured Iqbal's. What I found will be sampled in a moment and compared with the poetry and politics of Tagore in Chapter 12. With regard to the legal and political reading of (2) and (3), I also did as the wise contemporary statesman Asoka Mehta advised, purchasing and keeping near at hand in my legal and political library as many of Iqbal's political speeches and letters, available in English translation, as I could find, just as I have his poems and Tagore's either by my bedside or near by. My legal and political findings are those of Asoka Mehta and are recorded in a sentence or two in this book and more fully in *The Taming of the Nations* and *Philosophical Anthropology and Practical Politics*.

Upon Iqbal's death, Tagore said: "India has lost a poet whose work has a great universal appeal." The following verses from *The Tulip of Sinai* will suffice to show why.

> A beggar thou didst stand on Sinai,
>   For of itself thy soul is unaware;
> Stride boldly forth; be searching for a Man;
>   In that enquiry God Himself doth share.

> Those meadow birds are all to me unknown,
> Here by the nest I sit and sing alone;
>   Then leave me, if too tender is thy heart,
> For in my anthem all my life is gone.

To know this remarkable Muslim only through what he has written is more than enough.

Nevertheless, I feel that I have known him also personally. The reason is he and I both had McTaggart as the Director of our philosophical study at Trinity College on the Cam; he (Iqbal), in the first years of this century, I, two decades later. To have had the unforgettable spirit that is McTaggart in common is also to have one another in common. Perhaps the final two chapters of this book will help those who do not know both McTaggart's and Iqbal's philosophies of the person, nature, and religion to see why.

Robert Kimball Richardson had to be first on my dedicatory list. It was he who directed my undergraduate major in history at Beloit College. In most other subjects, except chemistry, botany, and the art of writing under Professor George Clancy, I was an indifferent student; so much so that I won my Phi Beta Kappa key there later "in life" rather than even coming near it in college. However, though few majored under him because of his well-earned reputation as the college's most ruthless and tough marker, under "Dickie" the grades on my term thesis and history Senior Essay were A's and even AA occasionally. Why? For the very good reason that, whereas the others stuffed me with information, which analysis showed me in later years they did not always understand, he sent me (1) into the library to read the source materials on the making of the unwritten British Constitution and (2) to my room to read in their entirety, reread, digest, and write term papers on my personally purchased copies of but four or five (not one hundred) of the classics of three of the Western world's most outstanding makers of history. Thus, I learned that there are no epochal historical periods or "facts" except as there are particular men with minds that contain important ideas—men such as St. Augustine, Boethius, Petrarch, or the makers and makings of the British Constitution. It was Richardson also (rather than the philosophy professor who put me back to sleep every morning as he talked about that dullest of all subjects, ethical abstract norms) who made it evident that there is no fully understood history without philosophy.

Charles Montague Bakewell appears next on our dedicatory page and quite necessarily so. It was he, during my first graduate studies at Yale before World War I, who acquainted me with the pre-Socratic natural philosophers. The naturalistic philosophy of this book stems from that experience. Equally important, he introduced me to his beloved Plato and to Plato's Socrates who tells those who can read, that one cannot arrive at "the idea of the good" except as one has first passed through "the hypotheses of the previous sciences," all of which, if one takes the trouble, as so few humanists do, to turn back a few pages in Plato's *Republic,* will be found to be mathematical natural sciences. Whitehead confirmed this judgment when he once humorously remarked that that silly old fellow, Jowett of Oxford, who knowing no mathematics translated Plato's works into English, did not have the foggiest notion of what Plato was talking about. Ever since then I have never been able to put any trust in a purely humanistic philosophy of the humanities; even that of my Trinity College teacher and friend, the late Professor G. E. Moore, or the 18th-century Kant, notwithstanding the fact that anyone who has not learned what each of these two honest men has to teach one about moral and other evaluative judgments will surely go wrong. Bakewell introduced me also to Aristotle. If I am greatly impressed with Aristotle, as I am, because (1) he is the founder of Western naïve realistic, descriptive, natural history, biological science and because of (2) what he wrote about Proposition 1, Book X of Euclid and his predecessors, but am not equally impressed, as this book will make evident, by his theory of knowledge or his physics, metaphysics, and part of his theology, the blame for the latter judgment must not be placed by the reader at Bakewell's door.

My present cherished friend and New Hampshire summer neighbor, Professor William Ernest Hocking, comes next for the same reason that McTaggart's name follows soon after his. Just as McTaggart was the Director of my philosophical graduate research at Trinity's Cambridge, so

Professor Hocking directed the philosophical part of my graduate thesis for the Ph.D. in philosophy at Harvard's Cambridge. From this occasionally (and always justifiably) severe and ever lovable wise man, I learned none too early that a genuine scholar has "to lose his life in order to find it." The point is that one must not prejudge the result of any investigation. If one knows the answer, there is no point in initiating the study; and if one doesn't know, then only the investigation can give a trustworthy answer.

He also, by example, made it clear to me that, although he could hold his own in ivory-tower philosophizing with anyone, such "philosophy" was not adequate philosophy. In this respect, he was like another friend, John Dewey, who reinforced this habit later in my life. Hence, one must not be afraid to get one's philosophical hands dirty and one's spirit disturbed by handling the unexpected brute subject matter of anything that may, and usually turns out to be, very important—be it neurophysiology, biochemistry, mathematics, symbolic logic, physics, religion, negative feedback mechanisms, morals in concrete decisions, painting, sports, practical politics, anthropology, poetry, and—yes!—that most difficult subject called law, or even Asia and Islam. As the wise Hocking put it many times: "Everything is grist for the philosopher's mill."

Today such philosophy is sometimes derogatorily and humorously labelled "service station" philosophy. The philosopher, whose Credo this book contains, is delighted to be a service station hand. There are two reasons: the first is that if the pre-Socratics, the mathematical Plato and his Socrates, the Stoic moralists and lawyers who transformed Western contractual legal science, Aristotle, Descartes, Leibniz, Kant, and Whitehead, did not believe that it corrupted the superb flour which they produced to have experts in other subjects bring technical scientific and humanistic grist to one's philosophical mill, who am I to do so? Second, my own independent study of natural science, mathematics, and other subjects for their own sake,

as well as for their philosophical significance, has made
me suspicious of the worth of a philosophical mill that
grinds little more than its own verbal philosophical gears,
as does so much of both metaphysical and ordinary language philosophy today.

Hocking, McTaggart, Whitehead, Iqbal later, and also
Einstein, with respect to the epistemological and even
religious linguistic meaning of science, showed me also
that a scientist or philosopher who is worth bothering
about is one who thinks the facts, problems, and mysteries
of life all the way through, taking seriously both (1) the
expertly determined facts and (2) logical constancy in
one's thoughts about them. To be either clear or thorough concerning even a piece of human knowledge and
experience, one cannot stop one-half or three-quarters of
the way through. This is why the present book ends with
religion, and "God" is the last word in its title. Whatever
this word may mean, and we shall try to find out, the last
chapter will show that, like the umpire in American baseball, His Word is always the last one.

Henry Sheffer's name follows Hocking's because of an
influence upon me which it is impossible to exaggerate.
It was he at Harvard, before I went to England's Cambridge, who made me aware that in contemporary man's
common-sense, philosophical, and scientific beliefs, there
are not merely the imageful words getting their meaning
where most laymen, scientists, and philosophers the world
over think *all* words get their meaning, but also concepts
present in recent Western mathematics and its physics
which are of a quite different character and which get
their meaning in a quite different way. Before this I had
supposed that the only mathematics, natural science, or
philosophy there is, is one in which its numbers, points,
and objects find their meaning purely inductively by looking, say, at one's five fingers and counting them off, one,
two, three, four, and five or by looking at their sensed
colored extension against the sensed differently colored

spatial extension of the sky. That they do in part get their meaning in this way is without doubt true. But it came as a revelation to me when Sheffer showed that in Western mathematical physics and its philosophy, there are concepts of number, space, events, and objects which are not thus known by radically empirical sensing or naïvely direct observation alone but get their meaning, instead, by imageless syntactical or formal postulational analytic construction. This Sheffer did for me in his advanced seminars when, without images either sensed or imagined, he constructed the "serial order" of Chapter 4, Boolean Algebra, and the equivalent intertransformable "postulate sets" of Euclidian geometry. Because, moreover, the marks which he wrote on the blackboard found their meaning in nothing that could be imagined, I also discovered that in addition to my two sensing eyes, I, or anyone who understands this kind of mathematics, have one imageless intellectual seeing eye.

It was "concepts by postulation" in this specific sense of Sheffer and not "postulates" in the generic sense of the assumptions of any scientific or philosophical theory, which abound in ancient Asia as well as the West, that I meant by "concepts that are in whole or part concepts by postulation" in *The Meeting of East and West*. Professor Joseph Needham in his voluminous books on classical Chinese science quite misunderstands the thesis of this book and, consequently, reaches an erroneous judgment of it, because he commits the error of confusing concepts by postulation in Sheffer and my specific sense with any set of postulates concerning science and philosophy in the generic meaning of the word "postulate." That *The Meeting of East and West* made this distinction clear is shown by two considerations: (1) Many readers, including some who are not trained in the imageless constructs of symbolic logic, pure mathematics, and Western mathematical physics, interpreted the words "concepts by postulation" correctly. This was because, otherwise, (2) it would have been mean-

ingless to set concepts by postulation over against concepts
by intuition, which do get their meaning after the manner
of the word "number" when one looks at one's fingers. If
the reader, therefore, is not to fall into the same error as
did the otherwise able Professor Needham and some Asian
philosophers, he must study with care the imageless construction of serial order and the 19th-century Western
mathematical concept of "number" and of the "limit" of
a series as sketched very briefly in Chapter 4.

Because such marks on the paper or the blackboard,
as sensed by one's two sensing eyes, have no sensed or
imagined meanings, but do, none the less, have precise,
syntactically constructed meanings as given only to one's
single intellectual seeing eye, I have in the latter half of
this book used the words "concept by intellection" as the
equivalent of "concepts which in whole or part are concepts by postulation." This has the advantage of making
it unequivocally clear that "concepts by postulation" in the
specific sense of Sheffer and me are not to be confused
with concepts of number, space, time, and other scientific
or philosophical entities, relations, and their theories, all
the concepts of which find their meaning by a linguistic
reduction analysis in concept by intuition data that are
given through the senses or in naïve (i.e., direct)
observation.

Lawrence J. Henderson must be included for two reasons. First, it was from his lectures and suggested reading
in his course at Harvard entitled "An Introduction to the
History of Science" that I learned most of what I know
about this fascinating, rich, and important subject. The
rest came from listening (i) during the same year to Richards' and Forbes' lectures on the history of chemistry and
(ii) later in England to occasional lectures by Smith and
Singer at the University of London, and a term's lectures
by Lord Rutherford at Cambridge, supplemented later by
the reading of Sarton. Second, just as Hocking directed
my philosophical, so Henderson directed the biochemical

part of my Ph.D. thesis in philosophy on *The Problem of Organization in Biology.* "L. J.," as everyone called him, is another reason why I am a naturalistic philosopher who insists upon having a scientifically verifiable and philosophically consistent and whole concept of a person that keeps some physiologically chemical red blood containing, *ipso facto,* plenty of hemoglobin in the self-buffering, oxygen-carbon dioxide, steady state that is one's living body. Otherwise none of us would be about for more than a few seconds. This is why, also, Henderson's nomogram of the blood and its accompanying imageless "concept by postulation" equations play a leading role in my first book, *Science and First Principles,* and why a self-buffering (i.e., teleologically mechanical) nervous system with, God willing, a brain with excellent association and higher centers, does in Chapter 1 of this book.

Alfred North Whitehead is listed next on the dedicatory page for countless reasons which will appear in what follows, not the least of which is the privilege which my wife and I enjoyed of memorable conversations beginning with the day he and Mrs. Whitehead put our eldest son, then not as tall as he is today, on the bed in their flat in Chelsea of Old London, to those two different moments when God's "primordial nature" under "the lure of his consequent nature" were soon to take them away from any terrestrial "present occasion." Three particular professional influences need be mentioned here.

(1) He directed my philosophical analysis of the theory and method of 20th-century mathematical physics in The Imperial College of Science and Technology in South Kensington where he was then located, while McTaggart at Cambridge directed my philosophical study of the British empiricists, Locke, Berkeley and Hume, and his own (McTaggart's) concept of the person, the temporal series as distinct from the "C series" and religion.

(2) Whitehead made it unequivocally clear to me that there must be a reconstruction of not merely the scientific

but also the humanistic, including the religious and aesthetic, philosophical assumptions of the modern world. He convinced me that unless one "spends one's days and one's nights with Hume" and also understands concepts such as the "limit" and $\dfrac{\text{"dx"}}{\text{dy}}$ in the infinitesimal calculus, one will certainly go wrong, as did Oxford's well-intentioned Jowett. Einstein later confirmed Whitehead's judgment that it is as important for a scientist and a philosopher to study Hume as it is for them to study both epistemology and the symbols and theories of mathematical physics. This Einstein did when he told me that it was his reading of Hume which first convinced him that Newton was wrong when he wrote that he had made no hypotheses and had, instead, deduced the assumptions of his mathematically physical theory from the [naïvely (i.e., directly)] observed experimental data.

Whitehead implemented this judgment the first time I was with him in his large office at the Imperial College, when he told me I must immediately buy and study George A. Gibson's *An Elementary Treatise on the Calculus*. A decade later I returned to England's Cambridge, on a Guggenheim Fellowship, to attend, during the fall and spring terms, Hardy's lectures on number theory and Littlewood's on the theory of functions of a real variable, while also going through with considerable care Hardy's book *Pure Mathematics* and Littlewood's on his lecture subject. The middle term I spent at the Mathematical Institute of the University of Göttingen where, thanks to its director, Hermann Weyl, I read the original papers by Weierstrass, Dedekind, Cantor, Gauss, and Riemann on these and other imageless, formal, mathematical subjects. Needless to say, in this academic year of undistracted study I found more than one imageless construct, or concept by postulation, which stubbornly refused to be analyzed away into vivid aesthetic sensed data or objects like one's naïvely observed fingers. In the latter concept by intuition meanings for "number," "five" and "finger" are present also. But by means of "number," "five" and "finger" in this radically empirical or naïvely observed concept by intuition sense, little, if any, mathematical theorems can be proved. It is by means of the epistemically correlated concept by intellection meanings of "number," "five" and public spatio-temporally located "finger" that rigorously deduced theorems are discovered and then proved. What has to be realized is that the predictive power of Western science arises not from the concept by intuition meaning of ordinary words, but from their epistemically correlated, imageless concept by intellection meaning. This is why radically empirical or naïve realistic science, such as that of the pre-Westernized Asia or of Aristotle's natural history biology, has very good descriptive, but very little predictive, power.

In 1932 at Cambridge, Hardy also taught me something which superficially appears to have nothing to do with pure mathematics but which, nevertheless, is of equal importance for the Credo of this book. This happened when we both found that we were conducting independent research on American baseball, and that he was an expert also, being an old Cambridge Light Blue in English cricket. Since I was able to put at his disposal some important research materials concerning the previous World Series, we decided to collaborate on our research. Of necessity most of the contribution had to come from Hardy, since I knew nothing about cricket. Under his expert tutelage and Babe Ruthian cross-examination, I did eventually learn a little about his science of cricket, and he told me as much, if not even more, about my own science of baseball. He was both a friendly and a hard taskmaster, insisting that we go out into the field at Fenners, just as he had done at Yankee Stadium a few years before while lecturing incidentally during such spare time as remained on pure mathematics at Princeton. The facts had to be sought out and then grimly faced. The most abstract theory, seen only with one's intellectual eye, was investigated and then correlated epistemically with the imageful events that one naïvely observed with one's senses on the playing field.

For hours he carried on this Ruthless cross-examination with respect to the facts and the intellectual subtleties of American baseball in his library, containing the books of both Gauss and Spalding, into the little hours of the night, after we had dined together drinking Madeira with its connoisseur Housman across the table from us in Trinity's dining hall. In fact, one night I barely succeeded in getting out through the gate before the porter at his lodge was about to lock everybody in. Nor was this the end of his inquisition, for the next morning when I arrived somewhat bleary-eyed and had seated myself in his lecture room in the New Lecture Hall, while listening to his first words on a complex theorem in pure number theory, a yellow sheet of foolscap, covered with equations, was handed by him to some young mathematician in the front row to be passed back to me. Upon perusal I found the equations to be crossed out, with the symbol "(Over)" below them. Upon following this instruction, my grim task was before me, for the page was headed: "Preliminary Questions." There followed ten by no means elementary queries on American baseball. The first one was: (1) Upon how many major league teams did Roger Hornsby play before he retired? That one was easy. Some of the others less so. Nor did this heartless director of my research relent. For at his next lecture down came another yellow sheet covered with more crossed-out equations, which the students were sure were a real frontiersman's solution of a previously unsolved problem in pure number theory. With fear and trembling I followed the imperative "(Over)." There I read "Advanced Questions." And advanced they were asymptotically in the distance, at least so far as this groggy research scientist was concerned.

Nor was my tutor completely assured himself, being not

merely a beloved but an honest mortal man. This showed when I handed in my answers to the earlier set of questions in the only Cambridge Duopos I ever took. He glanced at them with a seriously sober face and said: "Obviously these answers will have to be checked against the sources (Spalding's Baseball Guide). But judging merely superficially, it appears to be a reasonably good Pass."

Little did I realize then that this, as well as what he, Sheffer, and Littlewood told me about what I here call "concepts by intellection," would be grist for my philosophical mill, producing some of the flour which is part of the Credo in the present book. The reader of its last chapter will see why. Nor should either Hardy or I be blamed for the result. As I said at the outset: What comes to a focus here is one of those things that just happens.

But back to Whitehead. The third thing he impressed upon me, both the first time we met and the last time before he died, is that in either science or philosophy one cannot be too suspicious of ordinary language. In Chapter 11 we shall attempt to show the precise, vividly concrete, and more abstract mathematically linguistic sense in which he was correct.

While at Cambridge with Hardy and Littlewood I also called on Wittgenstein, telling him that the two mathematicians were my main concern, but hesitantly (because of previous reports concerning similar requests) asking if he would permit me to attend his lectures. He said that he could not see why anybody wanted to do such a thing, but if I wanted to, I would be welcome. This I did for the first fall and part of the third spring term. To my surprise he soon introduced me to one or two of his most intimate personal friends. This is the highest compliment that can be paid to any visitor in England. We soon became warm friends. It did not occur to me until recently that what he was trying to say in his way in those lectures was in many respects what Whitehead was saying about the pitfalls of language, in his quite different way. This is why Chapter 17 is in major part about Wittgenstein and why also his name has to be included in the list of those to whom this book is dedicated.

The reasons for Einstein's inclusion will be evident throughout this book. Our friendship began in his residence in Berlin in 1927. It was nurtured year after year, after he came to the United States, when he sat in his rocking chair in the back second-floor study of his Princeton house with his pipe in his hand and his frequent smile illuminating his face as he made a point concerning the meaning of common-sense beliefs and of mathematical physics, and of what men such as Hume and Bishop Berkeley have to teach us. The present book attempts to put at least part of this in print. To the partial but important extent that I find a different meaning in natural science, the way the mind gets its mathematical physical meanings, and in religion, than did Whitehead, my years of study of Einstein's classic scientific papers and those annual joyful hours with him at Princeton are the cause.

Junjirō Takakusu plays the same kind of role in this book as Sheffer, but on its concept by intuition Oriental rather than its concept by intellection Occidental side. Before his death he was Professor of Sanskrit at the University of Tokyo and probably the greatest authority on Buddhism. He was also a Buddhist himself. Certain of the English translations of some of the Buddhist classics in Max Müller's *Wisdom of the East* series are by him. He was a master of the Sanskrit, Pali, Chinese, Japanese, German, and English languages, to mention but a few. I have been told that he edited and translated or supervised the translation into Japanese of some one thousand Buddhist texts, thereby covering the entire history of Buddhism, from its moment of origin with the Buddha in what is now Bihar and then Sarnath near Benares in India, throughout its spread (1) southward over India and Ceylon, from where it went to Thailand, Burma, and Indochina, and (2) north and northeastward over Tibet, China, and Korea to engulf Japan. If anyone, therefore, is able to, authoritatively and impartially, decide whether what I came upon in the final chapter of *Science and First Principles* (1931), and later in 1939, and here call (1) "the undifferentiated aesthetic continuum," is identical with (2) what the Pali Buddhists call "Nirvana" and the non-dualistic Hindu Sanskrit Vedantists call "the Atman that is Brahman without differences," that man would seem to be Takakusu. In any event, this is what he did in 1939, as the immediate sequel will show.

That the Buddhist word "Nirvana" is identical with what the Vedantic Hindu means by "the Atman that is Brahman without differences" is demonstrated by what happened a decade later at the 1949 East-West Philosophers' Conference at Honolulu, when the Buddhist Suzuki tried to say what "Nirvana" means, and then added that it is unique in Asian philosophy and religion. Instantly, all the Indian Hindus present—the distinguished Indian lawyer and former political Dewan of Cochin-Travancore State, Sir C. P. Ramaswami Ayer, as well as Swami Nikhilananda and Professors D. M. Datta and P. T. Raju—vigorously protested, quoting verse and text from the Hindu Vedas and Upanishads to show, quite conclusively, that what the Buddhist means by "Nirvana" is not unique but is identical with what the Vedantic Hindu means by "the Atman that is Brahman without differences." The "without differences" is important, because Brahman's transitory body is differentiated, but the timeless Brahman *per se* is not.

The crucial question, therefore, narrows down to whether what the Buddhist means by "Nirvana" is identical with what I mean by "the undifferentiated aesthetic continuum." If the answer be "Yes!," then the aforementioned Hindu Indian philosophers and one lawyer are authority for the syllogistic conclusion that what I mean by "the undifferentiated aesthetic continuum" is also identical with what they mean by "the Atman that is Brahman without differences." In fact, the "without differences," which is the equivalent of my "undifferentiated," suggests an affirmative answer, as do the countless Vedic and Upanishadic Hindu texts.

It may help the reader who wants to take the trouble to find out what the present book means by its words "the undifferentiated aesthetic continuum," if I now describe the circumstances under which Takakusu's answer to the foregoing crucial question was "Yes." Without such understanding and the seeking out, in one's radically empirical continuum of immediate experience, that to which these words point but cannot say, one half of this Credo simply cannot be understood nor can its factual warrant be known.

Takakusu and I first met in 1939 at the first East-West Philosophers' Conference. Paralleling its daily closed sessions, he and I lectured in independent courses five days a week for six weeks in the University of Hawaii Summer Session. I attended his lectures; he mine. Both of us took elaborate notes. His lectures were on Buddhism. They covered its various systems and what is the meaning of the basic word "Nirvana" that is common to all the systems. My exposition of the dialectical development of the four major systems of Buddhism, as given afterwards in *The Meeting of East and West,* derives from these lectures and Takakusu's book, *The Essentials of Buddhism.*

I lectured, with Takakusu in one of the first rows, on the history and philosophy of Western scientific theory and especially its theories of mathematical physics. These began with Democritus, Archytas, Theaetetus, Eudoxus of Books V and X of Euclid, Plato, and Aristotle and passed, via the naïve realistic Aristotelian Scholastics of the medieval period, to Galilei, Descartes, Newton, Leibniz, and Kant and then on to Einstein and Whitehead. They ended with the thesis that if this concept by postulation—imageless, indirectly verified mathematical physical science, referring to external objects and a public space-time that is not directly sensed or naïvely observed—is to account for the sensed vivid imageful world of perishing particulars, as correctly described by Locke of the Essay and by Hume, then it is necessary to assume an additional, radically empirical and immediate, concept by intuition factor which, for want of better words, I (1) call "the undifferentiated aesthetic continuum" and (2) believe to be identical with what the Buddhist means by the word "Nirvana," and the nondualistic Vedantic Hindu means by " the Atman that is Brahman without differences."

In addition, Takakusu listened, during the closed daily sessions of the Conference, when I gave evidence from the Buddhist or Hindu texts in their English translations to support my thesis. Through all these Conference sessions for the entire six weeks, Takakusu sat, obviously attentive and reflecting, but with his Japanese face Maya-masking any sign of what his judgment was.

Two days before the Conference was to break up, with each of us going our several ways, he asked if I would dine with him the following and final evening. To my surprise, when I arrived at the appointed place, I was his only guest. It was a quiet, peaceful, Japanese restaurant with our reserved table set in the corner of the narrow arcade of a rectangular court, in which the sound of a tiny little fountain accentuated the impressively peaceful silence. Finally we relaxed over our cigars. Then he said, "The longer I listened to you trying to indicate to your occasionally critical colleagues what you believe the word 'Nirvana' and your words 'the undifferentiated aesthetic continuum' mean, the more and more I came to feel myself listening to my old Buddhist teachers decades ago. Moreover, today the present Buddhist monks, or at least many of them, have lost it. They have been more concerned with making Nirvana look like the Christian missionaries' concept of God."

I had come to the latter conclusion, previously, myself, when I saw a Honolulu Buddhist "temple" (which, when authentic, contains no congregational pews) filled with chairs, like a lecture hall with Methodist-like hymn books about the Buddha on each chair seat. As Professor Stella Kramrisch wrote in her classic two volumes, *The Hindu Temple*, "Congregationalism is completely foreign to Hinduism." It is equally so for Buddhism. The Buddhist meditates in his home before the Buddha or occasionally on his knees by himself before the statue of the Buddha in a temple.

The reader may now understand why, after returning to the mainland and, in 1943, making a trip to that remarkable, aesthetically vivid place which is Mexico, where my friend Justino Fernandez' authoritative knowledge of Orozco's paintings enabled me to understand one half of the Mexican game of bullfighting, and my friend Dr. Paul Fejos gave me the clue to the other half, I ventured to write *The Meeting of East and West*. Certainly it will be clear why Takakusu's name is on this book's dedicatory list, and why I prize a postcard which he sent me just before Pearl Harbor and a year or so before his death. On one side of this card, he himself had painted an approximately homogeneous undifferentiated color, which was differentiated only by the following marks in his own longhand: "Nothing to be said but everything to be wished. J. Takakusu."

A decade later, Suzuki reconfirmed this man's judgment. It was the first day of the second (1949) East-West Philosophers' Conference. Since I knew Suzuki only from his books, I called on him at his office near mine in the university. After mutually warm greetings he said: "I have read your *The Meeting of East and West* and have but one question to ask you. The answer which you give will tell me whether what you mean by 'the undifferentiated aesthetic continuum' is identical with what one who understands Buddhism means by 'Nirvana.' " His question was, "Is the undifferentiated continuum an object other than one's subjective consciousness of it, or not?" "Obviously not," I replied. "Otherwise, there would be a dualism or difference between my differentiable subjective consciousness and the undifferentiated aesthetic continuum. Then my subjective consciousness would not be undifferentiatedly identical with it." Instantly, Suzuki said: "Yes. That is Nirvana."

These autobiographical experiences have their scientific relevance. In a later part this book will quote Whitehead's description of the dramatic occasion when Eddington's report to the Royal Society confirmed Einstein's prediction of the bending of light rays in the neighborhood of the sun. Takakusu and Suzuki play the same role with respect to the thesis that the meaning of (1) "the undifferentiated aesthetic continuum," (2) "Nirvana," and (3) "the Atman that is Brahman without differences" is identical.

Some two decades later a Western philosopher, Professor H. J. Paton, read my chapter in the volume *Philosophy—East and West,* edited by Professor Charles A. Moore, which first stated this thesis. Afterward, in his published Gifford Lectures, *The Modern Predicament,* he wrote that this interpretation was the only one that, in his judgment, made any philosophical sense out of the words in the Buddhist and Hindu texts.

One other factor is essential to the total Credo of this book. It has to do with what the relation is between the unobservable, intellectually known, scientific objects and events in public space-time, known by means of concepts by imageless mathematical intellection, and the perishing, vivid, imagefully sensed qualities and relations denoted by concepts by intuition. The major error of traditional common-sense science and philosophy, as Chapter 11 will show in concrete detail, is that, due to the confusion of the two-termed subject-predicate grammar of any ordinary Aryan language with the nature of things, this relation is thought to be the predicate of a substance. As Chapters 2 and 3 will show, this error leads to such nonsensical combinations of words as "Electrons are pink," "Sweetness is square," or "Ticklishness inheres in the feather."

The correct solution, the writer came upon in 1938. It is what this book refers to as "epistemic correlations." I reported it at the first 1939 East-West Philosophers' Conference and then read a paper on it immediately afterward at the Unity of Science conference at Harvard with the physicist and philosopher of science, Professor Philipp Frank, in the chair. The latter paper, in an expanded form, is Chapter 7 of *The Logic of the Sciences and the Humanities.* This thesis also has been confirmed independently by competent mathematical physicists and philosophical analysts of the method and theory of knowledge of both common-sense and this science. Previously, in his *Philosophie der Raum-Zeit-Lehre,* the late Professor Hans Reichenbach had discovered these relations, calling them "Zuordnungsdefinitionen." Independently, my friend and Yale colleague, Professor Henry Margenau, came upon them, giving them the name "rules of correspondence." They are essential to the Credo of this book, as is also the writer's discovery, published first in Part I of *Philosophical Anthropology and Practical Politics,* that, whereas in the case of objects other than the knower, they are one-many or many-one, in the case of the determinate object known being one's determinate knowing self, they are one-one.

Any purely radically empirical or any naïve realistic philosopher can always be counted on to tell one that they do not understand these relations or see why they are required. They are not necessary in a purely radical empirical or in a naïve realistic abstractive theory of knowledge. We have already noted that concepts by intellection do not reduce either to radical empirical or to naïve realistic meanings. They are necessary, however, in any theory of knowledge which combines nominalistic radically empirical concepts by intuition with universally quantified concepts by intellection. It was the failure of the Democritean, Platonic, and Stoic natural scientists and philosophers to discover epistemic correlations, which made it impossible for them to give any intelligible account of what the relation is between (1) what they called "the real world" designated by their mathematical language and its constructs and (2) the perishing particulars of the sense world denoted by either radically empirical concepts by intuition or naïve realistic notions that purport to be definable in terms of the latter. It is also, incidentally, this failure which produced the existential *Da*-ness that is Heidegger. The result in his case is little but *Da*-ness, because of the absence of any concepts by intellection to turn the *Da*-ness into its epistemically correlated *Da-sein*.

Her Highness Princess Poon Diskul of Thailand had to be on the list for two reasons. First, our identical Nirvana self spontaneously enables us to contemplate one another's past, present, and future feelings without saying anything. This is the case, even though we have met only on three or four occasions and always with either my wife, who admires her equally, or some other proper chaperone present. Second, without what she pointed out to my wife and me in Bangkok, the Buddist-Hindu part of this book's final chapter would not be.

Finally, there is my beloved wife. Every step of the way through this quest for life's meaning, she has been at my side. Life with a philosopher who is perpetually immersed in the writing of books and brooding over scientific and philosophical problems is neither the most Buddhistically blissful nor vocally vivacious of human experiences. If the final meaning recorded here, at times at least, rings true, realistically, forthrightly, and honestly, then she is that meaning.

Two cautions remain to be noted: The first is that no authorities, even if they be the notable persons just referred to, suffice to warrant you, the reader, in believing anything that follows. Only you, yourself, can provide this warrant for yourself by doing both of the following two things: (1) Test what is said, if what is said refers to empirical evidence against the facts of your own discoverable, if not yet discovered, experience, or else trust the expertly tested reports of people such as Eddington, Michelson, Morley, Takakusu, Suzuki or Reichenbach, Professor Margenau or Professor Paton, to do it for you. (2) Test the beliefs or conclusions, which the facts are used to warrant, against the touchstone of their theoretical logical consistency. For both of these two things, you, yourself, must take the entire responsibility. Neither I nor any other authority under Heaven can do it for you.

The second caution is that the full Credo in its entirety which follows, however much some distinguished authorities may confirm or agree with each piece of it, is my responsibility. Even so, in another more important sense, this is not the case. For this final, total, beautifully typed Credo is not, at least in its last three chapters, the one I intended to write here when I started the focusing which is this book. Instead, after the manner of an author of a novel or a play who is captured by his characters, this Credo has taken its believer in hand, insisting that I write it, and that my harassed and besieged Helen of Northford type it and retype it, again and again, exactly in this way.

From here forward, therefore, you, the reader, proceed, if you are interested in doing so, at your own risk and responsibility. However, if the fact of error has the significance, with respect to both personal freedom and personal responsibility, that the sequel indicates to be the case, perhaps this also is as it should be.

1

KNOWING ONESELF

M AN IS a paradox. His knowledge of himself is more so. Nothing would seem to be nearer at hand than one's own self. Yet nothing is more difficult to know. It is not at all unlikely that there is at least one astronomer who, because of his concentration on his science, knows more about the inside of a distant star than about his own local self. In fact, as the sequel will show, a person may go through life knowing less about himself than he does about strangers. To be more of a stranger to oneself than is a stranger is, indeed, to be a paradox.

In *The Tulip of Sinai,* Iqbal sings:

> Thou reachest to the bosom of a star;
> Yet of thyself thou art all unaware;
> Grain-like, upon thyself open an eye,
> And thou shalt rise from earth a sapling fair.

Let us try.

Recent psychology has emphasized the importance of the unconscious portion of ourselves.* From psychoanal-

---

* Part of what follows originally appeared in *The Christian Register,* January, 1954.

ysis we have learned the value, if we would know ourselves, of bringing into the center of consciousness our
dream life and the vast portion of ourselves that goes
on unconsciously and automatically. Nevertheless, this
supplementation of introspective conscious psychology with
the psychoanalytic psychology of the unconscious does not
take us to the truest and fullest nature of ourselves.

In the last few decades there has been a new approach
to human nature, which has not received the attention
that it deserves. It aims to know man by shifting the
focus, but not the whole, of attention away from both the
conscious and the unconscious self to the objective cultural artifacts, which are the creations of every self. This
has the advantage not merely of a gain in scientific objectivity but also of forcing our knowledge of man to face
and comprise every objective manifestation of man's creative capacities. This is why, although objective, it throws,
perhaps, even more light on the subjective nature of man
than does a direct study of subjective man himself.

This new approach has occurred in cultural sociology
and cultural anthropology. Culture is the part of our experience that is the creation of men. The methodological
assumption, therefore, of this approach to the nature of
men is "By their fruits ye shall know them." [1]

This counsel is as sound scientifically as it is wise
morally. Whereas we cannot put ourselves in front of ourselves without distorting what we are in the very act of
looking reflexively at ourselves, we do have the fruits of
the creative activities of men before us in an objective form
in which they can be studied without distortion.

The first light which cultural anthropology throws on
human nature appears when we examine any specific culture and ask the following question: Is natural science as
a system applicable to cultural systems? One of the first
scientists to provide the clue to the answer is Professor
Emeritus Pitirim A. Sorokin of the Department of Sociology at Harvard University. He has pointed out that the

difference between the unity or integration of a cultural system and that of a system in inorganic nature centers in the difference between the two types of causality governing the systems. Whereas the systems of inorganic nature have their unity and changes through time determined by mechanical causality, cultural systems are governed by what Professor Sorokin terms "logico-meaningful" causality.[2]

Let us consider mechanical causation first. An isolated system is known to be governed by mechanical causation, if it is possible to specify a theoretically constructed, deductively formulated, scientific theory, empirically verified for the system, which is such that when the independent variables of the theory, defining the state of a system at a given present time, t_1, are determined empirically, the mathematically expressed laws of the theory permit one to calculate their empirically verifiable values for the system at any later time, t_2. Our own planetary system, as conceptualized by Newton's experimentally verified mechanics, is an illustration. The basic laws of Newton's mechanics and his law of inverse squares define the unity and inner order of the system. The two independent variables in these laws—the positions and the momenta of all the masses in the system—when found empirically, define the state of the system at the time they are determined. Given the empirical determination of the positions and momenta of the masses in our planetary system at a given time, t_1, and assuming the foregoing conditions to have been met, Newton's laws enable one to calculate the positions and momenta of all the masses in the system at any later time, t_2.

Consider now a cultural system governed by logico-meaningful causality. Let us begin with an illustration. If one introduces American law into an Anglo-American culture, such as that of Great Britain, the United States, New Zealand, or Australia, the law is effective. When, however, President Chiang Kai-shek introduced this same type of law into his Confucian Chinese culture of a few decades ago, the result, as one of his own followers, Chiang Monlin, has shown, was not merely failure, but also demoralization and corruption.[3]

Why this difference in the results of the introduction of a common stimulus into two different cultures? Chiang Monlin has given the answer. The writer's own investigations have confirmed his answer in the case of other cultures. The answer is that Anglo-American law presupposes for its effectiveness a certain way of thinking about themselves, their relations to one another, and to nature, upon the part of any people to whom this law is applied. The ways of thinking about themselves and their universe, which are necessary for the effectiveness of Anglo-American law, are present in an Anglo-American culture. They are not present in traditional Confucian Chinese culture.

The human beings in the two cultures have the same kind of nervous systems. The stimuli striking the sensory end organs of these nervous systems are also approximately the same. What is different in the two cases are the concepts used by the people of the two cultures to describe, unify, integrate, and anticipate the approximately common stimuli striking their similar nervous systems. In short, two cultures differ not so much because of the facts of experience or the structures of the nervous systems of their peoples, but because of the different concepts they use to classify, describe, and integrate the otherwise common facts.

Now concepts, by their very nature and definition, introduce meanings. It follows, therefore, that the unity and causality of a cultural system, unlike that of an inorganic system in nature, will depend upon and be a function of meanings. In other words, the causality of cultural systems is logico-meaningful. This was Professor Sorokin's very important discovery and insight.

The cultural anthropologist, Clyde Kluckhohn, came

upon the same fact quite independently in a different and perhaps more concrete way.[4] He made it one of the major concerns of his life to study, at first hand, the Navaho Indians of the southwestern United States. After many years of observation and lengthy periods of life with them, during which he supposed that he had come thoroughly to know and understand them, he awoke one day to the realization that for all his direct observations, he had not been understanding them. The trouble, he found, was that, although the sensed data which he observed were objective, the concepts which he used to describe, integrate, and understand his objective sensed impressions were, in considerable part, his own, rather than those of the Navaho. He saw, therefore, that objective knowledge of this culture and its people requires that one conceptualize what one observes with the concepts used by the Navaho themselves, rather than with the concepts of some white man's culture or school of social science. When he proceeded, therefore, to discover the Navaho way of describing, integrating, and evaluating the raw facts of their experience, he found himself confronted with a unique philosophy. Moreover, when one then looked at Navaho institutions and behavior from the standpoint of this philosophy, a novel, explicit set of moral and legal norms for settling disputes appeared, and facts in their behavior, which previously had seemed to an outside observer to lack meaning or to be even inconsistent with other facts in their behavior, immediately took on meaning and consistency.

Also, when this Navaho philosophy and morality were compared with the morality and legal norms of the white culture of the United States, incompatibilities appeared. Just as the philosophy of the Navaho is not that of the white man, so the ethical and legal norms for resolving disputes between the two peoples are different. Immediately, it became evident why behavior with respect to the Indians upon the part of the white man's courts and officials, which seemed very idealistic from the white man's standpoint, was demoralizing for the Navaho.

Another illustration from anthropology confirms this conclusion. A very famous French anthropologist, Lévy-Bruhl, was interpreted as affirming the thesis that there is a fundamental difference between the people of primitive cultures and those of our modern Western social groups. This difference, supposedly, was that primitive peoples are not troubled by fallacious arguments or logical inconsistencies in their thinking, whereas the modern sophisticated Frenchman is. No anthropologist today puts any credence in this thesis. The reason is that the lack of consistency has been found to have its basis in conceptualizing the facts of a culture not one's own in terms that are foreign to that culture. Further investigation of the culture shows that when one stays with it long enough to discover the mentality of the people, then everything they do has as much consistency and meaningfulness from the standpoint of their mentality as what we do has for us.

In fact there does not seem to be a scientific definition of the unity of a culture other than the conceptual one. Consider a small village in India made up of Muslims and Hindus who have lived side by side for centuries. Why must one say, if one speaks of elementary cultures, that there are two cultures rather than one in this village? The answer is that the Hindus in the village describe the facts of their behavior and experience in terms of the concepts and values of Hindu philosophy, religion, and morality, whereas the Muslims conceptualize the same facts from the standpoint of the philosophy and mentality of Islam. One other fact becomes clear. It is only as different men use the same basic common concepts for describing, integrating, and anticipating the facts of their experience, that they have a common culture.

The implications of these findings of cultural sociology, cultural anthropology, and the comparative philosophy of the world's cultures are important. It becomes evident that each one of us is very much more than a physical body moving around in space and time, subject to the natural laws of physical and biological science. To be sure, if we fall off a cliff, we fall according to exactly the same laws of gravity as does a stone. Moreover, each one of us is very much more than the Humean sequence of perpetually perishing sensations, images, and after-images, which introspective psychology exhibits, and which psychoanalytic techniques bring into the center of consciousness. Any person is all these things—physical, neurological, introspective, and psychoanalytic. In fact, neither any one nor all of these four factors in our nature give our essence. For what distinguishes man from any other system in the universe is not so much the facts—physical, neurological, introspective, and psychoanalytic—making up his nature, but his capacity to conceptualize these facts. It is because different men and groups of men conceptualize the facts of their own nature and the nature of all things in various ways, that there are separate cultures. Men alone have the capacity to conceptualize and symbolize what they are, what the rest of the universe is, and to have their objective physical behavior guided by such conceptual and symbolic factors.

This does not mean that behavior is purely rationalistic. Only that part of behavior is rationalistic which is guided by concepts that refer to the purely rational factors in human nature. But concepts can refer to any factors—rational and nonrational—alike. There is nothing rational about a stone, yet the concept of mass in mathematical physics embraces stones. There is nothing logically and mathematically rational about an introspected pain or a sudden burst of passionate rage. Yet the very concepts—pain, passion, and rage—refer none the less to these nonrationalistic items. Thus, insofar as our behavior is a function of a philosophy rooted in the emotional, the passionate, the unconsciously material and mechanical as well as in the logical and the mathematical, the behavior and culture of a people can express the irrational as well as the rational. In fact, a comparative study of the philosophy of the diverse cultures of the world,[5] as exhibited in comparative philosophical anthropology, forces one to the conclusion that a whole man and a full, complete, scientific account of human nature can be achieved only by a religion, a philosophy, a science, and a culture, which, in its basic mentality, is rich enough to describe, integrate, and give meaning to the physical, the neurological, the introspective, the psychoanalytical, the intuitive, and the emotional as well as the logical, mathematical, and more literally rationalistic factors in human nature and total experience.

This crucial and essential role of meanings and symbols and philosophy in human nature, experience, and behavior takes one not merely to the essence of human nature, but also to the heart of the moral life. Before any stimulus striking an end organ of the human nervous system is allowed to express itself in motor behavior, it has to fit itself into and pass the censorship of the system of symbolic representatives of past stimuli, which are trapped in the target area of the cortex of the human nervous system. Thus every human response is a function not merely of the stimulus of the moment, but of the trapped representatives of past stimuli. What is this but conscience?

What seems to be happening is something like this: The internal and external sensory end organs of every human nervous system are being continuously bombarded by stimuli. These stimuli are the effects upon the human individual of all the facts of his experience. If there were no way of retaining symbolic representatives of past facts, or integrating the countless number of present stimuli striking one's nervous system at any given moment of time, human beings would be knocked this way and that and torn to pieces in almost an infinite number of diverse and conflicting motor responses. It appears that the cortex traps representatives of these stimuli and stores them in separate areas of the brain, thereby making memory possible. From these storage areas, the association areas then freely abstract and permute the trapped representatives of particular stimuli, which seem to provide the key to all the others.

Put in terms of the methods of logic and scientific procedure, this means that certain factors in experience are taken as being more basic than others, because the latter can be defined in terms of the former. This suggests that the difference between one culture and another and between two men guided by different legal and moral principles centers in those factors in experience which are taken consciously and unconsciously as the more elementary and basic ones. Scientific method combined with philosophical analysis is the art of making this total conscious and unconscious process a systematic and completely conscious one.

But what is a set of primitive or basic concepts? The name given by tradition to the basic concepts of experience is philosophy. Since the foregoing considerations from cultural sociology and cultural anthropology indicate that the unity of a culture centers in the elemental concepts used by its people to describe, integrate, and anticipate the facts of their experience, it follows that every particular culture is the fruition of a particular philosophy. It follows, also, that the essence of man both scientifically and spiritually is that he is a walking philosophy, and that the cause of the unity of a culture is the philosophy which its people by intercommunication hold in common. In short, scientific anthropology is philosophical anthropology.

The reason why inorganic systems, such as our solar system, are governed by mechanical causation rather than by logico-meaningful causality now becomes clear. The behavior of the individual masses in inorganic systems is not the result of any concepts they use to conceptualize their behavior. What makes a human being unique is that he can respond not merely to stimuli, after the manner of the tides of the ocean responding to the pull of the moon's gravitation, but also to the way in which he conceptualizes these and all other stimuli.

Communism is one of the best examples of this. The difference between the Communists and liberal democrats fundamentally is not a difference in the stimuli hitting our respective bodies. The difference centers, instead, in the fact that they use the concepts of Marx, Lenin, Stalin, Mao, and Khrushchev for conceptualizing these stimuli, and we use those of Bacon, Locke, Newton, Jefferson, Franklin, and Lincoln. Similarly, Kluckhohn has shown that the natural and moral philosophy of the Navaho is different from that of the other people of the United States.

We referred above to the capacity of the neural cortex to trap present, persisting representatives of past facts or stimuli. It will be well to refer to certain developments in contemporary neural physiology, which make this reference more explicit. The crucial facts and theories have been revealed and constructed by several men of whom Dr. Lorente de Nó, Professors Rosenblueth, Wiener, and Bigelow, Doctors Warren McCulloch and Walter Pitts and the late John von Neumann are the most important.[6] These men, among others, have come upon two very significant facts. First, human nervous systems are goal-guided mechanisms, or, in other words, cybernetic, self-regulating, mechanical systems. Second, the neural paths in the human nervous system, leading from the sensory neuron to the motor neuron, which produces the behavioral muscular response, need not be linear in character. They can, in the cortex, also be ordered in a circle with these circles connected to form units of circles in a hierarchy.

Were the neural connections solely linear, once a sensory neuron had fired the intervening cortical neurons and the latter, in turn, had fired the motor neuron, there would be nothing remaining in the nervous system to represent the past stimulus. In short, memory would be impossible. Then man would literally have to be little more than a muscle twitch in response to an immediately antecedent stimulus.

Dr. Lorente de Nó and others have brought forth experimental evidence to indicate that neurons in the cortex may be ordered anatomically in a circle. Such a circular neural ordering, when the neurons are firing, is called a reverberating circuit. To one such circuit of neurons a sensory neuron may come, and from this circuit a motor neuron may go. Imagine that a stimulus from the environment fires the sensory neuron. Suppose also that the firing of the sensory neuron in turn results in the firing of one of the neurons in the cortical circuit, which in turn fires its neighbor in this circuit. If the time it takes the resultant impulse to be passed around the circuit is long enough to permit the metabolic processes of the body to restore the energy in each neuron in the reverberating circuit before its neighbor stimulates it a second time, then the impulse is passed continuously around the reverberating circuit as long as the human being lives. If there is no other sensory impulse coming to this particular reverberating circuit, it follows that its persisting trapped impulse represents the past stimulus which initiated the reverberation and only this past stimulus or fact. When something uniquely represents something else, it has the formal properties of a symbol. Thus, McCulloch and Pitts noted that the trapped impulses in reverberating circuits are formally equivalent to, or, to use the writer's epistemological terminology, are the neurological epistemic correlates of the introspected facts which we call ideas.

Neural anatomy tells us also that the trapped representations of specific visual sensations are sent to one particular area in the cortex and that those of auditory, tactual, olfactory, and other types of sensation are sent to other cortical areas. If these are all trapped in their respective areas, it is then easy to understand how class con-

cepts and classification arise. We have but to assume that
the impulses representing differing classes of past facts
are fed into an integrating area, as is in fact the case, to
understand how scientific and philosophical theories are
formed. All that is then required for human beliefs to determine bodily behavior and thereby generate, when
shared, the artifacts of culture is that there be a hierarchy
of impulses. These impulses, representing the philosophical
theory, are connected through motor neurons with the
many muscles of the human body. This is insured by the
anatomical fact that motor neurons run from the reverberating circuits to the muscles.

Before an external stimulus can influence motor behavior, it must, except in simple reflexes, pass the censorship of the system of trapped universals in the human
cortex. Since there is a common culture only when there
is a common set of universals held by at least a majority
of the people in the society in question, we now see why
religious and secular education, beginning in the mother's
lap at childhood and carried on to maturity, are present
in and a necessity of any culture. The essential connection
of religious and secular education with morality also
becomes clear. Without meaning, without a conceptualization of the facts of experience, or, in other words, without a philosophy, there is only a muscle twitch to a stimulus; there is no morality. Conversely, morality has its
roots, not in any single fact in experience, but in any fact
considered in its relation to all the other facts in experience. Only concepts can bring one fact of experience into
relation with all other facts. The basic concepts generating
the hierarchy of all concepts define a person's or a culture's
philosophy.

The point of cardinal importance is that the human
being does not come to the facts of his experience as a
blank tablet upon which the effects of the stimuli of the
sensory neurons of the nervous system are written. Instead, the human being brings to these stimuli and their

effects a hierarchically ordered set of memory organs for trapping universals in the human cortex. For a concise, authoritative, and exact account of this hierarchical ordering in the brain, which is also built into calculating machines, the reader is referred to *The Computer and the Brain* by John von Neumann.

It follows that the moral life of the individual and the unity of any culture is not a passive, purely receptive, mechanical process. With the almost infinite number of stimuli striking any human nervous system through the duration of a human life, the representatives of those stimuli which are basic and capable of being used to define, deduce, or anticipate others cannot be discovered by mere passive receptivity. Different possible candidates for the status of being basic are entertained and tried out through trial and error. In short, as noted above, the brain has association areas as well as storage areas.

There is a neurological basis for this also. Neurons connect the basic reverberating circuits with the motor organs of speech and writing. Otherwise we would not be able to express vocally, or visually write out, different scientific and philosophical hypotheses. Furthermore, the individual in certain rare cases—namely, those men of genius who constitute the sages of a culture—must have the creative imagination to propose fresh and original permutations of the raw data of experience. Thus the discovery of a philosophy for a people, adequate to account for the data of their experience and thereby capture their support, is a tremendous act of creativity. This is why a merely radical empirical positivistic philosophy, which would reduce all meanings in mathematical physics, religion, morality, and politics to the passively received sequence of perishing particulars which sense awareness exhibits, is so barren and poverty-stricken before the creative originality of the basic theories of mathematical physics, the intuitive subtleties of religion, and the rich diversity of cultures.

Philosophical anthropology makes it clear, therefore, that culture, which is the creation of the human spirit, is creative at two levels of creativity. It is creative, first, because its facts, being man-made, are artifacts—the fruits of men guiding conduct and building their cultural institutions in every dimension of experience, scientific, legal, religious, economic, technological and artistic, and in terms of a specific mentality or philosophy. It is creative in the second sense—achieved only by the sages of any culture— of discovering, expressing, and conveying this philosophy. Thus man creates not merely all the artifacts which are culture, but also all the diverse mentalities and philosophies which guide him in the creation of the artifacts. Furthermore, this philosophy defines his goal values.

This means that even contemporary behavioristic and neurological psychology is leading us to precisely the same conception of man as a creative being guided by ideas defining propositions and values to which introspective psychology led men centuries ago. In other words, the purposes, ideas, and ideals of men are not, as traditional materialistic philosophy has maintained, merely phenomenal. They are real and have causal efficacy with respect to overt bodily behavior.

There is, of course, a third sense in which creativity exists in human experience. Nature, as well as man, is creative. For the facts of nature are not man-made. This is why they are not called artifacts. Nevertheless, they are made. The creative source of their making is called evolution, God, Allah, Yahweh, Brahman, Nirvana, Tao, or the source of *jen,* the name varying with the philosophy of the culture in question.

It appears, therefore, that without knowledge and behavior guided by knowledge there can be behavior, but there cannot be moral behavior. This, I take it, is the point of the story of the Garden of Eden. Sin arose when Adam first tasted the tree of knowledge. This expresses the fact that without knowledge, which alone can be true or false and, hence, capable of error, there is no meaning to either good or evil; facts merely are; they are neither true or false, nor good or evil. The implication seems to be that good conduct is behavior governed by a conceptualization of all the facts of experience which is consistent with and true to all those facts. Evil behavior, conversely, is behavior guided by a conceptual system which is either false to the natural facts of experience or true only for some of them.

If the human being is capable of having, continuously within himself, representatives of the major classes of facts influencing the end organs of his nervous system as stimuli, and if these representatives of the facts of experience are ordered hierarchically so that basic or elementary concepts are distinguished from defined or secondary concepts, then nothing is more important in personal morality or national conduct than the adequacy of one's basic conceptual assumptions. The heart of the moral man is his philosophy.

This understanding of our deepest and most essential nature, to which philosophical anthropology has brought us, has important practical implications which the writer has described in more detail in his *Philosophical Anthropology and Practical Politics*. This understanding suggests that if a traditional culture, characterized by unity, homogeneity, and harmony, is confronted with a foreign ideology which contradicts and gradually eats away the indigenous beliefs, then the traditional culture will tend to disintegrate. Kluckhohn has shown this to be true in the case of the Navaho. Contemporary cultural sociologists and anthropologists find countless other examples throughout the world. In fact, what characterizes our time is such ideological conflict. The issue between Communism and traditional liberalism is, by no means, the only example. Every people throughout Africa, the Middle East, and the Far East now face the unsolved problem of combining the mentality, values, and instruments of modern Western cultures with the differing religions, mentalities, and ways of their indigenous traditions. Once it is recognized that these problems center in different mentalities and philosophies, the inadequacy of traditional political approaches to their solution becomes evident. Mere Western religious missionary activity, Voice of America propaganda, or economic Marshall Plan aid, even at the village level, will not do. All these methods have failed in Africa, the Middle East, and Asia, because the people introducing them have not realized that the native population will conceptualize them in native indigenous terms rather than in the Western terms necessary to understand and use them effectively. These practical problems of the contemporary world can be solved only by knowing that every factor in a culture presupposes the basic mentality and philosophy of its people, and by then seeing that the problem of foreign influence is, at bottom, that of relating and integrating in a fresh synthesis two rival basic philosophies of what life means.

As Chesterton has said, the question is not whether philosophy matters, but whether anything else does. Nothing is more important than that one has an adequate philosophy of contemporary, natural scientific knowledge, which takes into account the philosophy of one's own legal and political institutions and those of other people throughout the world.

What is the criterion of such a philosophy? Clearly its basic assumptions must be sufficient to take care consistently of all the raw data of experience. If this is to occur, the human spirit must be provided with a society in which all the data of experience have a chance to stimulate the individual and thereby effect and even bring about the reconstruction of his basic beliefs and assumptions. Otherwise, one will be describing, integrating, and guiding one's conduct with respect to experience only in terms of a part of what it is and of what is knowable about it. Here we have a second reason for the freedom of the human spirit and the human mind. *The essence of man as a moral and spiritual being is that he is a knowing being.* If, therefore, society makes it impossible for him to know afresh or keeps from him the factual data and various philosophical theories of experience necessary for adequate knowledge, it deprives man of the food necessary for his moral and spiritual sustenance.

But even in a completely free society all of the facts of human experience never stimulate or bring their conceptual requirements to bear upon any one person or even any one culture. This means that we can arrive at an adequate way of thinking about the raw data of our experience only if human beings pool both their experience and the diverse concepts to which they are led in describing and integrating their particular, limited portions of experience. This suggests that a philosophy which may be quite adequate for the facts of a single person's experience or a single culture may be quite incomplete as a philosophy of the totality of human experience. Only, therefore, by putting ourselves inside the basic mentality and values of the many cultures of the world and then pooling and integrating these philosophies to create, probably, a fresh philosophical synthesis which is a truly world philosophy can an adequate moral guide for the total personality and the contemporary world be approximated.

It is in this direction that contemporary natural and anthropological philosophy is now guiding us. The mentality of each culture must be seen from within and then related to the differing mentalities of the other major cultures of the world, precisely in the manner in which Kluckhohn's scientific studies have brought the philosophy of the Navaho Indians out into the open and then put it into juxtaposition with the different philosophy and legal codes of the Navaho's white neighbors. To do this for the entire world is one of the major tasks of our time. It is also, probably, the most effective way to an understanding and comprehension of the richness and complexity of the spiritual nature of man and to a realistic and practical politics.

At the present stage, the rich diversity and the pluralistic cultural relativism of the diverse cultural mentalities and value systems of the world are the factors most in need of emphasis. Only by learning from cultural anthropology and the comparative philosophy of the world's cultures what they are, can a realistic foreign policy be formulated. Also, notwithstanding the remarkable achievements of modern Western civilization, it now appears to have overlooked an entire dimension of human experience which the cultures of the Far East noted centuries ago. This neglected dimension may be appropriately described as intuitive, existential, aesthetic immediacy. Conversely, the traditional Far East has missed the purely formal, imageless, theoretically constructed type of knowledge of oneself and the universe in which the Greek mathematical physicists and the Greek and Roman Stoic lawyers and moral philosophers, with their law of contract, and the modern technological and legally contractual West are so proficient. These considerations suggest that to put oneself within the mental and moral standpoint of the philosophy of a foreign culture is to discover first-order facts in one's own experience which one has neglected and never dreamed were there.

Having done this not merely for the successive cultures of our own Western civilization, but also for the major cultures of the remainder of the world, we will then, for the first time, be able to talk objectively about the one true and adequate philosophy. Only then is it likely that we will have all the conceptual assumptions necessary to describe, integrate, and anticipate the totality of past and present facts, which have brought their conceptual influence to bear upon the countless sages and scientists of the many cultures of the world. If it is of the essence of the human spirit that it is a symbolic and a thinking animal, a creature not merely responding to stimuli but also conceptualizing these stimuli, then the human spirit will never be satisfied or be at peace with itself until it approximates that perfect or complete conceptualization of the totality of facts of human experience which religion has called the omniscience of God.

Such an approximation to a truly world philosophy must have at least two factors in it: One is the aforementioned intuitive component of oneself and things which the cultures and religions of the Far East have mastered better than any of the rest of us. The other is the theoretically constructed, indirectly known, logically and mathematically rigorous, deductively designated component of ourselves and things to which the mathematical physics and legal science of the West have pioneered the way.

Only if man first becomes as spiritually sensitive to the mentality and morality of other cultures as he should be with respect to his own, thereby doing unto others as he would have them do unto him, and then, out of this enlarged, intercultural, spiritual sensitivity, generates a fresh world-embracing creative synthesis, in which unity that respects diversity is achieved, can the full, rich content of one's own deepest nature be known. To see oneself objectively in the cultural fruits not merely of one's own creativity, but also that of all other people is part, at least, of what it means to know oneself.

2

THE COMMUNICANTS IN
COMMUNICATION ENGINEERING

To KNOW ONESELF is to realize that one is more than oneself. Hence, to be selfish is to be false to oneself. The reason is that communication between human beings is a major part of what it means to be a human being.

Without it, and the commitments to a common contract that it makes possible, there would be no commerce; nor would there be a family, a church, a legal and political nation, or, as we have seen in the previous chapter, a culture. Only in the case of the creative scientist, philosopher, saint, or artist of rare genius does the individual make the marital customs, the church, the university, the fine arts, or the legal and political community, instead of the customs, church, nation, and other cultural artifacts making him or her. In short, one is what others are.

Nevertheless, there is a sense in which any person is an original genius. The degree to which such is the case depends on the extent to which one is "from Missouri," doubting with Descartes all contemporary as well as traditional authority, weighing the evidence for, and the alternative theoretical possibilities with respect to past, present, or future claims upon one's allegiance and faith before further committing oneself.

If such originality is to occur, however, two things are necessary. The first is science. The second is philosophy.

Without the former to supplement ordinary observation, the facts necessary to enable one to judge the grounds for or against a given belief, allegiance, or commitment are not at hand. Without both word-watching analytic and world-embracing comparative philosophy, to acquaint one with the mature past and present novel possible ways in which the facts are to be analyzed and interpreted, the facts are likely to be conceived in entirely too piecemeal and dogmatically simple-minded, if not erroneous, a manner. Also some, at least, of one's provincial religious, political, and personal moral values may be given a universal validity that is not warranted.

But both science and philosophy, as well as ordinary discourse, involve language. It, in turn, entails communication. Consequently, if we are to understand ourselves and find life's fullest meaning, we must watch the instruments of communication.

When they are weak or short-range geographically, it is possible to suppose that one's own nation and its cultural philosophy and religion are enough. The speed and world-embracing range of today's instruments of communication make this no longer possible. An event in the Congo is on the front page, often in headlines, of our local newspaper. The events next door or in a distant state of one's own nation are on the back page, if they are in the paper at all. What President Mao says in Peking or Prime Minister Nehru affirms in New Delhi has to be reckoned with at No. 10 Downing Street, in the White House, or in Montevideo. In short, the world has become everyone's home yard. It is this cosmopolitan community in which each one of us now lives.

This elemental fact has several exceedingly important practical implications. It means, for every human being and nation, that foreign policy has become domestic policy. For example, the Federal Reserve Board in the United States cannot alter domestic interest rates without regard to what financial authorities abroad will do. Similarly, few domestic political decisions can be successful unless a judgment with respect to both short- and long-range foreign policy is made simultaneously. As Chapter 5 will show, this calls for a new religious as well as secular statesmanship.

The same is true of our recent legal thinking. In the Anglo-American world this thinking has been determined, for the majority of elder lawyers and legally trained statesmen in our midst, by the 17th-century British Hobbes, the 19th-century English Austin, and the early 20th-century American Thayer. According to this theory, the sovereign command of the local nation-state is absolute. The geographical range of contemporary instruments of communication has already rendered obsolete this theory of life's legal and political meaning. The spiritual home of this recent traditional Anglo-American legal and political philosophy was the Italian city-states of Machiavelli's continental Europe and the earliest Protestant nation-states of northern Europe. The present economic, legal, and political success of Continental European Union, and the fact that, as these words are being penned, Great Britain is becoming a part of it, means that the traditional, modern, Machiavellian power-political and Hobbesian, absolute nation-states are now being buried in the lands of their birth. Life today is finding its legal and political meaning in regionally federated, internationally legal, and political communities within the world community.

Much of our contemporary legal and political thinking and practice has failed to catch up with these developments. For a more detailed analysis and description of what is required, the writer's *European Union and United States Foreign Policy, The Complexity of Legal and Ethi-*

cal Experience, and *Philosophical Anthropology and Practical Politics* may be of some value.

Present instruments of communication have two unique characteristics—the one financial, the other military. Financially, they are very expensive and becoming more so every day. Militarily, in case of war, people communicate with missiles. Today's missiles are hardly the cave man's stones. Instead, they are such as to destroy not merely the enemy and ourselves, but also everyone else. Never, therefore, has the control of man's instruments, by life's ultimate values and meaning, been as necessary as it is today. To this end, let us consider the peaceful instruments of communication first, reserving the military and power-political for later chapters.

Communication engineering has slipped up so quickly on its human communicants that few of us are aware of what has happened. By the human communicants we mean two groups of the entire world's people—(1) those sending and (2) those receiving the messages transmitted by the expensive and persuasive contemporary instruments of communication.*

The senders are a very small class of human beings made up of two closely associated subclasses. The first of these is a very small group, since it includes merely the highest echelons of business executives who direct the manufacturing, management, and use of calculating machines and the communication networks. This subclass, because of stockholders' funds put at their disposal, has the wherewithal to purchase and then control these increasingly expensive cybernetic and communicative gadgets. The other closely associated subclass is composed of the highest military decision-makers and heads of sim-

---

* The first third of what follows originally appeared as "The Human Communicants in Communication Engineering" in *The Journal of Communication,* Vol. XI, No. 4, December, 1961, pp. 202–204.

ilarly "hush-hush" research corporations who, thanks to taxpayers' federal funds put either directly or indirectly via the military at their disposal, are also able to buy and direct the use of these expensive machines.

The receivers are a very large group. These embrace all the rest of mankind.

What has to be realized, also, is that the manufacturers of calculating machines are already at the major breakthrough point in their research at which these teleological mechanisms are being transformed from merely calculating into "creatively imaginative" problem-solving machines. What this may mean is that, whereas in the past we have had to wait several decades and even centuries for basic technical problem-solving men of genius, such as Eudoxus, Chrysippus, Aristotle, Newton, Maxwell, Gibbs, Einstein, and Heisenberg, to appear, these mechanisms, because of their even greater cost, are going to be put in the hands of these very few business and military men, subject only to the democratic control of that rubber-stamping farce called a stockholders' meeting and, in the case of the hush-hush military, not even to that; and these men are going to possess the most advanced and informationally confirmed ideas in the world.

That these developments raise moral, legal, and political problems that have yet to be even envisaged by the overwhelming majority of mankind who are on the receiving end of what is called communication engineering, hardly needs to be pointed out. It is to the credit, however, of at least some of the business and military leaders that they are sensitive to the human moral, legal, and political aspects of this situation and the human moral and legal responsibility, which they, personally, and their firms and military establishments, carry. The recent experiences of the executives in the electric utility manufacturing industries are likely to make them even more aware of this responsibility.

It must be said, also, in fairness to one, at least, of the

firms involved in this recent moral and legal scandal, that the research department of its management division has been working on a theory of management in which the latest research by philosophers and lawyers on the criteria of moral goodness and legal justice are being combined with the technological efficiency of the manufacturing division and high-pressure communication of its sales department. The plain fact probably is, therefore, that few manufacturing firms, whose moral and legal skirts are at present "clean," have such an advanced theory of management, even on the research planning board. Until such an approach to business, law, and ethics is both taught in our business and law schools and incorporated in the living practice of both our business and our military establishments and also in the foreign policy decisions of our federal government, it is unlikely that these moral and legal problems of our contemporary technological predicament will be resolved.

But this is only one piece of the problem. In addition to these narrowly controlled computing and creative thinking machines and their allied broadcasting networks, there are also the Pavlovian conditioned-reflex and Professor B. F. Skinner's learning-theory techniques of the behavioristic psychologists. These techniques are in the hands not merely of the aforementioned small group of top military and business decision-makers, but also in those of the not too morally scrupulous publicity officers of the successive Presidents of our federal government and the Madison Avenue advertising men whose offices are often, for obvious reasons, in the same buildings with the broadcasting corporations. The nature of the techniques of both Pavlov and Professor Skinner is that, unless one is a very sophisticated person with respect to the most difficult of all questions—the question whether moral, legal, and political decisions are significantly true or false —the users of these techniques are likely, quite innocently and unconsciously, to treat the human beings on the re-

ceiving end of the communication networks after the manner in which Pavlov treated his dogs, and American behavioristic psychologists treat their experimental guinea
pigs. In short, one treats each human being as if he or
she were a pawn or mere means; and this, as Kant saw, is
to be immoral. It is also to do something that is unjust
and illegal, even though our present laws do not make it
so. In other words, it is to behave toward people in a
way that is incompatible with the moral, legal, political,
and religious ideals of free men and women in the Free
World.

That such is the case is shown by the behavior of the
aforementioned business and military men and the behavioristic conditioned-reflex psychologists themselves. They
jolly well do not allow themselves to be put at the receiving end of the communicating process in the position
of Pavlov's dog or one of their guinea pigs. Hence, without realizing it or stating it consciously in their scientific
publications, they presuppose the existence of moral, legal, political, and religious, freely assenting and dissent-
ing human beings, so far as they themselves are concerned,
even though the rest of us have not yet awakened to this
fact.

The time, therefore, has come for the rest of us to
wake up and to awaken them to the overt consciousness
of the moral, legal, political, and religious standards of
free assent and dissent, which they themselves unconsciously practice and insist upon being applied to themselves. We, like them, are not Pavlovian dogs, but freely
assenting moral, legal, political, and religious human beings. Hence, the moment is here for all of us to treat one
another this way. In short, in communication engineering,
as in everything else, the individual person must be
treated as an end and not as a means.

If this is to occur, the two different kinds of facts, noted
in Chapter 1, must never be confused. They were: (1)
The nonman-made facts of nature and the naturalistic

part of any human being, and (2) the man-made artifacts of culture and artifactual human personality and bodily behavior.

The necessity of this distinction, let it be recalled, is that facts *qua* facts merely are, and are, therefore, incapable of being in error; error being meaningful only for beliefs which may be true or false with respect to what the facts are. Consequently, only for man-made cultural artifacts and the artifactual part of human behavior which is the causal effect of human cognitive beliefs that may be true or false, is it meaningful to hold a person responsible for what he or she does, or to say of any particular person's behavior that it is good or bad, legally or politically just or unjust, or religiously evaluatable as virtuous or sinful. This also is why it is nonsensical to say of the behavior of the planets, moving in their ellipsoidal orbits, that they are naughty and ought to be moving in orbits which are rectangular, doing a "squads right" at each corner.

Similar nonsense is unavoidable in our evaluative judgments of another person's or another nation's behavior, unless this distinction between naturalistic and artifactual behavior is kept constantly in mind. Otherwise, in criminal law, for example, one falls into one or the other of the two following errors: (1) Treating the culturally artifactual part of human behavior as if it were a naturalistic fact only, the conclusion is reached that there is no such thing as criminal guilt or innocence, but merely naturalistic sickness or health, and that, therefore, every defendant in a criminal trial should be sent to a hospital rather than to jail, just as if he had merely broken his leg due to having been swept off his feet by a tornado. Conversely, (2) treating the naturalistic, first-order factual causes of human behavior as if they were second-order, human belief-caused artifacts, defendants are judged to be guilty of crimes and are then sent to jail or even to the electric chair, when nature's temporally antecedent causal sequences, rather than the defendants' themselves, were responsible for what they did.

We shall find also, in subsequent chapters, that one of the major reasons why so many people are confused and demoralized in their personal moral or religious, as well as their legal and political, judgments and have, as a consequence, missed life's meaning, is that these two different kinds of facts have not been distinguished. Nor are lay folk the only ones to have fallen into this serious error. Since the time of Kant, the culturally artifactual humanities, including ethics, religion, law, and politics, have been treated autonomously, as if their "facts" were the same as those of the natural sciences. (Many cultural anthropologists still illustrate this same state of mind.) Then, as happened historically, the distinction arises between the *Naturwissenschaften* and the equally independent or autonomous *Geistenwissenschaften,* i.e., sciences of culture, society, and the humanities. Forthwith, it becomes impossible for modern man to get his moral, legal, political, or religious evaluative judgments into any meaningful working relation with his naturalistic beliefs or his nervous system and his body, since, on this "theory" they have no connection.

Also, when the present humanistic cultural artifact of incompatible moral, legal, political, religious, and anti-religious post-Kantian humanistic and national philosophies and their respective incompatible moral, legal, and political artifactual ways are faced, as today they have to be faced, the results are all too evident. Instead of these "autonomous," supposedly self-warranting subjects having saved morals, law, politics, and religion, everyone has been left either demoralized or self-righteously and dangerously dogmatic to, or beyond, the point of an atomic cold war.

Nor is the reason hard to find: an autonomous religion, law, politics, or humanism self-warrants these subjects, to be sure, but with every possible content that they have exhibited throughout the whole of human cultural history —the religious sexual orgies of a tribe in the bush equally with a "High Church" mass; the artifactual beliefs and national ways of atheists or agnostics equally with those of religious saints, and of nations that place their "trust in God"; the legal and political norms and practices of Communist nations equally with those of the free democracies; and theocratic, constitutional monarchies or Islamic caliphates equally with warring African tribesmen. The situation is not unlike that of the farmer who, after praying for rain through a long drought and finding not merely his parched crops but also their soil being washed away in a tempestuous cloudburst and flood, turned back to prayer, saying: "Yes, God, it's true I prayed for rain, but this has become ridiculous."

Clearly, the trouble with autonomous social sciences and humanities is that they are second-order artifactual subjects, and to treat such a subject matter as autonomous or self-warranting is to confuse second-order facts with first-order ones beyond which there is no appeal. The consequence is to leave one with no outside standard of reference for judging between the artifactual behavior and customs of one humanist, one nation, or culture, or one religious faith and another.

The pre-Kantian scientists and humanists of the ancient, medieval, and early modern Western world fell into no such personal, religious, moral, and cultural relativism and confusion, even though they may have committed other errors. This occurred because they realized the necessity of distinguishing the nonman-made facts of nature and the naturalistic part of human nature from the cultural artifacts and the artifactual man-responsible part of human behavior with which the religious or secular humanists, lawyers, judges, and politicians are concerned. In fact, their reference to any educational institution of higher education as a *University of the Arts and the Sciences* arose precisely in order to prevent confusing the artifacts making up the subject matter of "the Arts" with the non-man-made facts comprising the subject matter of "the Sciences." In pre-Kantian traditional usage, therefore, law, politics, ethics, literature, the fine arts, and cultural anthropology fell under "the Arts" rather than "the Sciences."

This did not mean, however, that "the Arts," including ethics, law, politics, and culturally relative religions, were autonomous. Nor did it mean that the religious or secular humanists who pursued "the Arts" were any the less factual, and, in this sense, scientific, with respect to their artifactual subject matter than the natural scientists and natural philosophers were with respect to their naturalistic facts. Quite the contrary. They realized, for reasons given earlier in this chapter which we, being "from Missouri," came upon quite independently, that there is no meaning for the normative words "good," "bad," "just," "unjust," "beautiful," "ugly," "sinful," or "virtuous" in their artifactual subject matter, except as these artifacts are the causal effects of human beliefs concerning the facts of the natural sciences and naturalistic philosophy, law, and religion, which may or may not be in error. Hence their name "the Arts," or what Aristotle called "Practical Wisdom," for what we today call the humanities or the cultural and normative social sciences, and their restriction of "the Sciences" to what we call the natural sciences and their naturalistic philosophy.

This is the reason why Aristotle and the ancients generally, whether Democriteans, Platonists, or Greek and Roman Stoics, affirmed that there were but three sciences: one, mathematics, which for them was an abstraction from physics; two, physics; and three, theology in the sense of naturalistic theology, i.e., the natural science which, by studying only the nonman-made facts of nature and of nonman-made human nature, determines whether there is any empirically testable naturalistic meaning for the claims of religion. The latter important question will be the major concern of our final chapters.

Since it is the generally accepted contemporary usage to apply the word "science" not merely to the subject matter of the natural sciences but also to the artifactual subject matter of the cultural sciences and the humanities, it is important that we have a more contemporary terminology for designating and distinguishing between (1) naturalistic facts and (2) the humanists' and social scientists' cultural artifacts. To this end we shall henceforth refer to the nonman-made naturalistic species of fact as first-order facts and to the artifactual species as second-order facts. This is appropriate since the latter are the causal effects in human personality and behavior of descriptive beliefs concerning first-order facts.

It is important to realize, if insoluble paradoxes are not to occur, that an indicative descriptive sentence about first-order facts is a sentence of a different type than one about second-order facts. This is the point of the chapter entitled "The Theory of Types and the Verification of Ethical Theory" in the writer's aforementioned *Complexity of Legal and Ethical Experience*. The failure to realize that the evaluative judgments embodied in second-order facts are meaningless, apart from an implicit cognitive statement concerning first-order facts, has resulted in several of the ablest philosophical analysts of our day, men such as Professors Charles L. Stevenson and A. J. Ayer in philosophy and Professor Alf Ross in law, concluding that ethical, legal, and political or religious sentences are hortatory or persuasive rather than meaningfully true or false indicative sentences. This leaves everyone in the aforementioned humanistic relativism.

There are some common-sense reasons for the distinction between first-order and second-order facts. First, nature and its earth were here before there were any human beings on it to eat of the tree of natural knowledge. Second, as my philosophical colleague, Paul Weiss, has emphasized in his recent books, *The World of Art* and *Nine Basic Arts,* all cultural artifacts are made of nature's raw materials, and all artists create with their naturalistic bodies. This is true not merely of the architects' buildings, the statues of the sculptor, and the pigments and canvas of the painter or the books of the poets and the Bibles and rituals of those of religious faith, but also of the speech with one's tongue and mouth of any and all humanists, be they atheists, agnostics, or men and women of religious faith. None of the humanists made his own tongue or the logic built into the neural net with which he was born and without which there would be nothing in which to trap the impulses that are the neurophysiological correlates, as we indicated in Chapter 1, of our humanistic beliefs. Nor did any one of us make the genes in our biological cells or the initially empty circular neural nets in our brains.

Moreover, the present chapter began, and its major concern has been, with the instruments of communication. These instruments also are made by men from nonman-made naturalistic materials. Without the first-order facts and man's true or false cognitive beliefs concerning what they are, there would be no instruments of the communication engineer, nor would there be any second-order factual evaluative or descriptive judgments to communicate by means of them. Hence, second-order facts presuppose first-order ones, logically as well as historically in geological time.

We conclude, therefore, that life finds its moral, legal, political, and sinful or virtuous religious meaning in man's self-responsibility for his own descriptive judgments of the part of himself and nature that is not man-made. If, therefore, life is to have moral, legal, political, and religious meaning, man must have the freedom to take on such a responsibility.

Here we have the naturalistic first-order factual ground

and warrant for life's free democratic legal and political meaning. Also we see why Kant was correct (even though the synthetic *a priori* and autonomous humanistic reasons he gave for his conclusion are erroneous) when he said that the communicators in any communication must always treat other human beings as ends rather than means.

For a precise analytic statement of what this entails with respect to the judicial interpretation of the principle of religious and civil liberties in the early Bill of Rights of the American Constitution and for an unambiguous formulation of Kant's categorical imperative, together with the grounds for its moral, legal, and political validity, the reader is referred to the final chapters of the writer's *Complexity of Legal and Ethical Experience.*

There, also, will be found the syntactical linguistic and the first-order factual descriptive reasons, determinable by anybody anywhere, why both the law of Status white Christian religious, legal and political racialism of the Old American South and "the dictatorship of the proletariat" and "the people's democracy" of the Marxist Communists are morally, legally, politically, and religiously self-contradictory and, hence, false theories.

The important point, however, is the positive one. Apart from human beings who are free to entertain human beliefs about first-order facts, error is meaningless. Consequently, apart from the second-order artifactual human behavior and its artifacts, which are the causal effects of such freely acquired and assented to human beliefs, there is no meaning for any moral, legal, political, or religious evaluative judgment. But to treat human beings thus as freely knowing human beings, whose first-order factual naturalistic human nature is such that they are capable of being in error, is to treat them as ends rather than as means. It is also to realize that the human quest for knowledge for its own sake, irrespective of its practical consequences, is not merely instrumental to other "values," such as money-making or military might or economic power, but is the *sine qua non* apart from which any evaluative judgment, and hence any other value, is meaningless.

Does this mean that beauty is not a primary and ultimate value also? Only if truth with respect to first-order naturalistic facts exhibits nothing aesthetic. To see that this is not the case, it is necessary to distinguish within first-order facts between two different species of them. There is no better way to see why this is required than by considering the themes of the next two chapters.

3

SCIENCE IS MORE THAN ITS GADGETS

IN HIS FIRST inaugural address, President Eisenhower said, "Science seems ready as a final gift to confer upon us the power to remove all human life from this planet." Can science give us nothing more in this atomic age?

There is no more appropriate place to have in mind when answering this question than Cleveland, Ohio. For it was there, in its Case Institute of Technology, that the first-order experimental fact was discovered which, when reflected upon by Einstein, led him to the theory which implied that the release of atomic energy would be practical. I refer, of course, to the experiment performed there in 1885 by Michelson and Morley.

This experiment shook modern physics to its very foundations. It did this by revealing a directly sensed image, having to do with what the physicists call "interference fringes." This fact simply should not be present if space and time are what traditional modern science and common sense suppose. It took twenty years before Einstein brought scientific theory into accord with this experimental fact by modifying the elemental assumptions of

63

both Newton's mechanics and Maxwell's electromagnetics in the manner specified by the Special Theory of Relativity.

Why was this speculatively discovered theory accepted? There were three very good reasons.

First, it was, and still remains, the only theory that the speculative intellects of anyone anywhere have been able to bring forward, which accounts both for the results of the Michelson-Morley experiment and the observable facts that the theories of Newton's mechanics and Maxwell's electromagnetics accounted for. In short, Newton's and Maxwell's theories come out of Einstein's Special Theory as special cases of it.

Second, there were certain astronomically observed phenomena which Newton's theory left a mystery. It followed logically from the speculatively discovered theory of Einstein that these directly observed images in the astronomer's telescope should be when, where, and what they are directly seen to be.

Third, it also followed logically from the speculative assumptions of Einstein's theory that, if an astronomer located his telescope and its camera at a certain point on the earth's surface and directed it at the sun during an eclipse, specific images would be found on the camera's photographic plate which would be different from the images to be expected, were Newton's theory the correct one. An English astronomer went to Africa, pointed his telescope and its camera under the circumstances prescribed, and returned to Cambridge to develop its photographic plate. The astronomer's name was Eddington. His report was first given before his fellow British scientists in London. Whitehead has described the occasion as follows:

> It was my good fortune to be present at the meeting of the Royal Society in London when the Astronomer Royal for England announced that the photographic

plates of the famous eclipse, as measured by his colleagues in Greenwich Observatory, had verified the prediction of Einstein that rays of light are bent as they
pass in the neighbourhood of the sun. The whole atmosphere of tense interest was exactly that of the Greek
drama: we were the chorus commenting on the decree
of destiny as disclosed in the development of a supreme
incident. There was dramatic quality in the very stag-
ing:—the traditional ceremonial, and in the background
the picture of Newton to remind us that the greatest of
scientific generalisations was now, after more than two
centuries, to receive its first modification. Nor was the
personal interest wanting: a great adventure in thought
had at length come safe to shore.[1]

Forthwith every informed natural scientist and naturalistic philosopher knew two things: The first was that the
modern world had to be reconstructed at its basic theoretical foundations in the manner prescribed by Einstein's
theory. They knew also that this was but a beginning.
Thus, Einstein added his General Theory of Relativity,
and Whitehead saw that the reconstruction would not be
over until the modern man's conception of the humanities
and its humanistic philosophy had been transformed also.
The second thing that informed scientists knew was that
mankind would have some novel and exceptionally dangerous gadgets.

How did they know this? In Einstein's original paper,
which stated the elemental theoretical assumptions or postulates of his Special Theory of Relativity, he logically deduced from them a theorem called the Mass-Energy Equation. It tells us that the Newtonian law of the conservation
of mass does not hold universally, nor does the law of the
conservation of energy. Instead, the product of mass and
energy is conserved. This, together with the Mass-Energy
Equation, means that it is possible to derive energy directly from matter itself as well as from other stores of

energy. Moreover, the equation specifies that if energy could be so derived directly from mass, a leverage involving the square of the number 186,000 would be at one's disposal, making possible the release from a very small amount of matter of a tremendous amount of energy exceeding in quantity anything practical engineers had imagined previously even as a possibility. The actualization of this logical deduction from the speculatively discovered assumptions of Einstein's Special Theory of Relativity is the atomic age and its atomic bomb.

But, as noted just above, the first effect of Einstein's Special Theory of Relativity, which the Michelson-Morley experiment made necessary, was philosophical rather than technological in character. Philosophers and theoretical physicists alike had to revise their conception of the universe. The general public sensed this also. This was confirmed by the books which were best sellers between the First and Second World Wars. These books were by Jeans, Eddington, and Whitehead, among others. They expounded, in a preliminary way, some of the philosophical implications of Einstein's Special and General Theories of Relativity and the Quantum Mechanics of Planck, Schrödinger, and Heisenberg. Einstein's *The World As I See It* instances the same philosophical state of mind.

The fact that the first impact of recent physical science was philosophical in character points up a prevalent error committed by people unacquainted with science who write about its ethical and social consequences. Many fact-finding social scientists, who apparently know little about the speculative character and the indirect method of verification of the theories of natural science, also fall into this error. It arises from equating science with only one part of itself, the applied, practical part, or its purely fact-finding portion. Science has its basic theoretical assumptions and its philosophical part also.

It is important to realize that two questions can be asked of any theory in natural science. The experimental physicist and the engineer ask one of these questions; the theoretical physicist and the philosopher of science the other. Given any scientific theory which has been experimentally verified, such as Einstein's Special Theory of Relativity, the engineer asks: "What way of putting the raw materials of nature together, different from any ways we have known before, does this theory indicate to be possible?" This question is answered by logically deducing from its fundamental theoretical assumptions, as formulated by the theoretical physicists, the theory's logical and mathematical consequences. Einstein's derivation of his Mass-Energy formula from the basic premises of his Special Theory of Relativity is an example. The engineer then used this Mass-Energy formula as a guide to new ways of putting matter together, so that energy is derived from mass by the relation and quantitative amount which the formula specifies.

The philosopher and the theoretical physicist, on the other hand, ask a different question. Their question is: "This theory being verified experimentally, how does it require us to conceive of ourselves and our universe?" Its answer is found, not by looking at the logical and mathematical consequences of the scientific theory, but by examining and analyzing its elemental theoretical assumptions and the method by which the theory is discovered, constructed, and experimentally confirmed.

In the case of the experimentally verified theories of contemporary natural science, these assumptions are exceedingly abstract or formal. As will be shown in the next and later chapters, the Theory of Relativity, for example, requires us to reject the concept of space, time, and mass as substances and to think of them as relationally defined entities and events. Moreover, it revises our conception of the relation of space and time to one another and to matter. The result is a conception of objects in a public spatio-temporal world different from that of Maxwell, Newton, Aristotle, and also ordinary common sense. This is why a new, experimentally verified theory in mathematical physics gives us a new natural philosophy, i.e., a new and more factually correct set of basic trapped universals with which to conceive of the first-order factual data of our experience. We shall return to this point in our essay on science and recent literature.

Even more remarkable, the philosophical analysis of these verified theories provides a philosophy of man and his mind as the knower of nature. Such is the case because the empirically verified scientific theory tells us that the mind of man must be such as to discover and construct the theory in question and to possess the kinds of ideas which it contains explicitly in its elemental postulates and their logically deduced theorems and, implicitly, in the operational definitions that make its experimental verification possible. As will be shown in the next chapter, and as has been described in more detail by the writer in his *Logic of the Sciences and the Humanities,* these ideas are of, at least, two different epistemological kinds. In other words, they get their meanings in two quite different ways. Consequently, every verified theory in mathematical physics is, *ipso facto,* a verified philosophy of the mind's cognitively meaningful ideas.

Nor does the fact that all explicit scientific statements are descriptive mean that they are not also necessarily, even though implicitly, evaluative. For there is no science except as human beings pursue truth for its own sake, and truth is a value. In fact, if the humanist's words "virtue" and "vice" refer for their meaning, as Chapter 1 suggests, to man's eating from the tree of first-order factual knowledge concerning nature and his nonman-made human nature, then the natural scientist's quest for truth with respect to first-order facts may well be not merely the primary value, but the only one in terms of which the humanist's man-made, second-order artifactual cultural values may be either meaningfully or cognitively evaluated and judged when they conflict.

The neurophysiological considerations of Chapter 1 support this conclusion. Because of the causal relation between the impulses trapped in the reverberating circuits of any human being's nervous system, and the motor nervous responses that determine the person's behavior, it follows that when the introspective psychological correlate of an impulse, trapped in the target area of the cortex, is one's philosophy of natural science and of mind, the latter impulse functions normatively with respect to the motor behavioral response of the person's nervous system to a particular stimulus of the moment, reinforcing that particular possible motor response to the given sensory stimulus which is compatible with this set of trapped universals in the cortex and inhibiting or weakening any other motor response that is not so compatible. Consequently, although no empirically verified, descriptive theory of nature or first-order factual human nature, as tested by appeal to the data given on the sensory side of the nervous system, logically implies a normative "ought-to-be," any theory with positive truth value, when assented to and trapped in the target area of the cortex, does *physiologically entail* an "ought-to-be" for the motor neuronic responses.

De facto human behavior is the product, therefore, not merely of the stimulus but also of the trapped epistemic representatives of ideas that the individual triggers in the target area of his brain. In this difference between the final *de facto* behavior which is (a) the product of (1) one's philosophy and (2) the stimulus of the moment, and (b) the behavior as defined by (1) alone, conscience and its distinction between what ought to be and what one's behavior in fact is, finds part, at least, of both its introspected psychological and its epistemically correlated neurophysiological meaning.

In any event, science is not the normatively neutral or positively evil thing which so many contemporary humanists affirm it to be. Such seems to be the case only when, concentrating attention on nothing but its practical instru-

mental by-products, one overlooks its speculatively discovered, indirectly and experimentally confirmed theory
and then neglects (1) the philosophical analysis of the
explicit assumptions of this theory, (2) the creative mental
as well as observational methods by which it is obtained,
(3) the implicit philosophy of both nature, the mind's
ideas, and even (4) that paramount value called truth,
which such philosophical analysis exhibits and makes
explicit.

That the mind and its ideas are involved becomes evident when one notes that scientists, like everyone else,
have to express their observations and theoretical inferences and conclusions in words. Moreover, words *qua*
mere marks on paper, or spoken noises, will not do. Instead, words having meanings are required, and meanings
involve the mind and its ideas.

Otherwise again, error would be impossible; a meaningful set of words, such as "President Abraham Lincoln is
alive today," or "The electron in the hydrogen atom is
stationary relative to the nucleus," could not be false. Consequently, for confirmability or falsity for any descriptive
set of words to be possible, and for error to be possible,
the idea of the meaning of the words must be one thing
and the facts to which they purport to refer, something
else. But even if this were not the case, science requires
meaningful words, and words of any kind have to be
watched. The reason is that meaningful words are frequently difficult to distinguish from words that are meaningless or nonsensical.

Such is the case because wordy nonsense is often more
vivid and apparently meaningful than scientific language,
which is both meaningful and descriptively the case. The
words of the sentence of Einstein's Special Theory of
Relativity, with respect to the simultaneity of spatially separated events, seem to be meaningless to the layman upon
a first reading and to many humanists after many readings.
Nevertheless, when one seeks out the source and character

of the meaning of each word in the sentence, one finds not only that the words of this sentence have a very precise meaning with surprising empirical consequences if this meaningful idea in one's mind be true, but also that empirical crucial experiments have shown it to be uniquely confirmed. The sentences "Electrons are pink," "Squares are round," "Sweetness is square," or "Physical might is politically right" are, on the other hand, much more vivid and apparently meaningful if one may judge by the frequent utterance of some of them by professors and politicians in high places. Nevertheless, if we take each word in any one of these vivid sentences and trace it to its specific kind of meaning, it turns out that each of these sentences as a whole is a meaningless combination of words.

Consequently, unless continuously watched and disciplined by meticulous semantic and epistemological analysis, words have a tendency, like carefree and undisciplined children, to start out in a meaningful manner and then go off on their own, getting both themselves and us into bad company. The sign of being in such bad company shows in each one of the vivid sentences above. Nonsense is the result. Each sentence has this character because it puts words in the same sentence, the meanings of which refer to different semantic or epistemological worlds of discourse.

The reason why the sentence "Physical might is politically right" is nonsensical should be evident from the distinction between first-order and second-order facts made in the previous chapter—the former being merely descriptive, the latter also normative. The words "physical might" are first-order factual, naturalistic words. They mean, therefore, facts of which it is meaningless to say that they are right or wrong. "Politically right," on the other hand, has only a second-order factual reference and, consequently, is meaningfully identified with, or predicable of, second-order artifactual human behavior, i.e., of human behavior that is the causal effect of first-order factual beliefs that may or may not be in error. Since physical might *qua* physical might is incapable of error, to say that might is right is as ridiculously nonsensical as to say that the planet Mars is right or that doorknobs are naughty.

But what of the sentences "Electrons are pink," "Squares are round," and "Sweetness is square"? Why are they also a meaningless association of words?

Clearly, the answer is not that one of the words in each sentence refers to a second-order fact and the other to a first-order one. Such is the case because second-order factual evaluative words, such as "right," "wrong," "good," "bad," "just," or "unjust," do not appear in any of these sentences. The answer would seem to be, therefore, that even with respect to nonevaluative words about first-order facts, there must be first-order factual words of different species referring to semantically or epistemologically different worlds of discourse. Otherwise, nonsense could never be the result of predicating one descriptive word of another.

Since the word "electron" in the sentence "Electrons are pink" is a concept in the mathematical language of mathematical physics, and the word "pink" is a word in ordinary language that is used by both a layman and a physicist when they refer to a directly sensed color, the words of the physicist's mathematical language and those of ordinary language must refer to semantically and epistemologically different worlds of discourse. Does semantic and epistemological analysis show this to be the case?

This question makes the topic of the next chapter important. It is of interest also in its own right.

4

KORZYBSKI'S SEMANTICS AND
MATHEMATICAL PHYSICS

IT IS EASY to overlook the degree to which the facts of our experience are mediated to us through language. Consequently, if our language does not fit the directly experienced or correctly inferred facts, we corrupt human experience in the very act of stating what it is. If, therefore, we are to find life's meaning instead of a linguistic distortion of it, we must watch words with as much care as we give to what they are trying to say. This is especially the case for anyone whose ordinary language is of the Aryan type. We now know that neither the immediately apprehended facts of our experience nor the scientific objects, events, and their relations which we correctly infer from them, conform to the syntax of any Aryan language, be it English, German, French, Spanish, Greek, Latin, or Hindu Sanskrit. The three people who have done the most to make us aware of this are Korzybski, Whitehead, and Wittgenstein. Whitehead's attempt to fit English prose to concrete experience will concern us in Chapter 11. Wittgenstein's genius will be analyzed in Chapters 11 and 17.

The first remark * which Count Korzybski made at the luncheon given in his honor when he came to New Haven for the Yale Semantics Colloquium was that he was honored to be there because Yale had produced Willard Gibbs. In saying this, he gave expression to the standard used by European thinkers in judging scientists. To the European, the outstanding scientist is not the mere fact-finder, nor even the experimentalist, but the theoretical, mathematical scientist who finds the basic, deductively formulated, axiomatically constructed entities and relations in terms of which the described particulars and the experimental data can be brought together within a formal mathematical theory. Democritus and Eudoxus were such scientists in ancient Greece. Newton was such a scientist of the modern world. One has but to read his *Principia* to see that it is a deductively formulated theory like Euclid's *Elements*. Clerk Maxwell did the same thing for electricity, magnetism, and optics, bringing them together under a single, deductively formulated set of basic assumptions. Einstein in our century has a similar rating because, in his Special Theory of Relativity, he reconstructed the theoretical foundations of both mechanics and electromagnetics and, in his General Theory of Relativity, he based gravitational and mechanical theory on novel, deductively formulated assumptions. Professors Schrödinger, Dirac, and Heisenberg have done the same thing for contemporary quantum mechanics.

These scientists did their creative work in Europe. In the late 19th century Willard Gibbs achieved, for the science of physical chemistry, what they accomplished later for mechanics, electromagnetics, and quantum theory. This is why L. J. Henderson and European thinkers regarded Gibbs as America's greatest scientist.

One remarkable thing about Gibbs' accomplishments is —the story goes—that he never studied a physical or

---

* The first part of what follows was printed in the *General Semantics Bulletin,* 1955, pp. 1–8, under the title "Mathematical Physics and Korzybski's Semantics."

chemical system more complicated than ice water. His famous phase rule came from an observation and the axiomatic mathematical formulation of the gaseous, liquid, and solid phases of water. He formalized mathematically these phase relationships of any physicochemical system. He also noted the central importance of the second law of thermodynamics and related his physicochemical reflections to that cardinal principle. At the same time, he inaugurated the shifting of the concept of law in physics from the absolute to the statistical type. So remarkable was the genius of this man that today many contemporary mathematical physicists, as for example Professor Norbert Wiener, believe that no scientist's ideas have stood the test of time, during the revolutionary changes in scientific theory which have been made in this century, as have those of Willard Gibbs.

The fact that Count Korzybski singled out Gibbs must be significant for a proper understanding of Count Korzybski's semantics. He could hardly have paid such tribute to this great American scientist had he not approved the type of cognitive scientific concepts which Willard Gibbs used. But, if this be true, then the frequent expositions of Korzybski's semantics, as entailing the clarification of the meaning of any word in terms of the inductively given, concrete images of particulars, must be rejected as a false, or, at the very least, an excessively partial account of his semantics. Certainly to attempt to understand the axiomatically constructed, mathematically formulated, statistical mechanics and physical chemistry of Willard Gibbs in terms of sensed water[1], sensed water[2], sensed water[3], sensed water[4], would be ridiculous. Yet it is precisely this which those expositors who talk about Cow[1], Cow[2], Cow[3], etc., have attempted to do with Korzybski's semantic theory of conceptual meaning. Were the latter interpretation correct, we would be at a loss to explain the frequent quotations in his books from Gibbs, Newton, Einstein, and Poincaré.

This does not mean that there are no concepts whose

meanings are exhausted in concrete images or in immediately sensed particulars, after the manner of "Cow" in the sense of the immediately apprehended image Cow^1, the immediately apprehended image Cow^2, the immediately apprehended image Cow^3, etc. Clearly, all concepts in science which refer completely for their meaning to immediately apprehended things must be analyzed in this nominalistic, existential manner to clarify their meanings. Count Korzybski knew that there are such concepts, since he was aware of the natural history sciences which describe flowers or birds in terms of their immediately sensed shapes and colors. He also knew that we possess the ordinary words "yellow," "blue," "red," "green," etc., where by these words one means the immediately sensed, particular images which bear these nominalistic names.

But Korzybski's respect for scientists like Gibbs, Newton, Maxwell, Poincaré, and Einstein shows also that he was aware of the axiomatically constructed, deductively formulated concepts of mathematical physics which are of a quite different type. Their meanings are obtained in a novel way. They cannot be clarified by reduction to particular images, such as Cow^1, Cow^2, Cow^3, etc.

The problem, therefore, of understanding Korzybski's semantics is much more complex than many of his simple-minded expositors have supposed. It requires a clarification of the type of conceptual meaning which appears in mathematical physics, as well as of that which is present in the more purely inductive, natural history sciences, in impressionistic painting, and in so much of common-sense experience.

In order to carry through this enlarged and more complicated clarification of meaningful concepts, the writer has found it necessary to have different names for the two foregoing types of concepts, which appear in science, and which Korzybski's semantics includes. Let us call them "concepts by intuition" and "concepts by postulation." The definitions of each species, which follow, are important.

The type of concept of which the immediately sensed color denoted by the word "yellow," and the Cow[1], Cow[2], Cow[3] images are examples, is appropriately called a "concept by intuition." *A word is a concept by intuition if its entire meaning derives from something that can be immediately apprehended inductively.* Since what we apprehend with immediacy inductively is always a concrete particular succeeded by another perhaps similar, but in some sense different, concrete particular, such concepts, when they are class concepts, are nominalistic rather than real universals. To assert that a concept is a nominalistic universal is to say that the all-ness or universality of the commonness of the particulars which the class concept conveys, belongs to the symbol and not to the things that are symbolized. What the symbol refers to is a set of successive, particular images, each one of which is unique; not merely unique in itself but also unique in the sense of being relative to the particular percipient who senses it. Since concepts by intuition refer, therefore, to such unique particulars, their meaning becomes clarified only when the succession of particular, immediately apprehended or apprehendable images is specified. For concepts by intuition in the radically empirical sense defined above, the semantic analysis in terms of temporally successive Cow[1], Cow[2], Cow[3], Cow[4] unique particular images is correct.

Since the concepts of mathematical physics are axiomatically constructed in the postulates of a deductively formulated theory, it seems equally appropriate to call them "concepts by postulation." *A concept by postulation is a concept whose meaning in whole or part is proposed for it imagelessly and syntactically by the axiomatically constructed postulates of a specific, deductively formulated theory.* "Red" in the sense of the constant number of a wave length in the deductively formulated theory of electromagnetics of Maxwell is an instance. The concept of electron in the deductively formulated, mathematical electromagnetics of Lorentz is another example. Clearly, the meaning of such concepts will be completely missed if one attempts to clarify them in terms of temporally successive, concrete, immediately apprehended images. Instead, to understand the meaning of any concept by postulation one must turn to the axiomatically constructed postulates and theorems of the deductively formulated theory in which the concept by postulation in question occurs.

I venture to introduce my own terminology, with its concepts by intuition and its concepts by postulation, in the present exposition of Korzybski's semantics because, at the aforementioned Yale luncheon, Korzybski turned to me and said that he had made a thorough reading of my *Logic of the Sciences and the Humanities,* in which this terminology was expounded, and found himself in complete agreement with it. He added that it is impossible to clarify conceptual meaning without paying attention to epistemology and to the different types of concepts to which the different epistemological ways of knowing give rise.

In order, therefore, to understand his semantics and the solution of many baffling problems in modern psychological science, philosophy, and popular thinking which it provides, it is necessary to distinguish a concept by intuition from its correlated concept by postulation in a concrete example. Consider a pitcher of ice water. It serves as the instance of a concept by intuition since we have our immediately apprehended images of it. It also suggested to Gibbs the concepts by postulation of his phase rule and his mathematical physical chemistry. In the sense of a concept by intuition, it is a set of sensed particulars. These particulars are its brightness, shininess, its sensed operational heaviness and shape, and its sensed coolness and wetness. Each one of these particular sensed images is relative not merely to the perceiver but also to particular sense organs of any given perceiver. For example, one cannot feel the shiny brightness of the water, and one cannot see its wetness. Furthermore, if one feels the water with a left hand which comes from touching a solid cake of ice, the water feels warm, whereas if one touches it with a right hand which comes from the ordinary temperature of the room's atmosphere, the water feels cold. Berkeley expressed this relativity of any immediately sensed object or image to percipients and to particular sense organs by saying that for them *esse est percipi,* i.e., to be is to be perceived by a particular perceiver. This is the nature of the subject matter of any concept by intuition.

Were concepts by intuition the only meaningful words which we possess, it follows that there would be no meaning for the ice water being here in the pitcher, when no percipient or particular percipient's sense organ has an immediately apprehended image of it. Yet you and I certainly believe that the pitcher and water would be here on the table if no one were present in the room. We believe also that the stars and planets move on in their courses during the night and would continue to do so if everyone were asleep. An analysis of the meaning of words, which reduces all meaning to particular images, leaves one with a semantics which provides no meaning for these common-sense beliefs.

Is it possible to make the common-sense belief in external objects semantically meaningful? In the beginning of his *Principia,* Newton answers in the affirmative. After pointing out that sensed objects and sensed space and time are relative to particular perceivers and to their particular sense organs, he added that there is a space and a time which is the same for all perceivers and which would exist were no one present or looking. Public space and time, Newton called "mathematical space and time." This was but another way of saying that public space and time are known only by means of the axiomatically constructed concepts by postulation of Euclid's geometry and Newton's *Principia.*

What do we mean by a scientific object in such a theory? The mathematicians and the mathematical logicians, who know the methods by which the entities of mathematical physics are given their precise scientific meanings, provide us with the answer to this question. For a mathematician or a mathematical logician an entity, when considered by itself in isolation, is a bare x. x by itself means "any one." But how, then, is the entity x, which is to signify any one electron, to be distinguished from other kinds of x? The answer is to be found in the formal, imageless properties of the relations within which x functions as a term. To be an electron is to be an entity which can be an x in relations which have the formal properties of the postulates of the electron theory of Lorentz or his successors. To understand a scientific object which is a concept by postulation in deductively formulated mathematical physics, one must concentrate not on the object but on the formal properties of the relations in which it is a term. Hence to grasp the meaning of entities which are designated by concepts by postulation, it is of the essence that one must *think relationally,* imagelessly and, therefore, by means of the intellect, rather than the images of the senses or the sensuously nourished imagination.

But how is such imageless relational thinking to be achieved? Consider the following elementary example of an axiomatically constructed relation R. For any entities x and y let it be asserted that R relates x to y. Expressed in the symbolism of mathematical logic, this gives:

Postulate I (x, y) : $x \, R \, y$, where the x, y in parentheses are called *universally quantified variables.* This means that *any* two entities in the entire subject matter of the science are connected by a relation, the other relational properties of which we do not yet know. Even so, Postulate I entails that the scientific events and objects are not chaotic, disconnected atoms. Instead they are terms in an organic relatedness. To grasp fully this elementary point, which few did, as a later chapter will show, until Ernst Mach in the 19th century, is to understand field physics and to realize also, as Mach and Einstein later were the first to do, that Newton's so-called "particle physics" is field physics. When a relation R has the formal property of Postulate I, then all the many-termed relational entities x, y, z . . . , whether they be "infinite" or "finite" in "number," comprising the field of R are *connected* and R is a universal field equational or connective law.

The additional postulates of any scientific and philosophical theory *of this concept by postulation* type then give the scientific objects and events in the field of R their additional scientific properties. This is done, not directly by predicating properties of them (as does naïve realistic substance-property, Aryan ordinary language thinking and describing), but indirectly by relationally assigning additional imageless formal properties to R. Let us now illustrate this by means of a simple elementary example which the writer learned first from Professor Sheffer at Harvard University in his seminar on The Logic of Relations.

Postulate II (x): not (x R x), where (x), being universally quantified, means "for all x in the field of R."

Postulate II asserts that R is an inreflexive relation. A relation is inreflexive when it does not hold between any entity and that entity itself. "Father of" is an example. No man is father of himself.

Let Postulate III assert that for any x and any y, if x R y, then not y R x. Expressed in the symbolism of mathematical logic, this gives:

Postulate III (x, y): (x R y) and not (y R x).

Postulate III asserts that the relation R is an insymmetrical relation. A relation is insymmetrical if, holding between x and y, it does not hold between y and x. "Wife of" is an example.

Let Postulate IV assert for any entities, x, y, z, that if R holds between x and y and R holds between y and z, then R holds between x and z. Expressed in the symbolism of mathematical logic, this gives:

Postulate IV (x, y, z): (x R y) and (y R z): implies: (x R z). Postulate IV asserts that R is a transitive relation. A relation R is transitive if, holding between x and y and between y and z it also holds between x and z. "Earlier than" is an example.

What scientific properties does the relation R, as axiomatically constructed by the four foregoing postulates, give any entity in the field of R? The answer is unequivocal and may be put concretely as follows: Consider a group of bare entities having no specified relation to one another. What happens to these entities when they become terms in an axiomatically constructed relation which has the formal properties of Postulates I, II, III, and IV above? The entities become ordered in a series. Postulates I, II, III, and IV, therefore, define a serial relation. They also have the effect of turning any entities of such a relation into serially ordered entities.

By making the formal properties of R more and more complex, the properties of any scientific objects which have R as their relation to one another become more and more complex and restricted. In this way, scientific objects of any degree of complexity can be constructed.

It is to be noted that nowhere in their scientific meaning is any appeal made to immediately sensed objects, relations or images. It is by this means that man is able to arrive at the concept of an object which exists independently of sensed images which are relative to perceivers. It was by this means also that Newton provided meaning for a public world, the same for all perceivers. Einstein follows Newton in this regard. This will be shown in Chapter 14 where the meaning of the Principle of Relativity, which is common to Newton's and Einstein's physics, is made evident.

The concept of serial order in its imageless, many-termed relational concept by postulation meaning is very important. Without it, the Democritean, Platonic, Stoic, and modern concept of (1) "number" and (2) a mathematical "limit" cannot be understood. It is necessary to say something about these two words. Both involve the imageless, relational concept of serial order.

The latter concept is a many-termed, not a two-termed, relation. This fact will turn out to be of great importance when we attempt, in Chapter 11, to find a language that will not distort the facts of our immediate concrete aesthetic experience in the very act of stating what they are. Furthermore, the relata of such a many-termed relation may be, and in mathematical physics usually are, infinite in number.

This does not mean, however, that relations are defined in terms of numbers. Quite the contrary. Instead, numbers are imageless, concept by postulation, relationally and serially ordered entities also. Otherwise, the distinction between natural, rational, irrational, and real numbers, and the different species of infinites in which they fall, would be meaningless.

The concept of serial order is an elementary idea also in the concept of limit. Even Newton, who was aware that his mathematical theory of nature required this concept, failed to give a relationally clear concept by postulation analysis of what the word "limit" means. This remained for 19th-century mathematicians, such as Weierstrass and Dedekind, to accomplish. Although the aforeshown concept of serial order is part of what the word "limit" means, any term in the serial order is not the term that is the limit. Instead, within the field of any serially ordered relation, its entities may be divided into two classes, which we shall call A and B. When class B has a first term and is approached asymptotically (i.e., never reached) by the unending serially ordered entities in class A, then the first term in class B is the *limit* of the series of terms in class A. This many-termed relational concept of limit will take on climactic importance at the end of this book.

The three postulates above are preceded by entity variables in parentheses. These entity variables in their parentheses are called by mathematical logicians "universally quantified variables." This amounts to the assertion that the relation R holds not for some of the "epistemic correlates" of these entities, but for all of them. This means that to be a scientific object in axiomatically constructed mathematical physics is to be an instance of a universal relation or law. Such entities are real, rather than nominalistic, universals. They are not unique particulars, since the sole scientific meaning which they possess is a meaning prescribed by being an entity in a universally quantified relation or law. Their theoretical scientific properties have nothing to do, therefore, with inductively sensed images, nor with unique particulars.

Expressed in the language of ancient Greek and medieval natural science and its philosophy, this means that the Aristotelian and Thomistic dictum that there are no ideas in the intellect, which are not first in the senses, is erroneous. It entails also that Kant's dictum, to the effect that concepts without percepts are empty, while, in part, true, needs serious qualification. Instead, the logically realistic theory of knowledge of the Democritean, Platonic, and Stoic natural scientists, philosophers, lawyers, and natural theologians is not merely the one required and present in the concepts and method of modern mathematical physics, but it is also the only one, as subsequent chapters will show in greater detail, that gives empirically confirmed meaning to our common-sense belief in external objects in a public spatio-temporal world. This Democritean, Platonic, Stoic, and modern semantic theory is that there are concepts in the intellect (i.e., concepts by postulation that, in whole or part, are imageless concepts by intellection) which are neither given first in the senses nor definable or conceivable imaginatively as associations or sequences of such imageful (i.e., nominalistic concept by intuition) ideas.

Stated in terms of the way we gain human knowledge, again using classical language, this also means that "the sense world suggests but does not (by abstraction) contain the real world." Here, the expression "the real world" means humanly knowable, public objects, events, and their relations and laws, which are invariant or the same for all knowers. Today's language for stating the same thesis is that science and its method of knowing use speculative and theoretically introduced hypotheses which are tried out, by trial and error, and confirmed only indirectly, via their deductive consequences, as tested in crucial experiments, against imageful, directly sensed (i.e., nominalistic concept by intuition) data.

This recent way of describing the hypotheses and method of first-order factual naturalistic descriptive knowledge has one serious limitation. It fails to make clear that the concepts in the hypotheses are (1) imageless relational constructs which do not derive their meaning from the images of the senses, rather than (2) concepts, the meaning of which is first in the senses or in some other factor that is experienced empirically with equal immediacy. It was precisely in order to avoid confusing the descriptive concepts of species (1) of Democritean, Platonic, Stoic, and modern mathematical physics, with those of species (2) of classical Asian and Aristotelian Western empirical science and philosophy, that the writer first introduced in *The Meeting of East and West* and in *The Logic of the Sciences and the Humanities* the expression "concepts by intuition" to denote descriptive words of species (2) and "concepts by postulation that are in whole or part concepts by intellection" to designate descriptive scientific and philosophical theories or hypotheses of species (1).

Misled, in all likelihood, by the present practice of suggesting that the semantic meaning and method of modern Western science is completely specified when its indirect method of empirically confirming its hypotheses is noted, the otherwise able student of Chinese science, Professor Joseph Needham, then fell into the *non sequitur* of concluding that because classical Chinese texts exhibit countless empirical scientific theories, Chinese science also pos-

sessed "concepts by postulation" in the writer's meaning
of these words. This led Professor Needham to affirm that
he had shown the main thesis of *The Meeting of East and
West* to be false. This erroneous inference upon his part,
resulting from the failure to distinguish between hypotheses
whose concepts are of species (1) and those of species (2),
is not surprising to anyone who is acquainted with Professor Needham's scientific work, since he made his reputation
as a biochemist largely because of his imageful, naïve
realistic "pattern theory" of organic compounds; he tends
also to be imagefully naïvely realistic in his political thinking, being like Feuerbach in this respect.

The necessity of distinguishing scientific theory built out
of concepts of species (2) from that constructed in terms
of descriptive words of species (1) is equally important if
we are not to misunderstand what Korzybski meant when
he attacked what he called "Aristotelian thinking." This
becomes evident when one notes that such thinking is a
special case of imageful thinking in which directly sensed
qualities, such as wet, dry, hot, cold, yellow, or pink, are
thought of as the persisting predicates of supposedly directly sensed substances or external objects.

To see why, one very frequent confusion must be
avoided. This confusion consists in supposing that the relatedness of axiomatically constructed scientific objects is
the relatedness of inductively given, concept by intuition,
sensed relations. For this to be true, the relatedness, for
example, of sensed images in sensed space and time would
have to be identical, or isomorphic, with the relatedness of
axiomatically constructed scientific objects in mathematical
space and time. Newton has already pointed out to us that
this is not the case. Our ordinary experience confirms his
judgment. The relatedness of sensed space is fuzzy. It is
one thing with one's glasses on; it is another thing with
them off. It is blurred and distorted before breakfast; it
becomes sharper after one or two cups of coffee. Sensed
space, furthermore, does not extend beyond the local

horizon. The relatedness of the space of mathematical physics is infinitely extended and in Newton's mechanics, Maxwell's electromagnetics, Gibbs' physical chemistry, and Einstein's Special Theory of Relativity, it has the same Euclidean mathematical properties everywhere and always. This makes it clear, therefore, that one cannot identify the relatedness between scientific objects of mathematical physics with the sensed relations of sensed objects of inductive natural history science or of common-sense awareness. In short, the concept by intuition relations are not to be confused with concept by postulation relations.

What, then, is the relation between the axiomatically constructed relatedness of the scientific objects of deductively formulated mathematical physics and the relativistic sensed relatedness of sensed objects in imageful natural history science and ordinary sense awareness? To clarify this point is to get to the heart of Korzybski's criticism of Aristotelian thinking.

According to Aristotelian thinking, sensed objects are related to the scientific objects of mathematical physics by the two-termed relation of predication. In Aristotle's physics, for example, the chemical and physical element "water" was defined as anything which is sensed to be wet and cold. "Air" was that which is sensed to be both wet and warm. Galilei had no difficulty in showing that such an "object" is not objective in the sense of being an external object that exists independently of its being perceived. He could have demonstrated this, as we have done previously, by pointing out that if one's hand comes to the water in the pitcher from the atmosphere of the room at its ordinary temperature, then to that sense organ coldness with wetness and, hence, water is present; whereas if one's hand comes to the contents of the pitcher from a cake of ice, then the substance in the pitcher is wet but not cold and is, therefore, not water but air. This relativity of all sensed qualities or objects to the perceiver, and even to different sense organs of the same perceiver, was the major semantic

consideration which led Galilei and Newton following him
to reject sensed qualities as the properties which define
either common-sense or scientific objects and the public
space-time in which they are located. It also put an end to
what Korzybski meant by Aristotelian thinking—whether
this thinking be indulged in by Aristotle, St. Thomas, the
Asian Charvakian materialists, Hobbes, Locke with his
directly sensed or introspected material and mental substances, Feuerbach, Marx, President Mao, Professor Needham, or you and me.

This is the point of the Korzybskian reduction of "Cow"
in its imageful concept by intuition meaning to the proper-
named, successively perishing images of Cow^1, Cow^2,
Cow^3, Cow^4, etc. This prevented any one of these images
from becoming thought of as permanently attached to a
purportedly sensed underlying substance called "the cow"
conceived as an external object in public space and time.

But if the relation between sensed imageful qualities,
objects, and events, denoted by nominalistic and personally
relativistic concepts by intuition, to the public objects and
spatio-temporal events, designated by imageless, intellectually known concepts by postulation, is not that of a
predicate of a substance, after the manner of Aristotelian
and the even more widespread Aryan linguistic type of
thinking, what, then, is the relation? Recent theoretical
physicists and philosophers who have analyzed the theory
and method of mathematical physics have come to a notable
agreement on the answer to this question. They have arrived at the answer in the following way. This relation
must be present in the method of mathematical physics itself. This method, in its postulates, involves, as we have
noted, imageless, axiomatically constructed relations which
are universally quantified with respect to the entities which
they scientifically define and relate. As such alone, however, the method of mathematical physics gives merely a
possible world; it does not designate an indirectly and ex-

perimentally confirmed theory of the actual world. Yet the theories of mathematical physics are experimentally confirmed theories. Consequently, in the experiment there must be implicitly present an unobservable relation joining the nominalistic concept by intuition images, which the experimenter directly senses, to the unobservable, purportedly present, concept by postulation designated objects and events of the theory being tested. Analysis has shown that what is required is a two-termed relation that is not always a one-one two-termed relation. As we have noted, however, it is not the two-termed relation of predication of Aristotelian and Aryan linguistic grammatical thinking. Instead, it has to be a two-termed relation which epistemologically joins the imageful entities, events, and relations of the concept by intuition world of discourse to the relational universally lawful entities of the imageless intellectual concept by postulation world of discourse.

Professor Henry Margenau has called these positive two-termed relations "rules of correspondence." The late Professor Hans Reichenbach called them "coordination-definitions" *(Zuordnungs definitionen)*. Because they are epistemological relations joining two semantically and epistemologically different worlds of discourse, the writer prefers to call them "epistemic correlations." The name is irrelevant, except as one name is more suggestive than another in indicating what is meant. A rose is a rose, whatever it be called.

In Part I of *Philosophical Anthropology and Practical Politics* the writer has given reasons for believing that, whereas when the object of knowledge is other than the knower, the two-termed epistemic correlations are many-one; in the case in which the knower is knowing himself, they are one-one. Hence, in the latter case only is the concept by intuition relatedness and its concept by postulation correlate isomorphic and, therefore, an identity. The manner in which this resolves the traditional modern body-mind problem and the problem of reconciling its concept of causality with self-initiating personal freedom and responsibility is to be found in the aforementioned book.

The question raised at the end of Chapter 2 can now be answered. It arose when we came upon descriptively worded sentences such as "Electrons are pink" and "Sweetness is square," which are clearly nonsensical; or, in other words, an association of words which independently are meaningful but which together are meaningless. Such sentences suggested that just as first-order facts must be distinguished from second-order artifacts, so within first-order facts, two different species of them with their respective languages referring to different worlds of discourse must be distinguished. The question at the end of Chapter 2, therefore, was: Does semantic and epistemological analysis show this to be the case? The answer is Yes.

5

POLITICS IS MORE THAN ITS POWER

WE COMMUNICATE with other people as nations, through the official acts of our politicians with respect to foreign policy, as well as person to person. Also, as shown in Chapter 2, life's contemporary meaning is inescapably and incurably international. Quite apart, therefore, from the danger of annihilation, due to a political bad judgment that sets off an atomic world war, our conception of foreign policy is very important.

It is well to approach this subject at the domestic level. The ancient nations were patriarchal joint-families, between whom there was no law, or they were warring tribes. The original meaning of the word "nation" is "tribe." Gradually, however, tribal international war was replaced by intertribal (i.e., international) law. So effective was this international law that its community soon regarded itself as domestic, and the word "nation" took on a new meaning. The Roman and the Holy Roman Empires were such new nations, as were the modern Hobbesian absolute nation-states which followed upon the decline of these empires. It is notable that in this decline, the Western world did not return to its original tribal nations. Hence, even the modern Hobbesian absolutely sovereign nations were in fact international legal and political communities.

Today, however, we are seeing the remarkable reversal of the traditional modern fragmentation of the Europe-embracing international legal, political, and economic community of the Empire period of Western artifactual history, into the traditional Machiavellian and Hobbesian absolutely sovereign and warring nation-states. Moreover, this reversal, which occurred first in the Continental European Union of the Six, and which is now engulfing Great Britain, has been achieved in a contractually democratic manner. This, Great Britain has learned the hard way. After trying to stand aloof from the legally and contractually constructed Continental European economic, military, atomic energy, and political community, she is now finding this to be a political impossibility. Faced also with possible runs on both the pound and the dollar, Great Britain and the United States are already pooling their currency reserves with other members of the Continental European and the Atlantic Communities. In fact, for all practical purposes, we are already operating our currency under an internationally federated reserve board. Hence, as the *Economist* of London suggested some months ago, whether we call these recent political developments by these words or not, effective international law and world government are already here, regionally, so far as Western Europe and, in part, even the wider Atlantic Union, are concerned. But where Great Britain goes, Canada, New Zealand, and Australia are likely to go also.

Need one wonder that Premier Khrushchev sees the point and has indulged in a minor fleabite, by way of a barbed-wire fence and a short, stone wall, in the futile attempt to divide the Western European federated legal and political community in the hope of turning back this remarkable movement which is now spreading to other parts of the world. The time has come for us to open our

eyes, look at what is before them, and get a realistic sense
of proportions concerning the obsolescence of the traditional Machiavellian and Hobbesian absolutely sovereign
nation-states, and the similar lack of realism in the unilateral power political theory of foreign policy that was
their instrument.

Traditionally, the latter theory had two versions, one of
which, in recent American politics, was represented by
former Secretary of State Dulles, the other by Ambassador
George F. Kennan. The former is appropriately called the
unilateral morally and religiously based power-political
theory of foreign policy; the latter, the unilateral morally
and religiously neutral power-political theory. The words
"unilateral" and "power-political" express the fact that the
two theories are more identical than different, as events
have proved. Both are unilateral, because each assumes
the absolutely sovereign Machiavellian and Hobbesian
nation-state in which justice is, by definition, the command
of an absolute national political sovereign. From this it
follows, as Hobbes, Austin, and their Anglo-American
legally positivistic followers affirm, that the expression
"international law" is a self-contradictory notion and,
hence, is a meaningless association of words. Consequently,
when the foreign policy commands of such absolutely
sovereign nations conflict, physical power, rather than law,
is the only meaningful court of appeal. Hence, the unilateral power-political theory of any nation's foreign policy.
The only question then becomes, whether, in "playing the
game" of unilateral power politics, one bases it on the
cultural morals and religion of one's own faith and nation
or not. The unilateral, moral, and religiously based theory
of foreign policy answers this question in the affirmative;
the alternative unilateral power-political theory, in the
negative.

If our choice is limited to one or the other of these two
theories, the decision has to be in favor of the latter al-

ternative. The reason, as experienced diplomats have seen, is that when one bases a Hobbesian nationalistic power-political foreign policy on the cultural moral customs and religions of one's own faith or nation, moral and international crusades generating war become likely. To what in practice is pure unilateral power politics, religion is added. Thus, instead of bringing foreign policy under moral and religious control, the effect is to prostitute morals and religion by making them the instruments of power politics.

Because many career diplomats and students supposed these to be the only possible theories of foreign policy, the *non sequitur* was inferred that to base foreign policy on the moral and religious beliefs of men is an error. Hence, the only realistic and practical policy for achieving even a temporary semblance of peace—long-run peace, because of power politics being impractical and unlikely—is to base our relation to foreign peoples and their cultures completely on something that is morally and religiously neutral, such as physical force. Hence, the one hundred percent power politics of this theory.

We have said that this prevalent contemporary notion is the result of a *non sequitur*. Why? The reason is that there is another alternative, as contemporary international political events are proving.

Its theory of foreign policy has two parts—the one regional, as we have just noted; the other world-embracing. Both parts derive from a lesson which the sciences of sociological jurisprudence and cultural anthropology have taught us. This lesson is that legal and political decisions are not likely to be effective unless they give expression to the underlying cultural customs of the people. It follows that where several modern nations, for all their differences, have cultural norms in common, an effective international, federated legal, and political community can be built, and the Hobbesian power-political European wars, repeating themselves in every generation, have a real chance of being eliminated. Hence, if one will seek out the common cultural norms, bringing them legally, economically, militarily, and atomic pool-wise into the foreground, a viable international political community can come into being. This is precisely what the elder political statesmen of Continental Europe—Schumann, De Gasperi, Spaak, Chancellor Adenauer, Jean Monnet, Guy Mollet, and many others—did. Part of the story is told in the writer's *European Union and United States Foreign Policy*. The present political results speak for themselves.

What of the peoples of Asia, Islam, and Africa, whose still persisting cultural customs and traditional philosophies are different from those of the Western world? We shall answer this question in more detail, so far as India is concerned in Chapter 12. Here several things are to be noted. First, Pakistan, Free India, and Ceylon, as well as several of the present new African nations, are members of the British Commonwealth of Nations. The only common political language in each of these Asian nations is English. The pull, therefore, toward the English-speaking international legal, political, military, and economic community of Australia, New Zealand, Canada, the United States, and, now, Continental Western Europe may well be like the centrifugal pull of Britain into the Continental European Community of the Six. Moreover, the free democratic content of the legal, political, and economic education and aims, and even the legal constitutions of the African as well as Asian nations of the British Commonwealth, make such a move the most natural one. This is especially likely if unilateral power politics, with the neutralism into which it tends to drive weaker nations, is dropped and replaced with our alternative theory.

Even so, cultural differences and their diverse cultural mentalities have to be reckoned with in any realistic foreign policy. Here the way is indicated by the Canadian constitution, which gives culturally different French Quebec

and British Canada a very great states' rights legal and
political independence within an over-all constitutional federal government. Pakistani India and New Delhi India
might well create a similar federal legal and political system, thereby fitting their positive law to the single rail
transportation system which was left by the British, the
shared comradeship of their Sandhurst-trained top military leaders, and the physical geography of their situation.
The present geographical anomaly becomes evident when
one notes not merely that the border between Free India
and Pakistani India is an unnatural and a militarily inde-
fensible one, but also that the border of Free India alone is
longer than that of Pakistani India and Free India combined. Such a movement from the present unilateral power
political Hobbesianism to an international over-all federated India on the Canadian model would also automatically solve the Kashmir problem. Moreover, it is
probably the only realistic way in which this political issue
can be solved. Cultural differences, therefore, require a
pluralistic internationally federated legal and political
theory of foreign policy, both regionally, where there are
cultural differences, and for the world as a whole.

This culturally pluralistic international legal theory of
foreign policy and world law agrees with both traditional
power-political theories in noting that peace is rarely
maintained in any domestic community, even the sleepiest
village, without the policeman and the policeman's physical power. It agrees with Sir Arthur Goodhart in his *English Law and the Moral Law* when he shows that, instead
of the Hobbesian materialistic club giving the positive law
its sanction or obligatory character, it is the moral content
of the positive law as expressing the cultural values of the
community that brings the club into being and makes its
use legal.

Our theory agrees, therefore, with the unilateral morally
and religiously based power-political theory in observing
that any nation's military men and policemen are never

given their physical power, nor are the politicians paid the taxes necessary, to provide domestic economic aid, unless they use this military and economic power domestically according to legally specified rules, which must not run counter to the shared moral values of the community. This applies equally to military or economic aid sent abroad. Unless such aid takes into account and conforms itself to the cultural customs and philosophical mentality of the people to whom it is sent, it is likely to be opposed and to fail, thereby defeating its own purpose. How to avoid such self-defeating failures in foreign policy is the major concern of the practical part of the writer's recent *Philosophical Anthropology and Practical Politics*.

This pluralistic philosophically anthropological and international legal theory of foreign policy entails three things: First, a guarantee, implemented with police power by the legally constituted world community, of the right of each people or regionally international federation to build their domestic institutions in their own way in the light of their own cultural and moral traditions and upon such foreign values and ways as they may choose freely to import, just so long as they do not force their particular ways by military or subversive means on other people. This, incidentally, is the only policy that has a practical chance of restricting the Marxist Communist philosophy of culture and politics to the relatively few on the earth's surface who really want it.

Second, since there is never a legal right or protection without a correlative legal or moral obligation, there must be the automatic responsibility of each member of the world community to contribute to any legally processed community-authorized police action. The policing of the peace of the world as pluralistically authorized, legally and politically, is not merely every people's right, but also every people's responsibility. When the cultural values and philosophy of every nation and culture in the world community are realistically allowed to express themselves and taken into account in the community's official legal and political decisions, the members are then more likely to accept their responsibilities to protect others as well as the right to be protected by others. Provided a majority do, this is sufficient. For no breaker of the law can stand up before a morally committed and responsible majority in any political community.

Third, since military men, policemen, engineers, and economists are the instruments of politics, rather than its ends, decisions with respect to foreign policy need to be restored, in accordance with the philosophical ideals of the founders of the government of the United States, not merely to control by the civilian members of government, but also to the direction of civilians who possess expert diplomatic and anthropological knowledge of the diverse cultural mentalities or philosophies of the world's nations, *including their own.* This requires a planning board in the United Nations and in each foreign office or state department made up of career diplomats who know foreign cultures and the mentality of their peoples at first hand and other experts who are trained in the methods of sociological jurisprudence, cultural anthropology, and the comparative philosophy of the world's cultures and their respectively different traditional legal and political institutions and ways. Only if both long- and short-range foreign policy is planned in the light of such objective knowledge, can it claim to be realistic or avoid being self-defeating. Moreover, as illustrated in the writer's *Philosophical Anthropology and Practical Politics,* the design of foreign policy must be tailor-made to fit each particular culture or regional cultural community.

In any event, one thing would seem to be clear. Just as science is more than its technological instruments, so politics is more than its economic and political power.

One final question suggests itself. We have noted how contemporary Europeans have sought out cultural norms, untapped in modern times, common to the recently warring

Western European nations, to create a viable regional international legal and political community. Are there worldwide norms of this kind? More specifically, has human altruism been underrated?

6

SOME REALISM ABOUT ALTRUISM *

A<small>RE THERE</small> facts in human nature and in nature generally which make all men one? Or, to put the matter negatively, are the obvious facts, which uniquely differentiate one person from all others and which exhibit all animals as competing with one another to obtain the food and clothing necessary for their very existence, the only facts about nature and first-order factual human nature? More specifically, is the self-centered or class-focused struggle for existence and its battle for the control of the materialistic means of production what "really" characterizes human existence and gives life its meaning, however much we may turn to religion or morals as an "opium" to disguise the fact or however much we may wish it were otherwise?

We do not answer these questions, as most contemporary religious or secular humanists suppose, by saying that there is more to human nature than this and then, in support of one's statement, pointing to all the evident facts of cultural

---

* Originally published as "Scientific and Philosophical Foundations for Altruism" by P. A. Sorokin, *Explorations in Altruistic Love and Behavior,* Beacon Press, Boston, 1950, pp. 194–202.

history which are presented in literature, the fine arts and comparative religion and moral, as distinct from natural, philosophy. No! The answer "There are human evaluative judgments and their values" as well as dogs seen eating dogs will not do. For, as shown in Chapter 1, all these "values," precisely because they are the product of human judgments, may be in error due to one's eating of the tree of knowledge with respect to nonman-made, first-order facts, and whether or not this is the case is precisely the point at issue in the foregoing questions. In other words, all three of these questions admit the existence of every cultural artifact and their humanistic values and ask whether they are not the products of wishful thinking rather than of correct knowledge concerning nature and first-order factual nonman-made human nature.

In considering any such question, it is exceedingly important to keep in mind two different usages of the word "fact." As shown in Chapter 4, there is first-order fact in the sense of something directly inspected, the knowledge of which can be obtained without inference or recourse to speculatively discovered theory. The ineffable, aesthetic quality, blue, as immediately sensed, is an instance. Fact in this sense of immediately inspected or inspectable datum, we shall call pure fact.

The word fact is also used by common sense, science, and philosophy to designate that which is inferred from immediately inspected pure fact by logical methods. Scientific objects, such as electrons with diameters smaller than our senses can detect, or, such as the electromagnetic waves of the electromagnetic field with their velocity of 186,000 miles per second in vacuo, are examples of fact in this second sense. Since fact in this sense, because of its very nature, can be known only by logical inference and by recourse to theory, it may be appropriately called inferred or theoretically known fact.

It appears, therefore, that human nature and nature generally have two components—the component which is immediately experienced, pure fact, and the component which is theoretically known, inferred fact. The latter component we have called the theoretic component of nature and human nature; the former component, the aesthetic component.

The appropriateness of the adjective "aesthetic" to designate pure fact becomes evident when we examine its character. In such an examination, great caution must be exercised if a most frequent error is to be avoided. Most people suppose that knowledge of tables and chairs with a fixed geometrical shape the same for all observers, existing during the night when nobody is observing them, is knowledge given as pure fact; they believe also that one's own self, conceived as a determinate entity existing when one is not conscious of oneself and persisting through the night when one is asleep, is also knowledge guaranteed as pure fact. The slightest examination of the situation will indicate, however, that this is not the case.

Consider, first, the belief in persisting public, external tables and chairs and planets, believed to possess the same geometrical shape for all people notwithstanding the different shapes and images of them which various people have from their respective standpoints. The very distinction between the diverse directly inspected images and the public, external object with its form and properties, believed to be the same for all observers, exhibits the error of identifying knowledge of the existence of public external objects with nothing but pure fact. The pure fact is the immediately apprehended sequence of present, successively perishing images which differ from person to person and from standpoint to standpoint as sensed within the all-embracing continuum of immediacy. The public external object, with a constant geometrical shape the same for all perceivers, and for one perceiver over many moments, is a theoretically known, inferred fact; it is not immediately apprehended pure fact.

Let me become more specific and even personal. It

is necessary to become personal when one deals with pure fact, since it is, in considerable part, what a specific person immediately senses or inspects, and this is a private thing varying from one person to another and from moment to moment. At the present I believe myself to be sitting beside a wooden desk, the top of which has four right-angle corners. The actual image, i.e., the directly sensed datum or pure fact, which I have of "one of its corners," is the image of an acute angle. The latter is the immediately apprehended fact. The theory that the top of the desk, conceived as a public object, has right-angle corners, notwithstanding the directly observed fact that I sense it from the point where I am now sitting as having an acute angle, is obviously something not given as pure fact but something inferred from what is given as pure fact.

It is inferred, moreover, in an indirect rather than a direct way. Certainly one cannot deduce directly the existence of a desk with a right-angle corner from the directly inspected fact of an acute angle. The formal logic of the situation operates in the converse direction. It is necessary first, by a speculative leap of the theoretical imagination, to postulate a public three-dimensional wooden desk, the top of which has four constant right-angle corners, and then to assume that the right-angle corner of this desk is related to the acute angle image which I have of it from this particular standpoint at this moment by the laws of perspective of geometrical optics. In other words, assuming the inferred theoretically known rectangular, public, material desk and the laws of geometrical optics, one can, by formal logic, deduce the acute angle image which I inspect at this point.* In other terms, whereas one can infer pure fact from inferred fact, when, by a trial and error leap of the imagination, one hits upon the hypothesis concerning inferred fact which permits the deduction to be

---

* It is necessary also to assume certain relations termed "epistemic correlations," but these can be neglected without error for our present purposes. They will concern us in later chapters.

made, one cannot deduce inferred, theoretically known fact from directly inspected pure fact.

This is the reason why no scientist or philosopher has ever been able to give a proof of the existence of the external world. This is also the reason why, if one insists, as did Bishop Berkeley, that nothing exists but pure fact or what the senses and immediate apprehension give, one must, as he demonstrated, deny the existence of public, external material objects conceived as having a geometrical form the same for all people and persisting through time.

Consider now the common-sense belief in one's own self as a determinate thing different from that of any other person in the universe, and conceived to exist when one is asleep or has one's attention upon other matters. Clearly, direct inspection cannot tell one what is present when one is not inspecting. Thus, the belief that one's determinate self exists when one is not directly inspecting it is an inference beyond pure fact; it is not mere pure fact itself.

But consider what one finds when one attempts to turn one's attention upon one's self and notes what is immediately introspected or apprehended. Again, as in the case of external objects, it is a sequence of differing, sensuous images and aesthetic qualities, not a persisting, determinate entity with constant properties. Thus, even the belief that one is a determinate being, the same through time, is inferred fact; it is not immediately apprehended pure fact. This is the reason why Hume, who, like Berkeley, denied all knowledge which is not empirically immediate as pure fact, was forced to deny the existence of a determinate persisting self, notwithstanding that he believed "in practice" that the determinate persisting self and determinate persisting external objects exist.

The character of pure fact may be made evident in another way. We can immediately apprehend as determinate fact only what the senses or introspection exhibit to us. No one, upon reflection, would maintain that one's sense of sight picks up the heavy grand piano on the far side of the living room and conveys it through the observed empty space to the retina of one's eyeballs and then up the optic nerves to the visual area of one's cortex and then across, in some mysterious manner, into the immediacy of consciousness. All that the sense of sight conveys is a sense datum which is a colored shape. A sensed, colored shape is an aesthetic quality. It is not a three-dimensional material object.

Dr. Johnson thought he proved, when he kicked the stone, that the senses gave him the stone as a material object of pure fact; but all he got for his trouble was a sensation of pain and an abrupt noise in addition to his momentary visual images. Now, an association of a grayish angular shape, a pain, and an auditory sound or noise is a group of aesthetic qualities; it is not a three-dimensional material stone. Dr. Johnson's kick missed the point.

Let us turn our attention to the immediacy of nature. As given now as pure fact, it is ablaze with colors. Nature appears to sight like the qualities which the impressionistic artist paints upon his canvas. This, rather than nature theoretically conceived as spherical, astronomical bodies, moving about one another as they radiate electromagnetic waves travelling with a very high velocity, is nature as immediately apprehended. Similarly, the warm, felt flow of ineffable images and sensuous qualities is one's human nature or self as pure fact. In short, pure fact, whether in nature or in human nature, is made up of the kind of thing which can only be known by feeling it and which cannot be conveyed to anyone who has not experienced it. A directly inspected blue cannot be conveyed to Helen Keller. A directly inspected green cannot be conveyed to the writer, since he happens to be color-blind with respect to green. He has no idea of the sensed quality denoted by the symbol "green," which many other people say they inspect. Such is the nature of the factors making up pure fact. They can be known only by being shown with immediacy to those who have the capacity to apprehend them. They are ineffably qualitative and intuitive in character. In short, they are the kind of materials with which the artist works—sensuous colors, sensuous sounds, sensuous flavors—all imageful. They are not the material objects upon which common sense and science and much Western theoretically formulated philosophy concentrates its thought. Being thus the qualitative kind of material which the impressionistic artist presents, it is appropriate to designate the component in nature and human nature which is pure fact as the aesthetic component, where "aesthetic" means impressionistic art rather than Euclidian metrical geometrically proportioned classical Western art.

Having noted that nature and human nature are composed of the imageful aesthetic component, which is pure fact, and the imageless, intellectually known theoretic component, which is inferred fact, our basic question falls into two parts: Is there, in the aesthetic component of man and nature, a factor which makes all men one, as well as the obvious factors which make men different from one another? Also, in the imageless, intellectually known theoretic component of all men and nature, is there a common factor as well as a differentiating factor?

It has been the tendency of most modern thinkers, who have been positivists and radical empiricists, restricting nature and human nature to radically empirical pure fact, to conclude that pure fact is made up of nothing but local, private, transitory, perishing, sensuous qualities succeeding one another in time. On this basis, different men represent different associations and sequences of determinate, transitory, sensuous qualities. Since these qualities, by their very nature, are one thing for one person and another thing for another and, since as Hume pointed out, there are no sensed necessary connections relating any given sense qualities to other sensuous qualities, it follows that the only factors which constitute human nature are those local and private to the "flow of consciousness" of the particular individual. Since one person cannot directly inspect the introspections of another person, one's conduct has nothing to base itself upon except one's own private, and, in this sense, selfish, directly inspected preferences, wants, and pleasures. Because these are different from person to person, the pursuit of nothing but private interest and feeling would seem to be the essential and, hence, inevitable first-order factual nature of man.

One can, to be sure, by means of symbols, obtain the idea that other people have their preferences, wants, and pleasures which they apprehend immediately as pure fact. Thereby, in a symbolic way, one can get the idea of deferring to their wants as well as one's own. Thus a certain amount of altruism and *laissez-faire,* live-and-let-live, comes in.

It is important to note, however, that it enters merely by way of symbols and not by way of experience and feeling. Experience and feeling being, on this theory, determinate and private, one cannot know the other person's determinate consciousness. One knows him or her only in the dull, dry, unmoving form of symbols—not in the vital, emotive, affective form of impulses, moving preferences, and feelings. This is why a utilitarian, empirical, social hedonism, for all its emphasis upon sensation, is so frightfully verbal, dry, and dull in its social philosophy; more like the heartless mechanics of the countinghouse than the warm, felt immediacy of the impressionistic artist's materials.

But is the aesthetic component of all men and nature a mere aggregate of solipsistically isolated islands of associated, determinate, perpetually perishing, sensuous qualities? An examination of what we immediately apprehend forces us to answer this question in the negative. As William James put it, only the focus of consciousness of what we immediately apprehend is sharply differentiated into determinate, sensuous qualities. The periphery of immediately apprehended fact is undifferentiated and undeterminate, yet none the less immediate and real as pure fact. In other words, as William James pursuing his radical empiricism and the sages of the Orient practicing their methods of intuition or immediate apprehension and contemplation have emphasized, pure fact or the aesthetic component of man and nature, is an immediately felt continuum common to everyone and everything, only partly differentiated into solipsistic islands of associated, sensuous, localized data.

We arrive, therefore, at the following conception of the aesthetic component of nature and human nature. It is an immediately apprehended continuum, in part differentiated and in part indeterminate and undifferentiated. The differentiated part differs from man to man and, hence, makes men different from one another, thereby tending to cause each to behave from the standpoint of his own private wants, preferences, pleasures, and self-centered interests. The undifferentiated continuum or field factor in all men and in nature, however, makes all men one with one another and with nature, giving each a felt impulse—not a mere symbolically designated but unfelt toleration—to act with felt sympathy for all men and from the standpoint of all men and all nature, rather than from the standpoint merely of one's own local determinate, partial, and self-seeking self. It appears, therefore, that there is a positivistically immediate and, hence, scientific and philosophical basis for altruism in the radically empirical, aesthetic component of nature and human nature.

What about the imageless, intellectually known, theoretic component? Here two factors are relevant. One, the method by which it is known; the other, its character as known.

The method for knowing it has been designated already in connection with the distinction between the speculatively inferred, imageless, theoretic component and pure fact, and the specification of the way in which the former is in-

ferred from the latter. As shown in Chapters 3 and 4, the
imageless, theoretic component is known by a trial and
error method of hypothesis, in which the formal logic or
deduction runs not from pure fact to inferred fact, but
in the opposite direction, from inferred fact to pure fact.
In other words, the logic of verification is always of the
following form: if *a* then *b, b* is the case, therefore, *a* is
the case, where *a* is theoretically designated, inferred fact
and *b* is immediately apprehended pure fact. Any argument of this form commits the fallacy of the hypothetical
syllogism called "affirming the consequent."

The presence of this fallacy of "affirming the consequent" in all knowledge of the inferred imageless, theoretic component in man and nature has a very important
consequence. It does not mean that such knowledge is
invalid. Note that the two premises of the hypothetical
syllogism are as follows: (1) If *a* then *b* and (2) *b* is the
case. These two premises insure that the conception of the
inferred theoretic component designated by *a* has been
confirmed. Hence, instead of showing the conception to
be false, the presence of the fallacy of affirming the con-
sequents indicates it to be, in part at least, confirmed
through its deductive consequences. It tells us, in other
words, that, if the speculatively inferred, imageless, theoretic component in man and nature is what *a* specifies,
then all the facts described as *b* in pure fact, or the aesthetic component of nature, are accounted for.

What then, it may be asked, is the meaning of the statement that a method of verification of this logical form
commits a fallacy? The meaning is that such a method of
verification has not proved the uniqueness of *a*. It has not
proved that the conception of the inferred theoretic component of man and nature, designated by *a,* is *the only*
conception which has the capacity, through its deductive
consequences, to account for the data observed to date in
pure fact. Nothing prevents the possibility that some

other conception of the inferred theoretic component, *c,* may also have the capacity through its deductive consequences to account for the observed facts, *b,* also.

This means that any conception of the theoretic component of man and nature, by virtue of the very method by which the conception is obtained and significantly said to be empirically confirmed, cannot be said to be the only possible conception. The possibility of other conceptions than *a* must also be admitted. In other words, to understand the method of knowing the inferred theoretic component in man and nature is to be forced to realize that one's specific beliefs about this component must be taken with a certain lightness of touch and with consideration for the different beliefs of other people. To have such an attitude is to possess the spirit of toleration, open-mindedness, avoidance of dogmatism, and consideration for beliefs and theories other than one's own. In short, the basic beginnings, at least, of a spirit of altruism are present.

What of the content of our knowledge of the inferred theoretic component of man and nature? We shall deal with this question in more detail in the final chapters. Here we note that this content has one specific, inescapable characteristic. Because this inferred theoretic component of man and nature is by definition not immediately apprehended, it can be designated and known only by means of theory. Furthermore, as has been noted, the theory which specifies it can be achieved only by a trial-and-error, creative leap of the imagination. If this unseen factor is to be even conceived, the concepts and propositions which designate what it is must be specified. The minimum number of propositions necessary to specify this inferred factor are called, by scientists and logicians, "postulates."

But before one has the right to assert a specific conception of the inferred theoretic component, arrived at by a leap of the intellectual imagination as designated by its postulates, to be the true theoretically designated conception, one must determine the consequences of its postulates and check these consequences against pure fact and find them confirmed. In order to determine the consequences, one must deduce other propositions called theorems from the postulates which designate one's belief or theory. The resultant totality of propositions made up of postulates, and of theorems logically deduced from these postulates, is called a deductively formulated theory.

Knowledge specified by such a deductively formulated theory is, by its very nature, systematic in character. It is also knowledge composed of propositions which are universal propositions.

This universality is twofold in character. First, it applies to all the primitive entities which the theory asserts to compose the theoretic component of man and nature, and it applies as far as its meaning is concerned for all time. Secondly, it applies for all men.

The latter fact is especially relevant to our basic question. It tells us that, in experimentally verified, deductively formulated, scientific knowledge designating the first-order, factual, theoretic component of man and nature, we have knowledge of something designated by propositions which are meaningfully the same for all men. The theoretic component of all men and nature, when brought to propositionally expressed articulation in human knowledge, gives men a belief for the true understanding of themselves and nature which is the same for all. It gives meaningful common knowledge and a common guide, and in this sense makes all human beings one, rather than merely many.

It appears, therefore, that in both man and nature as pure fact and man and nature as speculatively discovered, imageless, intellectually known, inferred fact, there are scientific and philosophical grounds for altruism. In the aesthetic component, which is pure fact, there is the all-embracing, in part indeterminate, aesthetic continuum of felt immediacy which insures that all men, notwithstanding their determinate differences, are, to this extent, in fact, one. In man's knowledge of the theoretic component of himself and nature, which is inferred fact, there is the basic toleration and attendant altruism prescribed by its indirect method of knowing, and the common faith and resultant altruism sustained by the universal and verified character of the propositions which designate this component as known.

7

WHY A COLLEGE NEEDS A CHAPEL *

This chapel has been the place where, in my years here and I trust also in yours, the members of our college have met together in unity, in peace, and in the serious attempt to give deep and lasting meaning to our personal and collective lives. The football games have united us also, but usually with some distressingly noisy and unnecessarily aggressive outsiders present on the other side of the field whose spirit, like that of this belligerent partisan on our side, was often hardly conducive to a spirit of unanimity and peace or to a concern with lasting values rather than with the immediate partisan gain of the moment.

The point is not that the playing field and the debater's contest do not teach their valuable lessons. I am too passionate an admirer of the skills of Cobb and Rizzuto and those of Lincoln and Douglas to lay myself open to such a misinterpretation. The point, instead, is that even vic-

---

* Address delivered at the rededication of the Edward Dwight Eaton Chapel, Beloit College, December 12, 1954. Reprinted from *The Christian Century,* Vol. 72, No. 37, September 14, 1955, pp. 1050–1052.

tories on the debater's platform on Friday evening or on the gridiron on Saturday afternoon fail to leave a good taste in one's mouth afterwards if something of the spirit of peace and unity of a Sunday afternoon in this chapel is not embodied in their achievement. Such, I take it, is part, at least, of what this chapel and this occasion signify for every son and daughter of our alma mater.

But this building is more than the physical and spiritual focus of Beloit College; it is also a temple of religion. Religion is something universal to mankind. Because of this universality of what it symbolizes and is dedicated to sustain, this occasion has significance not merely for ourselves but also for the world, especially the contemporary world.

Of what does this signifiance of religion in its universality consist? Clearly, it comprises religions in addition to our own—Hinduism, Buddhism, Confucianism, Taoism, Jainism, Shintoism, Judaism, and Islam as well as Christianity, Greek Orthodox, Roman Catholic, and Protestant. The history of the religious life of this college supports this conclusion. This is a chapel, which, in its cultural and historical origins, is a Protestant, even a Congregational Protestant, Christian chapel. From the beginning it enriched and enlarged its initial Congregational spirit in word and deed so that men and women of any Protestant denomination felt at home here, and Roman Catholics and Jews came to sit beside them equally at ease, later to be joined by Chinese of Confucian mind and Indians with the Hindu's intuition of the all-embracing formlessness which is Brahman. Both the historical trend here and the present facts elsewhere are therefore clear: religion in its universal import is not merely universal; it is also a diversified universality. Hence, the import of this occasion for others as well as for ourselves is that it signifies the impact not merely of religion but of comparative religion upon the contemporary world.

What this entails by way of a modification in missionary

practices and in courses on religion in college, graduate school, and divinity school is yet to be fully understood or implemented. Part of what is involved will become evident if we shift our attention, momentarily, to the contemporary world and note the challenge which it presents to religion and, in particular, to comparative religion.

Two outstanding facts make the contemporary world unique. One is the rise and resurgence of Israel, Asia, Africa, and Islam. The other is the release of atomic energy.

The first of these two events means that the Judaic-Christian West no longer dominates the world. As a consequence, the peoples of Asia, the Middle East, and Africa are demanding a position of equality beside the nations of the West. This resurgence of the East and Middle East and Africa is not merely political and economic in character. It is also cultural, spiritual, and religious. The fact, therefore, is that other peoples are now demanding that their respective religions be treated on a basis of equality with ours. This shows in the fact that whereas Asians can now write about the recent political domination of their countries by Western nations without rancor and with objective understanding, they find it very difficult to refer without bitterness to what they often call the "cultural imperialism" of Western Christian missionaries.

Nor should this surprise us. If one conquers a people politically and exploits them economically while leaving their basic religious and philosophical beliefs intact, one has restrained and harmed their bodies but has not touched their spirit or their souls. When, however, by missionary endeavor, one shifts them from their traditional basic religious and philosophical beliefs, one may destroy their cultural and spiritual tradition in soul as well as body. Clearly, a Christian religious leadership capable of meeting this challenge of the contemporary world must be one that makes comparative religion central and faces the seriousness of what one is doing when one asks a person of a different cultural and religious tradition to replace his religious beliefs and practices with one's own.

This does not mean that there is no place for Christian missions in the contemporary world. The need is perhaps greater than ever before. Nor does it mean that part of the impact of Christian missionaries has not been exceptionally beneficial. The contemporary reactions abroad in favor of political self-determination and modern Western, tolerative, free democratic legal and political institutions are, in considerable part, the result of the influence of Christian missionaries. Moreover, non-Western peoples everywhere are demanding the higher standards of living which they see their neighbors in the modern West enjoy. These economic advantages cannot be achieved without scientific technology which entails large capital expenditure —a larger capital expenditure than even the richest of Asian joint families or African tribes can provide. Thus, if the Asians, Middle Easterners, and Africans are to achieve their economic aim, they must introduce not merely Western technology but also an interfamily and an intervillage raising of capital. This is impossible without financial integrity at the national level and without resort to the Western law of contract. This Western law of contract requires the ethics and religion of the West for its effectiveness. Thus, the economic problem in Asia is at bottom an ethical, legal, and religious problem, which involves the deepest philosophical understanding of Western law, ethics, and religion for its effective practical solution.

The same is true of Western technology. To operate these Western financial, medical, mechanical, and agricultural ways effectively, not merely the nationally raised capital but also the mentality required to understand the theoretical, scientific principles upon which the technological instruments depend for their effectiveness, is essential. This means that the philosophy of science of Western physics, medicine, and engineering, as well as these applied sciences themselves, must be comprehended. This philosophy of science is essentially related to the three Semitic religions: Judaism, Christianity, and Islam.

The Asians' and Africans' occasional bitterness over our Christian missionary zeal, and their insistence on having their religious as well as their political and economic life treated on a par with ours, mean that the introduction of our political, legal, economic, technological, and religious ways in these nations must be envisaged—if it is to be a vital, effective transplantation—not as the replacing of their traditional political, economic, and religious ways with ours, but as the harmonious merging of the two diverse religious traditions, each of which has something to contribute, into a fresh and original creative synthesis. This means that comparative religion must become the key factor in religious teaching and religious statesmanship.

The second unique fact of our time is the release of atomic energy. It means that war is no longer a practical way to settle disputes between nations. Professor Roscoe Pound, the former dean of the Harvard Law School, reminds us that history gives no evidence that, in any domain of human relations, disputes are settled without recourse to force except as these disputes are brought under the rule of law. This entails, if we are to remain sane and be practical enough to survive in an atomic age, that we must have an effective international law. Is this possible?

The answer to this question is to be found in the factor on which law depends in those cases in which it has been effective. Legal science has investigated this factor. The conclusion is as follows: Positive law is effective when the norms which it specifies for ordering human relations and settling disputes are supported by the living beliefs and habits of the people to whom it is applied. This means that if we are to build an effective international law we must seek out, sustain, and build on those living beliefs in the hearts and minds of men which are of a character such as to support and sustain the new international law which we would construct and so desperately need.

Where, other than in religion, are the living beliefs of the requisite universality, goodwill, and content to be found? Since Christian religious beliefs are those of but a minority of the people in the world, it follows that we must root our international law in the living beliefs of *all* the religions of the world, not merely in those of our own. Again we come back to the crucial challenge to comparative religion and to collaborative team-play between the believers and leaders of the major religions, which the contemporary world presents.

But even if this collaboration occurs, something more is required. The religious sources of inspiration in our own particular religious tradition must be drawn on so that the religious content of our own lives is intensified. Also, the norms for ordering human relations of all peoples under God, which each and every religion in different ways specifies, must be brought to bear on the decisions of our political leaders. What doth it profit a people if their President or Minister of Foreign Affairs is a Christian or a Hindu but orders their foreign policy by the materialist's principle of power politics? What doth it profit a college or a university to teach and affirm the religious concept of human relations in its chapel if its Institute of International Affairs or its political science professor affirms the power-politics theory of foreign policy that might makes right internationally, and if its law school teaches the legal philosophy that law finds its sanctions not in its moral content but in the amount of physical force its sovereign political agent can attach to himself?

The times call for a law that makes world-community-authorized police power its instrument and the diversified spiritual resources of mankind its inspiration and its sanction. If such a lawfully run world is to be, national and international policy must root itself in the basic philosophical and religious beliefs in the minds and hearts of men, and these beliefs must become so vital and so practical that they direct and control our military men, our lawmakers, and our statesmen. Religion makes the same practical demands on us. Did not Jesus teach us to pray: "Thy will be *done* on earth"? Belief alone is not enough; deeds in accord with these beliefs are also required.

But if deeds are to flow forth thus from our faith, this faith must become something more than a merely precious inner feeling. Its inner meaning and grounds and its basic principles must be made articulate. For this the philosophy of religion is required. Similarly, if law is to embody within itself the diversified spiritual resources of the world necessary to make itself effective, more than its positive legal statutes must be studied; their grounds also in the living beliefs of men must be sought out. For this philosophy of law and the philosophies of the world's cultures are essential. Likewise, if law and political policy are to meet the contemporary demands of mankind for an equitable and higher economic standard of living for everyone everywhere, modern physical and chemical science, including agricultural chemistry and engineering, must come to the aid of common sense. Experience with these Western scientific ways in Asia and Africa shows that they are frequently misused and ineffective once the Western advisers depart, unless the people grasp the mathematical and relational way of thinking about natural phenomena, or, in other words, the philosophy of physics from which modern technology derives and on which it depends for its efficient operation. To implement faith through deeds, therefore, faith must articulate itself philosophically and then embody that philosophy in law and implement itself with technology—a law and technology which can convey to Asians and Africans not merely our political constitutions and technological mechanisms but also the mentality, or, in other words, the philosophy necessary to operate them with comprehension and efficiency.

It is because law, economics, political science, engineering, and the other applied sciences need the spiritual resources of philosophy and religion, if they are to be truly practical, that a college needs a chapel. It is because religion requires philosophy to articulate its faith, and law, literature, and science to transform that articulated faith into deeds, that a chapel needs a college—a college, moreover, such as this one, where students and faculty are free not merely to believe but also to seek out the scientific evidence and philosophical reasons for what they believe.

Such, in part at last, is the import of this place and of this occasion. Such also is the challenge which comparative religion and the contemporary world present to you and to me. It is appropriate therefore that, as we dedicate this newly reconstructed chapel of Beloit College, we rededicate ourselves to all it stands for—to the universal as well as the personal component of its religious life and to the practical and political demands which religion places on us. At the same time, let us give thanks for its gifts to us of unity and of grace.

8

THE RELIGIOUS AND THE SECULAR
IN CONTEMPORARY EDUCATION *

Previous chapters have shown that today
the world is everyone's oyster. Domestic, fiscal, military,
legal, and political decisions are self-defeating unless they
are interculturally and internationally minded.

To see this, any teacher, especially if he be in a graduate or professional school, needs but to look at the color
of skin and to recall the nationality of the students in his
courses. They are of every race and almost of every nation. Moreover, if one teaches over a brief period of years,
they are of every religious faith—Buddhist, Confucian,
Hindu, Shinto, and non-Semitic, religiously African as well
as Judaic, Muslim or Greek Orthodox, Protestant or Roman Catholic Christian. This situation requires an education that is world-embracingly cosmopolitan in its content.
It calls also for exceptional religious as well as secular
educational statesmanship.

The task will be misconceived if it is thought of as the
chance merely to acquaint foreign students with the secular

* Originally published in *Religion and the State University,* edited
by Erich A. Walter, University of Michigan Press, Ann Arbor,
1958, pp. 269–281.

and religious subject matter and skills of one's own culture and nation. Nor does it suffice to provide, in addition, as has the Massachusetts Institute of Technology, facilities for nurturing the respective religious faiths of students from abroad. What is required is the education of domestic and foreign students alike for the professional decisions they will have to make after they receive their diplomas. As previous chapters have demonstrated, these decisions are inescapably international, intercultural, and interreligious in character, whenever they are not self-defeating. A few considerations suffice to show why.

The masses of Africa, the Middle East, and Asia are rebelling against Western imperialism. This development includes insistence upon their own indigenous cultural values. Since the separation of politics from religion is foreign to any people who have not passed through the Protestant Reformation or come under modern Western secular political philosophy, this native cultural renaissance is also a resurgence of their own religion. Note the recent Islamic religious reaction in Turkey against Atatürk's modern secular reforms. Read the Burmese Premier U Nu's exposition of Buddhism in *An Asian Speaks*.[1] Consider the similar synthesis of Buddhist religious and aesthetic values with constitutional democracy in Thailand. Recall Gandhi's statements, "Such power as I possess for working in the political field [has] derived [from] my experiments in the spiritual field" and that the Hindu *Bhagavad-Gita* is "the book *par excellence*"[2] spiritually. Read Esther Warner's *New Song in a Strange Land*[3] and hear the contemporary Liberian say, "All we got to live under two laws. We got to live under the Liberian government [Western] law. They got plenty soldier. We don't give our heart to that law. The other law is the law of our people where the chief is the big man. That one we give heart to."

Clearly, the era in which religious statesmanship is conceived in terms of converting the world to one's own religion is over. The prevalent notion that sufficient economic aid alone will enable Western contractual, legal, and political ways and technological instruments to take root in African or other non-Western cultures is equally unrealistic and also morally and politically misguided. It is by cultivating a respect for one another's differing cultural and religious traditions and customs that religious or economic statesmanship in today's world will find itself. As the Hindu Swami Akhilananda has suggested, "Teachers should not attempt to convert students from one religion to another." Nor should economic "experts" press secular ways from one culture on the different economic ways of another people without any knowledge of, or sensitivity to, the aided people's traditional economic and other customs. The deepening of each student's insight into the richness of his own religion and the expansion of his imagination, intellect, and heart to enter sympathetically and with understanding into the spirit and novel merits of other religions and other people's secular customs is the wiser course. In any event, it is the only practical one, the mood of non-Western people being what it is.

In fact, their present tendency is to affirm that the Judaic-Christian West, however inspired may have been its founders, is obsessed with material wealth and instrumental gadgets at the expense of the intrinsic religious and moral values necessary to control them. Vice President Radhakrishnan of India, speaking out of his Hindu-Buddhist background, like Iqbal of Lahore speaking for a reconstructed Islam, concludes that the hope of the world centers in the religions of Asia, or of Islam, which, not drawing such a sharp division between the religious and the secular, keep the details of daily life more continuously and intimately rooted in the spiritual. A recent study of Indian students on an American university campus shows that they leave, even after three years, including visits in religious homes, with a conviction that Americans lack a proper appreciation of spiritual values.[4] Even European students often share this opinion. One need not accept these judgments in order to see their practical consequence, which is that the West, and especially the United States, is on the defensive with respect to its morals and religion and also, it may be added, its education.

Another fact points in the opposite direction. The people of Africa, the Middle East, and Asia are demanding both (a) the right to build their social institutions in the light of their own indigenous religious traditions and also (b) the higher standards of living and the democratic political control of their lives, which they see the peoples of the modern West enjoy. These two demands generate spiritual conflicts and raise problems which must be understood if the needs of foreign students on American campuses are to be met, or, if American students are to make correct judgments concerning the introduction of Western legal and political institutions and aid abroad.

The ways of native non-Western people, before the modern Western imperialists and Christian missionaries came, were not those of liberal democratic, constitutional democracy. As Sir Henry Maine showed in his *Ancient Law*[5] and as the comparative philosophy of the world's cultures confirms, any people not influenced by Western law or religion live under the religion and ethics of "the law of Status," and not under the religion and ethics of "the law of Contract" from which liberal constitutional democracy derives. In a perfect law of Status society, the selection of political leaders is not made in an election guided by a contractually introduced constitution, to which all people have in principle given their consent and before which they are all equal, after the manner of the religion and ethic of a perfect law of Contract community. Instead, all leadership is set by status of sex and temporal priority of birth within the ancestral family and by color-of-skin familial or caste status *vis à vis* the tribe as determined by whether one is biologically bred in the line of the predominant sex from the first family of the tribe.

For example, in a purely patriarchal law of status religious community, the head of the nation or tribe is the eldest son, by way of the eldest son in each intervening generation, of the first family of the tribe, according to the rule of primogeniture. In a purely matriarchal society, the eldest daughter is both the political ruler and the head of the family by the same principle of biologically bred status. Consequently, family, caste, and tribal loyalty become the primary moral, religious, and political obligations. Furthermore, religious worship is not congregational but focuses around the privacy of the family hearth and the ceremonies of the tribe.

Such was the religious, political, and personal ethic of the ancient cities of Rome before the creation of Western legal science by Roman jurists who were Stoic Roman philosophers or heavily under the influence of this philosophy. The African in Esther Warner's Liberia spoke truly when he said that he gave his heart to "the law of our people where the chief is the big man." In this statement he showed that their morality and religion is that of a law of Status community in the biological and racial sense of Status of Sir Henry Maine. The laws of ancient Hindu India are called the Laws of Manu because Manu symbolized the founder of the Aryan-Hindu tribe. Under the laws of this Hindu religious community, only biologically bred, patrilineal descendants of the first Manu enjoyed political, moral, or religious leadership. The same law of Status ethic operates in Shinto Japanese society, the Caliphate, and in many local families in unreformed Islamic society and to a predominant, though lesser, extent for families in Confucian and Buddhist societies.

This is why the people of Islamic Turkey and Pakistan and of Hindu-Buddhist Thailand, Burma, and Free India have had to introduce a law of Contract constitution and a legal system imported from the West in order to bring their domestic affairs under their own democratic control and to introduce the reforms necessary to begin to lift their standards of living. But this is to initiate the shift in Western civilization, following the Stoic Romans, from the religious ethic of biologically bred and defined Status to that of Contract. The effect of this shift is to break moral, political, and religious man free from color-of-skin, ancestral-family-centered, and tribally bred man to identify him with universal or cosmopolitan man, i.e., any human being whatever standing equally with all others before contractually constructed and freely accepted universal legal principles.

In the West, with the decline of the Roman Empire, this new religious ethic of the law of Contract passed, on the one hand, to the Eastern Empire and Justinian and, on the other hand, into the Roman Catholic Church thereby creating Western Stoic Roman, Judaic-Christian civilization. In fact, the literal meaning of the adjective "catholic" in the Christianity of the Roman Catholic Church is "universal." Kant's categorical imperative, to the effect that only that conduct is good which can be expressed as a universal law for everyone, is identical. The Declaration of Independence of the American colonists and the Bill of Rights of the Constitution of the United States and Free India are other examples.

Because the shift from Status to Contract cannot be made instantaneously, the Stoic Roman Catholic, Judaic-Christian ideal tended historically, in considerable part, to be filled in with law of Status content. Consequently, Roman Catholic Christianity became associated with hierarchically ordered aristocratic and regal institutions rather than with democratic and egalitarian ones. The same is true of the Protestant Christianity of Luther's and Bismarck's Germany, of Calvinism, and of the Church of England of Hooker, Elizabeth I, Sir Robert Filmer, and the latter's biological descendants, the First Families of Virginia. Hence, if the Stoic Roman Christian ethical ideal was to be achieved, it became necessary to reform not merely the Roman Catholic Christianity of Saint Augustine and Saint Thomas, but also the Protestant Christianity of Luther, Calvin, Hooker, and Sir Robert by means of the more democratic values of (a) Nonconformist Protestantism and (b) modern secular natural and moral philosophy, particularly that of Newton, Locke, and Jefferson.

In their zeal, however, to locate the source of religious and political authority in the conscience and freedom of the individual, Nonconformist Protestant Christians tend to lose the Roman Stoic factor in Judaic-Christian civilization. Consequently, for them, unlike Roman Catholic Christians or followers of Islam, legal norms seem to be merely instrumental and to be irrelevant for intrinsic personal moral values or for the religious life; also, political nationalism tends to be fostered at the expense of lawful universalism and of faith in the need for, or the spiritual foundations of, international law. It is no accident, as the writer has shown elsewhere,[6] that many of the major leaders in the achievement of the transfer of some national sovereignty to the Western European economic, military, and political community have been vital, Stoic Roman, legal thinkers and Roman Catholic Christians.

These considerations point up the fact that Protestant and Roman Catholic Christians need one another. Inter-religious understanding and collaboration on the university campus is as important, therefore, domestically as it is internationally.

Both Christian groups also need modern secular natural and moral philosophy. Witness the stand of many Southern Nonconformist Protestants for the color-of-skin law of Status ethic (derived, as Peter Laslett has shown recently, from Sir Robert Filmer through the First Families of Church of England and Calvinist Virginia) and against the application of the universal ethic of the law of Contract by the Supreme Court of the United States in its recent unanimous decision on segregation in education. Clearly, the reform of Roman Catholic and Conformist

Protestant Christianity by Nonconformist Protestantism is
not sufficient to achieve the religious and moral shift from
biologically bred Status to a society in which Judaic-
Christian man is universal man. All too often, the Nonconformist Protestants, taking the Bible as the literally
dictated word of God, go to the patriarchal and tribal
ethic of the God of certain parts of the Old Testament for
their criterion of the Divine and the good. Boyd Smith's
play, "The Patriarch," portrays a recent West Virginian
example. A third factor has been necessary, consequently,
in order to approximate the initial ideal of Stoic Roman,
Judaic-Christian civilization. This third factor is modern
secular natural, moral and political philosophy, especially
that of Newton, Locke, and Jefferson and the Kant of the
categorical imperative.

The foregoing role of the Old Testament in this story
shows that Jews as well as Christians need the reforming
influence of Stoic Roman legal science and modern secular
science and philosophy. Otherwise, more and more Jewish
students, persuaded by the latter subjects and convinced
of the validity of the universal ethic of Western contractual,
legal science, while they see many of their fellow religion-
ists pursuing the religion and politics of the law of Status,
are going to be increasingly alienated from their religion.
This, in fact, is the domestic problem of the secularized
leaders of contemporary Israel from Western Europe
when, in their introduction of a law of Contract constitution, they are confronted with the religiously orthodox
Jews from Morocco and the Arab peninsula who out-
number and outbreed them.

It appears, therefore, that if the natives of Africa, the
Middle East, and Asia want to retain their indigenous religious and cultural traditions while also achieving the
democratic control of their own affairs and the more
democratically distributed higher standards of living which
they see peoples in the West enjoy, they must amend the
law of Status religious and social ways of the masses in

the light of a deep understanding and acceptance of the quite different law of contract religion and ethic of the Roman Stoic Judaic-Christian, the Nonconformist Protestant Christian and the modern secular West. Clearly, the modern West has not merely its efficient instruments, but also its unique intrinsic spiritual values. A wise religious and secular educational statesmanship on the American university campus will insure that American and foreign students alike have the chance, inside as well as outside the curriculum, to learn what these spiritual values are.

The Africans, Muslims, and Asians must master these values also if they are to achieve their present insistence upon the more universally spread standards of health and wealth which they see the modern West achieve even imperfectly. These medical and economic aims require the introduction of scientific medicine, agriculture, and machinery and the latter's high capital investment. Such finance requires (a) the introduction of law of Contract control of banking and investment at the federal level and (b) the moral integrity in the handling of finance by public officials who, abhorring nepotism, give greater loyalty to the law of Contract norms of a dull legislative statute or an abstract constitution than to the concrete blood ties to the members of one's own family and to the first families of one's tribe—a type of financial integrity on the part of public officials which a family-centered and tribally-centered law of Status morality and religion does not provide, and which only the universalist ethic of the Stoic Roman law of Contract religion and society insures.

The latter ethic, as the Stoic Roman jurists and philosophers made clear, goes back, as does modern scientific technology, by way of Greek philosophy to Greek mathematical physics with its conception of any truly known individual thing as an instance of a formally universal law. This frees the essential properties of any truly known individual from such sensed properties as color, thereby preparing the way for the Stoic Roman jurists, and the Roman Catholic Judaic-Christians following the jurists, to break moral, religious, and political man free from color-of-skin, family, caste, and tribal man and identify him with cosmopolitan man. It follows that if non-Western people want the widely distributed standards of health and wealth, they must introduce not only Western scientific instruments, but also Western law of Contract religious and moral values. Similarly, if Western religious and educational leaders are not to betray their spiritual heritage, they must radically reform their present conception of the relation between the humanities and natural science, breaking down departmental lines by revealing the common philosophical and scientific way of knowing from which both derive and upon which both depend for their validity and effectiveness. This is as important for American as for foreign students.

Countless Americans are emotionally disturbed and spiritually empty to the point of sickness. This is the case, frequently, notwithstanding a religious upbringing and even attendance at Jewish synagogue or Christian church. Every state government is plagued with the endlessly mounting cost of providing care for the insane and the mentally sick. It is difficult to escape the conclusion that this points to something spiritually lacking in the religion of the Hebrew-Christian world and in the ethic of the modern secular West.

The central place which emotion occupies in these ills suggests that it may be here that, for Western man, the more intuitive religion of the African negro, the Islamic Sufi, the meditating Buddha, the nondualistc Vedanta Hindu, and the warmhearted Confucian *jen* come into their own. In any event, Swami Akhilananda of the Ramakrishna Hindu Society of Boston reports that American students, professors, and businessmen, who are eminently successful, come to him spiritually unsatisfied and emotionally at odds with both themselves and their mates. May it not be that the religious worship in which they participate, in synagogue or church, is too much concerned with group sermons, group ceremonials, and pastoral visits and confessionals and not enough given to nonverbal, private meditation and direct intuitive communion in silence, which religions such as Buddhism and nondualistic Vedantic Hinduism provide? Perhaps, also, the modern West needs those psychological techniques discovered by Asian spiritual investigators, which so shift and transform the content and focus of a person's emotive experience that he becomes one with the existentially immediate, undifferentiated, and, hence, timeless and infinite component of himself and of all things. If so, the provision on the university campus of the religious symbols and practices of Africa, Islam, and Asia, beside those of the Judaic-Christian West, may be as important for Jews, Catholics, and Protestants and even agnostic secularists as it is for enabling foreign students of other faiths to sustain and deepen and discover what is still valid, after the reform by the ethic of the law of Contract, in their own religious traditions.

In this connection, the new modernistic chapel at Massachusetts Institute of Technology is very much to the point. In this building there is but one chapel completely devoid of symbols from any religion whatever. On the floor below the chapel there are several little rooms, each containing the symbols of one of the major religions of the world, Oriental as well as Western. When one religion is scheduled for the main chapel, its symbols are taken there.

In one respect, however, this admirable practice leaves something to be desired. It makes the error of supposing that all religions are congregational, bringing people together to worship as a group. This is true of Judaism, Christianity, and Islam and also of Westernized forms of Buddhism and Hinduism. In her book, *The Hindu Temple,*[7] Stella Kramrisch reminds us, however, that congregationalism is completely foreign to [non-Westernized] Hinduism. The same is true, in major part, of Buddhism, Jainism, Confucianism, and an important part of Roman Catholicism, as the presence, at any moment of the day, of a person worshipping alone before a side altar in a Roman Catholic church demonstrates. Consequently, if the authentic religions of the Orient, in their non-Westernized forms, are to bring their intrinsic intuitive emotive values to their own adherents or to others on the American campus, special permanent rooms with their respective symbols, isolated from all outside noise, must also be provided for each of them.

For followers of Islam, the chapel at the Massachusetts Institute of Technology, with its blank, modernistic interior, is ideal. To a Muslim, the presence of any symbol whatever within the place of religious worship is regarded as idolatry and as religiously shocking. Also, the floor of any chapel should be level throughout. Otherwise, the Muslim worshipper runs the risk of being unable to return his body to an erect position when, with his knees on the floor, he swings his trunk forward and touches his forehead to the floor. All pews or seats must be removed if followers of Islam are to worship there. At most, only a huge rug or many rugs should be in the room. Before the single chapel for all congregational religions is built, an astronomer might well be called in to orient it so that its front interior points toward Mecca. At campus meals or invitations to luncheon or dinner, where Hindus are included, the provision of an adequate meal containing no meat and composed largely of vegetables is of equal importance.

Such attention upon detail may seem overdone; yet their neglect may produce unnecessary embarrassment and result in more harm than good. Also, Oriental religions should be presented in their pure, non-Westernized, authentic forms. This does not prevent Westernized versions of Oriental religions from holding congregational forms of service, after the manner of the Ramakrishna Hindu Mission and certain Westernized Buddhist groups. Probably, however, the modern West has enough of such religious worship without going to Westernized Hindus and Buddhists for more. What we, in our hectic overwordy, overpreached, and overlectured world, need is the more private, silent type of intuitive meditation and contemplation that brings the emotive fulfillment and spiritual equanimity which the statue of the meditating Buddha, his eyes half open, half closed, or of the meditating Ramakrishna conveys. The Oriental philosophical and psychological methods of analyzing and directing attention and modifying its content, described in part by Premier U Nu of Burma in his aforementioned article, need to be introduced by Asian experts and studied by Western analytic radical empirical philosophers and psychologists. French philosophers and scientists are always doing this.[8] Such study might revive an interest in, and a respect for, religion upon the part of faculty and students for whom religious philosophy means merely Hume or Wittgenstein and religious psychology suggests merely Pavlov, Freud, or Jung.

Cultural anthropologists and philosophers have found that the behavior and ceremonies of one culture seem meaningless and even silly to an observer from a different culture, unless the observer learns to understand what he sees in the observed culture's terms. Because very few religious people have learned how to do this, the observations of the missionary of one religion upon the meaning and merits of another religion are, with rare exceptions, of little worth. The same is true of most politicians and laymen in their judgments of a foreign nation's secular behavior. Contemporary social scientists who describe a foreign culture in terms of the concepts of recent Western behavioristic or Freudian psychology commit the same error. If we do not want students on the campus to react similarly to modes of worship or meditation other than their own, the religious and educational leaders must learn from the philosophical anthropologists.

The latter have found that to understand the people of a foreign culture one must think about what one sees or hears them do from the standpoint of their own way of thinking about it, rather than from the standpoint of one's own culture. As Chapter 1 has shown, when anthropologists such as Paul Radin and Clyde Kluckhohn did this, even for people who have no written language, they found themselves confronted in each case with a complete and novel philosophy. Recently, the anthropologist Professor E. A. Hoebel has made a study of the legal norms of seven different so-called primitive peoples. So different are the norms of any one of these seven peoples from those of the others that he finds it necessary to set up seven sets of basic postulates to describe them.[9] Interreligious understanding requires the same approach.

Practically, this means that the authentic presentation of the major religions and their practices, on or near the university campus, is not enough. The mentality or philosophy behind each must accompany the presentation. To appreciate and understand Roman Catholic worship, one must interpret what one sees in terms of Roman Catholic doctrine and philosophy. To evaluate and gain respect for Islam, one must, in addition to observing Muslims at worship, read the Koran and some of the Sharia (laws) while also having some appreciation of the Greek, Arab, and Persian philosophy of a very high order, which has gone into their interpretation. Likewise, to understand the Buddhist's Nirvana, the verbal and nonverbal practices of its Zen sect, the Hindu's Brahman or the psychological and gymnastic techniques of a Hindu Yogi, something of Buddhist and Hindu philosophy and, especially, its epistemology must be comprehended. To present the authentic practices without the indigenous theory necessary to understand them is to fail practically.

It follows that ministers, priests, and lay religious leaders must be closely associated with the faculty. The resources in the departments of anthropology, philosophy, area studies, comparative law, and religion must be drawn upon. Perhaps all of these departments will have to be expanded, becoming less culturally provincial in the philosophy, law, and religion which they teach. Also, foreign and American students who are authentic representatives of their respective faiths should be encouraged to expound to one another the inner meaning of each religious tradition.

Since the major point of the presence of foreign students in the United States is to obtain an authentic understanding of its culture, it is best that they live as far as possible, with American students. Otherwise, the differing spiritual mentalities of the different foreign cultures which they represent will tend to reinforce them in the error of judging the United States in spiritual terms other than its own. Then, instead of achieving an objective understanding of our particular spiritual values, they will leave, after the manner of the Indian students in the aforementioned University of Pennsylvania study, with their initial provincial religious and political prejudices concerning the United States reinforced. Hence, the regular university union should be used to bring students together, and a *residential* international house is probably unwise.

The education of foreign students in our modern Western graduate and professional schools requires new procedures also. The present pedagogical practice of having them concentrate the whole of their time on the courses and materials, which a domestic graduate student studies, runs the grave risk of so Americanizing or Anglicizing them that, when they go back to their native lands, they will fail to appreciate and be able to come to realistic political or educational terms with the customs and differing cultural mentality and values of their own people. Instead, the need, for native and visiting students alike, is to envisage one's graduate and professional school education anywhere as entailing the understanding of the mentality and customs of both one's own people and those of other nations and cultures in terms of their respective, deepest humanistic, and naturalistic philosophical assumptions and beliefs. For this, courses and research in the world's comparative law, comparative medicine, comparative politics, and comparative religion and their respective naturalistic and humanistic philosophies are indispensable.

9

RECENT LITERATURE AND SCIENCE *

THE QUARTER of a century between World Wars I and II was notable for the intimacy of literature and science. This manifests itself in two ways: one, the literary quality and imaginative appeal of the writings of many scientists; the other, the remarkable manner, differing radically from what happened in the 19th century, in which prose, poetry, and criticism have first absorbed and then been transformed by the new insights of science.

Sir Arthur Eddington's *Stars and Atoms* and *The Nature of the Physical World* are examples of the writings of the scientists. These works are as happy in their frequent literary allusions and in the refinement of their style as they are successful in opening new vistas for the imagination and the intellect, while also confronting us with the scientific and philosophic issues of our time. Sir James Jeans in *The Mysterious Universe* and *Mathematics and Music* similarly combines a lightness of literary touch with a notable capacity to bring science, art, and the meaning of human existence together.

---

* Originally published as *Literature and Science* in *The Saturday Review of Literature,* Vol. 27, No. 32, August 5, 1944, pp. 33–36.

What poet in our time has exhibited the creativity of the human spirit and the unplumbed ranges of the human imagination while, at the same time, jolting us out of a stultifying spiritual complacency, as has J. B. S. Haldane in *Daedalus* and *Possible Worlds*? In a more somber vein, restricting itself to biology and psychology, but none the less readable and of high literary quality, was Julian Huxley's *Essays of a Biologist*. Cruder both in form and content, but equally potent in its popular appeal, was Lancelot Hogben's *Mathematics for the Millions*. More important and profound was Alfred North Whitehead's *Science and the Modern World* with its insight into the romantic movements of the literature of the 18th and 19th centuries, wedged as these movements are between the old mechanics of Galilei and Newton and the new philosophy of contemporary science.

In a quite different vein, but equally important, is Earl (Bertrand) Russell's *Mysticism and Logic* with its "Free Man's Worship." This is fine writing. It also strikes an unequivocal contemporary note—one which is to re-echo again and again through the pages of I. A. Richards' *Principles of Literary Criticism* and *Science and Poetry*. Then, in a somewhat similar iconoclastic, yet more positive mood, with a freshness and incisiveness of style which has caused one observant reader to remark that our biologists write better English than our professors of literature, there was Hans Zinsser's *Rats, Lice, and History* and *As I Remember Him*. In a comparable manner, the scientific Lynd's *Middletown* pushed the literary Sinclair Lewis' *Main Street* into the background. It would seem almost that if today one wants what literature has always given previous generations—namely, a living rather than a studied prose and the poetry of a quickened imagination, a freed mind, and a sensitive spirit which has not confused honest feeling with shallow sentiment pursued at the expense of knowledge and thought—then it is to our scientists rather than to our humanists that we must turn.

But this is only part of the story. During this period in which the scientists have been taking on more and more of the traditional functions of the man of letters, the poets, novelists, and critics have been absorbing and, as a consequence, have been transformed by the suggestions of a new science. This science has given us not merely a more imaginatively open universe into which to breathe, but also a more emotionally released man to do the breathing. Poems, novels, and criticism could hardly be insensitive to such a change. The result is a contemporary poetry deviating in form and content from that of previous centuries and a new criticism equally different from its predecessors—as different, in fact, as James Joyce and the early T. S. Eliot are from Shelley and Browning, and as I. A. Richards and John Dewey are from Ruskin and Matthew Arnold.

The effect is sufficiently arresting and significant to warrant a more detailed designation of its cause. Contrast usually heightens vision. Hence, we shall understand the 20th century the better if we set it against the background of the 19th. It will be well also to note the source of the more open universe first and come to our concept of the more emotional and contemporary man afterwards.

Two factors have contributed to the placing of man in a universe more congenial to the expression of his moral and aesthetic nature. In passing from the 19th into the 20th century, mathematical physics replaced biology as the science of predominant importance. Nothing has happened in zoology or botany in our time to compare in significance with the discoveries of Planck and Einstein in mathematical physics. This is as true for the popular as it is for the scientific mind, as the news value of Einstein's name and the sales of the books of Eddington,

Jeans, Whitehead, and Lancelot Hogben clearly demonstrate. This change was significant not merely for what it said, but for the human faculties which it called upon for the saying of it. The more open world in which we now live is the product of the one as well as the other.

What science said is personified in the replacement of Newton, Laplace, and Darwin with Einstein, Planck, and especially Heisenberg, with the latter's *principle of indeterminacy*. Pauli's *exclusion principle* is also equally important. These names signify that the old, rigid, cast-iron universe, in which man seemed to be nothing but a mere cog in a vast cosmical machine, has evaporated. The field of space-time, the cosmical constants, and the organic recognition upon the part of one electron of the presence of others even in the organization of the atom, represent something quite refreshing. No longer is nature to be conceived as a mere collision of individualistic *laissez-faire* atoms, nor man merely as a collocation of such atoms, struggling for existence. In this new physical universe of Planck, Einstein, Heisenberg, and Pauli, even Darwin begins to take on a new aspect. Schrödinger's most readable and imaginative little volume, *What Is Life?*, expresses this transformation.

Let no one suppose that this is significant merely for science and natural philosophy. It now enables us to see the literature of the 19th century in a new light, as literally an escape literature. It enables us also to see why this had to be its character.

Darwin's man in Newton's universe was not a creature who could function as a free moral agent or as one who could regard the intuitions of the artist as anything more than mere phantasms. Thus the 19th century's Keats, Shelley, and Rossetti had no alternative but to run away from their own universe and their own home to Greece and medieval Rome and Spain; also Byron and Carlyle, even like Kant, when, in his humanistic philosophy, he separated the natural from the spiritual sciences. Poets

and critics alike sought a "sweetness and light" not their
own, thereby providing an escape literature because their
own conception of the natural universe did not permit
them to have literature at all.

Nevertheless, notwithstanding the undeniable magic of
its verse, the more exuberant and exaggerated in its preciousness because of the very desperation which called
it forth, this literature did not satisfy. Even pure humanists, such as F. L. Lucas in *The Decline and Fall of the
Romantic Ideal,* found it wanting. Also the so-called
"idealism" and "moral freedom" which were behind its
romanticism turned out in the hands of the politically
romantic Germans who created it, because of its very release from the sobering effect of scientific knowledge, to
be not only a goodness which was too good to be true, but
also a set of practical demands which were too arbitrary
to be tolerated. Similarly, the classicism in its return to
the beauty, however sublime, which was Greece and Rome
became so much not one's own that there was little of
one's self left for the appreciation of it. Consequently,
when following the first war of this century, mathematical
physics gave the modern man a universe of his own,
which, if not yet fully reconciled with moral and aesthetic
values, at least gave promise of becoming so, the poets,
novelists, and critics were quick to move in and inhabit it.

But the faculties of the human mind necessary for the
understanding of this new universe of the scientists were
as significant as its objective character. Even the most
superficial acquaintance was sufficient to indicate that it
cannot be known merely by looking at it. Nor can it be
grasped even by the intuitive images of the poet's imagination. For not only the neat, billiard ball-like, physical
models of the physics of the 19th century, but any images
whatever, which even the most fanciful poet's imagination might devise, are incapable of representing it. Only
the quite different, purely formal imagination of the
mathematician can lay hold of it. Thus it is, that in our

time, the realm and the limitless ranges of the human imagination, necessary even for an adequate and experimentally verified science of the actual, have been discovered to be in a new place—a place, moreover, at which the poet, provided he follows the mathematical physicist, can hint vaguely and metaphorically, but into which, literally, he cannot enter.

This is the real reason why the prose of our scientists has replaced the verse of our poets in stimulating and extending the human imagination. The cause is not that the scientists have been active and the poets imaginatively indolent. It is, instead, that the richest sphere of the imagination is one that can be entered only by the formal "imagination" of the mathematician, not by the concrete, sensuous imagination of the poet.

But science has altered man's conception of himself as well as his conception of his universe and the faculties necessary to comprehend it. Put more concretely, Darwin has been supplemented with Freud.

It was Freud who replaced Locke's essentially blank, aesthetically and emotionally empty, puritanical Protestant soul and Hume's notion of the self as a mere association of vivid and faint sense data and Darwin's merely biological behavioristic man, with an emotional human being, of whom, like the soul of the Spaniard as defined by Salvador de Madariaga, passion is the essence. This is the kind of scientifically conceived person with whom the arts, and their emotional and vivid aesthetic materials, can function. With such a science of man, it is not necessary for poets, novelists, dramatists, and critics to run off to Greece and Rome, or to indulge in an intoxicated romanticism, in order to find something aesthetic to say. Within such a contemporary intellectual climate Eugene O'Neill's dramas, James Joyce's *Ulysses,* Aldous Huxley's *Point Counter Point,* I. A. Richards' *Principles of Literary Criticism,* Ernest Hemingway's *Death in the Afternoon,* and the poetry and novels of the early T. S. Eliot, Ezra

Pound, Conrad Aiken, W. H. Auden, E. E. Cummings, Stephen Spender, Marianne Moore, Gertrude Stein, and Jean-Paul Sartre can be born. Also the painting of Rudolf Ray, the choreography of Erick Hawkins, and the music of Lucia Dlugoszewski acquire this freshness and aesthetic meaning.

This literature shows that the psychological science of our century has given the arts a richer subject matter and a wider domain than they previously enjoyed, even though this domain does not extend as far in its imaginative range as that of the mathematical physicists. For as Edwin Muir has written of James Joyce, "he has revealed the swarming world of sub-conscious and half-conscious thoughts which constitute three-fourths of our life, and he has shown that it has a magical and excessive beauty." Similarly, in the hierarchy of interests of the new psychology and the resolution or easing of its conflicts by emotive rather than merely cognitive means, I. A. Richards in *Science and Poetry* finds a new future for poetry, as John Dewey in *Human Nature and Conduct* and Charles L. Stevenson in his *Ethics and Language,* find a new and added meaning and technique for the good life. Thus, although the science of the 20th century, by the imaginative appeal of its mathematical physics, has shifted from literature to science the function of providing the most extensive stimulus to the human imagination, this science in its psychology of the emotions and the subconscious has amply repaid literature and the arts for this loss by providing them with richer materials, a wider domain, and more novel functions than they possessed previously.

It might seem that this is the end of the story. Literature and science having again joined in holy wedlock, one might suppose, after the manner of the ending of the American movie, that they live together happily ever afterward.

Unfortunately, the participants themselves prevent so facile a conclusion. Aldous Huxley started, to be sure,

with the Freudian biological man of *Point Counter Point,*
but he has not ended there. This *Brave New World* gave
birth, as its author continued to live with it, to the thoroughly disillusioned "hero" of *Eyeless in Gaza.* T. S. Eliot
wrote "The Waste Land," but he has since written "The
Idea of a Christian Society," and even I. A. Richards has
departed from the psychological irrationalism of Freud
and the excessively positivistic and mechanical theory of
meaning of Ogden and Richards' *The Meaning of Meaning,* at least sufficiently to admit in his Bergen Lecture at
Yale University that even literary criticism must have a
metaphysics. Clearly, all is not well in this new utopia, as
in some others that might be mentioned.

Where does the plot take one? Neither the contemporary
literature nor its critics provide an answer. T. S. Eliot and
Aldous Huxley suggest that we return to the old faith—
not that of the 19th or even the 18th century, to be sure,
since this is too recently known to permit its fatal weaknesses to be forgotten, but that of the 14th century and
the Middle Ages. But surely this will not do. The new
literature and the new criticism is not nothing, even
though its most devout adherents have discovered that it
is not everything. Because a modern science and philosophy, as conceived by literary men, has revealed its very
disillusioning shortcomings, is no reason for supposing
that a medieval science and philosophy, which, as the
doubting Descartes can testify, exhibited equally disillusioning and fatal inadequacies in the 16th century, will
be any the less untrustworthy.

But a more important consideration remains. There is
more to contemporary science, even its psychology and
biology, than Freud's psychoanalysis and I. A. Richards'
excessively positivistic and mechanical initial theory of
meaning. To this fact the writings of the scientists, considered earlier in this essay, clearly testify. Also the contemporary sciences of psychology and psychiatry have
found the Freudian theory to be as misleading at many

times in its dogmatic diagnostic and therapeutic predictions as it has been at other times suggestive and illuminating. This has caused contemporary psychologists to attempt to put the Freudian theory on a less verbal and metaphorical and more controlled scientific basis. To this end, they have asked themselves how factors like "unconscious drives" can be verified. This question has guided them to the method of mathematical physics, which, as we have noted, also deals with unobserved events and processes. But to understand this method of exact science is to become aware of the limitation of the Freudian irrationalism as the sole measure of scientific procedure in psychology and to become equally aware of the limitation of I. A. Richards' original theory of meaning. Thus, it may not be contemporary science which has failed our contemporary humanists but their excessively psychological and uncritically Freudian conception of what this science means.

Under these circumstances, those, like Whitehead, who approach their theory of symbolism from the standpoint of the mathematical rather than merely the psychological science of our time, are likely to be better guides. Also an analysis of the method of mathematical physics may be expected to provide a more embracing and sound basis for literary criticism than a further pursuit of the method of psychoanalysis. To be sure, the method of mathematical physics seems utterly foreign to literature and aesthetics, when it is examined initially and superficially. Nevertheless, it contains within itself the formal, intellectually known factor in the nature of things which only mathematics can literally show. And, let it be remembered, this is the factor which has inspired the distinctly literary and imaginative quality of the writings of our contemporary scientists. The method of mathematical physics also contains within itself the immediately apprehended factor in the nature of things laden with its emotional aesthetic content, with which art is concerned and which our contemporary literature has so greatly extended, at the suggestion of Freud, to include "the sub-conscious and the half-conscious." What the astrophysicist sees when he looks at the sky is not the internal constitution of the sun but the color and the form of the sunset in all its beauty. The inner molecular organization of this star is an inference from the aesthetically immediate materials—an inference which only the formal mathematical intellect, not the aesthetic intuition, can fully grasp. Moreover, did the method of mathematical physics not contain within itself the emotionally laden, aesthetically immediate materials, this method would be totally unable to verify its mathematical and imaginative theory of the chemical make-up of the sun.

Similarly, as Chapter 1 has shown, contemporary anthropological science has recently led us to the same conclusion. The psychologist also confirms this judgment as he gains a more accurate understanding of his method. He is finding that what we immediately apprehend in man is the emotional, aesthetically vivid factor in human nature with which the novelist, and especially contemporary impressionistic literature and art, are most expert. By contrast, the behaving Darwinian man with a cortex and nervous system responding to a stimulus from his environment and the Freudian man with his unconscious and, hence, unseen conflicts and drives are imaginatively and theoretically known factors in human nature which only the method of hypothesis of mathematical physics, checked by meticulously controlled experiment against the immediately apprehended, more aesthetic data, and introspected ideas, can adequately handle.

It appears, therefore, notwithstanding the recent temporary disillusionment and suggested estrangement, that the new science and the new literature of our time both stand, and both need each other. Each contributes something unique in the nature of things and at the heart of human nature. In fact, man and nature alike are each constituted of the theoretically known component which only the formal intellect of the mathematical scientist can designate and the aesthetically immediate component which only the concrete, imageful, and emotive intuition of the artist can adequately convey.

Consequently, the division of labor between science and literature is not that the former is purely scientific and the latter purely literary. The literary and imaginative quality of the writings of the scientists and the natural history, empirical, scientific content of the psychological works of the contemporary poets, novelists, and critics, give the lie to any such thesis. Instead, both science and literature are each both scientific and literary in different ways. Contemporary science is more poetic than poetry with respect to its capacity to raise the human spirit to the envisagement of new possibilities and to extend the reaches of the human imagination and intellect. Contemporary poetry is more scientific than science in its power to convey both nature and man as pure fact in all their radically empirical, aesthetic immediacy. But contemporary science is more scientific than poetry with respect to the capacity to understand and control the data which the poet experiences, and, similarly, contemporary poetry is more poetic than even the most imaginative mathematical physics in its capacity to make us feel and enjoy what the scientist understands and manipulates.

But before a poet can make us feel and enjoy the world and man which the scientist's verified imaginative theory reveals to us, this poet must understand the theory. Such an art for our time does not exist, although one of our talented younger contemporary poets, Muriel Rukeyser, in her biography, *Willard Gibbs,* has recognized the need for the meeting of the artist and the mathematical physicist, which is a prerequisite for its existence. Recently, creative musicians, such as Lucia Dlugoszewski and Professor John Spratt, have realized this also. The creation of such an art is one of the major tasks of tomorrow. Its second opportunity is to be found in exhibiting the immediately apprehended factor in nature and man in all its aesthetical immediacy and purity, apart from any theory either contemporary or traditional.

Until both of these forms of art are pursued independently and then combined harmoniously, our knowledge and our feelings will be at odds with each other, and there will be no genuine peace in either our culture or our souls. It appears that the happiness of man and the possibility of a more enlightened and humane society are intimately connected with the capacity of science and literature to maintain their individual integrity while also supplementing and sustaining each other.

10

GOETHE'S ARTISTIC AND
NATURALISTIC GENIUS *

Mᴏʀᴇ ᴛʜᴀɴ any other modern creative thinker, Goethe foresaw two major movements of contemporary culture. They are: The pursuit of relational, organic factors as well as atomic, analytic elements in science; and the harmonious synthesis of aesthetic and scientific knowledge. Only in one respect did Goethe fail to envisage the novel scientific and philosophical conception of man, nature, and culture, which is gradually coming to articulation in our time. Contemporary events in Israel, Africa, Islam, and Asia cannot be understood unless it is realized that the Orientals are insisting upon placing the political control of their destiny in their own hands in order, among other things, to apply the scientific knowledge of the West to their natural resources to lift the economic well-being of their people generally. These Western scientific instruments derive from the experimentally verified theory of modern mathematical physics. Consequently, the unique cultural phenomenon of our

* Originally published in *Goethe—UNESCO's Homage,* Bericht-haus, Zurich, Switzerland, 1949, pp. 83–98.

149

time cannot be understood without recognizing the key role of mathematical natural science in world culture.

But mathematical physics was the one thing which Goethe never understood. As Ernst Cassirer has pointed out,

> Goethe's theory of nature was one continued attack on Newton and Newtonian physics. During the course of his life, this attack grew sharper and sharper, and it finally led to a tragic climax. Everywhere—among philosophers, physicists, biologists—he looked for allies in this contest, but he was able to convince scarcely anyone. Here he stood alone and this isolation filled him with a growing bitterness.[1]

In this respect, Goethe no more fits our contemporary world than he harmonized with his own.

Nevertheless, there are two respects in which contemporary developments in mathematical physics and the philosophy of nature give expression to Goethe's theory of nature as well as to Newton's. These two respects have to do with the emphasis upon relational as well as atomistic factors in contemporary mathematical physics and with the relation between the inductively given aesthetic component and the mathematically designated theoretic component in the contemporary scientist's knowledge of nature.

The entire topic may best be approached by way of Goethe's relation to Kant and Kant's analysis of Newton's physics. An excellent account of the relation between these three men appears in Ernst Cassirer's *Rousseau—Kant—Goethe*. In this study Cassirer writes, "Kant demanded that mathematics should enter into every part of the theory of nature, Goethe energetically rejected any such notion. 'Physics must be divorced from mathematics,' he said."[2]

But if contemporary thought in mathematical physics

and the philosophy of nature is on Kant's side against
Goethe upon this point, it is, none the less, on Goethe's
side against Kant upon another, perhaps even more important, point. Kant, it will be recalled, introduced a
sharp gulf between the philosophy of the arts and the
humanities and the philosophy of nature—a gulf which
all of Kant's efforts in his *Critique of Judgment* never removed. Goethe, on the other hand, insisted that human
values derive from and have their roots in nature. In other
words, Goethe was a naturalist in his theory of value.
Thus, upon this crucial point, Goethe foresaw a major
development in the science and philosophy of our own
time. In fact, it was precisely Goethe's insistence upon
rooting the source of the arts and of all human values
in nature, which led him to a concept of nature so alien
to that of the Newtonian mathematical physicists.

Goethe's approach to the essential connection between
art and nature is a most obvious one. The arts, whatever
else they may be doing, are always working with immediately experienced materials. The painter puts immediately sensed colors before us. The musician presents
immediately apprehended sequences. The poet, to be sure,
gives us words, but words, which, if they are effective as
poetry, conjure up in our imagination the same vivid
images and sensations which the painter achieves by
means of his pigments on canvas, and the musician creates
by means of the sounds from his instruments.

But Goethe saw also that nature, as immediately sensed,
presents to us precisely the same kind of materials. When
we look at nature, we see it ablaze with sensuous qualities
like those which the painter puts upon his canvas. We
hear the brook babbling when we walk beside it in the
woods in the same way in which the poet conjures up the
babble for us in our imagination by the magic of his verse.
Thus Goethe saw the very obvious error in Kant's theory
of value—the error of supposing that human values are
alien to nature as directly observed and, hence, as sci-

entifically known. Only a person who is deaf, dumb, and blind could escape the obvious fact that nature itself presents to our senses at every moment, perhaps in a different order to be sure, the same ineffable, sensuous materials and images with which the humanist as artist concerns himself.

What Goethe saw was that it is because the traditional mathematical physicist's conception of nature, upon which Kant reared his philosophy of nature, ignored this aesthetically immediate component of nature, that it failed to account for aesthetic and other human values and thereby drove Kant to an autonomous ethics and to a philosophy of the humanities, having little or nothing to do with one's scientific knowledge of nature. Goethe's only error was in concluding, by a *non sequitur,* that, because immediately sensed nature is scientifically and philosophically evident and real, therefore, the theoretic component of nature, designated by the experimentally verified theory of the mathematical physicists, is not also real.

This problem is cleared up when one realizes that, in man's scientific approach to nature, his scientific inquiries pass through two stages. One, the inductive stage in which nature is presented and described as in Goethe's vivid, emotional, qualitative, and intuitive morphological terms; the other, which comes after the inductive natural history stage, in which the scientist passes to mathematical, deductively formulated theory, the primitive entities and relations of which are not directly observable. Both types of scientific knowledge and stages of scientific method contribute to the final total of one's scientific and philosophical theory of nature.[3] The natural history approach gives nature or any natural object in Goethe's aspect of felt qualitative aesthetic immediacy, in which only the form or morphology of the object in its aesthetic unity is evident, and the analytic parts of the whole are present to awareness only potentially and vaguely—often even unnoticed. The stage of deductively formulated theory gives nature in Newton's and Kant's aspect as theoretically designated, with the analytic components and relations in the center of thought and the morphological unity of the whole expressed, to be sure, by the totality of propositions of the deductive theory, but—because of the finiteness of the human mind—present to thought, piece by piece, rather than as a whole. It is not an accident that Goethe's approach to nature was of the inductive, sensuous, natural history type, and that the modern scientific concept of morphology arose with him.

Kant's scientific conception of nature brushed this natural history aesthetic component of nature aside as mere appearance, making the theoretically known, imageless, mathematical metric of the forms of sensibility and the theoretically designated categories of the understanding, e.g., substance, causality, etc., the significant philosophical content of the scientist's knowledge of nature. That this *is* philosophically important, Kant saw quite correctly. That the immediately sensed, aesthetic component of nature is also valid scientific and philosophical knowledge, and as important for ethics and art as it is for natural history biology, it was the genius of Goethe to see and to emphasize.

The weakness of both Kant and Goethe is that each saw the factor in scientific knowledge and nature, which he himself emphasized, as the only significant one. Thus Kant, notwithstanding his unsuccessful attempt to retrieve the situation in his *Critique of Judgment,* tended to regard Goethe's felt qualitative aesthetic immediacy as mere superficial appearance, and Goethe found it necessary to attack the theoretic component of nature of the mathematical physicists with a fury which eventually embittered his spirit.

One of the most important results of the philosophy of natural science of our own day is its demonstration that the sensuously and aesthetically immediate natural history knowledge of nature, which Goethe emphasized, and the theoretically designated, experimentally verified, mathematical knowledge of nature, which Newton and Kant emphasized, are both equally ultimate, irreducible, and real.

The cause of the supposed opposition, assumed in common by both Kant and Goethe, between these two factors is to be found in the second of two assumptions, underlying traditional modern thought, made by Galilei and Newton in their statement of the conception of nature of modern mathematical physics. These assumptions are: (1) Sensuously immediate qualitative data in sensed space and time must be distinguished from mass particles in theoretically designated public, mathematical space and time. (2) The former is related to the latter by way of the scientist as observer, as appearance to reality.[4] It is to be noted that it is the second of these two assumptions, made by Galilei and Newton, which leads to Kant's conception of Goethe's aesthetically immediate component of nature as mere appearance, and, hence, as a superficial type of knowledge so far as science is concerned and a selfish and superficial basis for conduct so far as moral philosophy is concerned.

More recent studies of the relation between theoretically designated factors and sensuously immediate, inductively given, natural history factors in scientific knowledge have shown, however, that the aesthetic component of nature of Goethe's natural history inductive science is related to the theoretic component of nature of experimentally verified, modern mathematical physics, not as appearance and reality, but as two equally basic components of a single thing. Put in more technical terms, it has been found that aesthetically immediate factors are related to theoretically designated factors in scientific knowledge not by the three-termed relation of appearance but by the two-termed relation which may be appropriately called "epistemic correlation."[5] Of this, more in later chapters. The substitution of the latter relation for the former has the consequence of making aesthetic immediacy as ultimate a component of scientific and philosophical knowledge as is the theoretically and mathematically designated component of nature. Thus, Goethe's natural history, aesthetically immediate component of nature, which, as he saw, provides a basis in nature for art and human values and for morphological biology, combines with Newton's and Kant's and the contemporary mathematical physicist's mathematical concept of nature, without conflict. Goethe can keep his remarkable insight without becoming embittered.

It would be a mistake, however, to suppose that art and the humanities find in nature only this sensuously immediate, aesthetic component of nature designated by Goethe's qualitative, natural history, morphological science and by the intuitive impressionistic artist. The art of the Western world, which restricts itself to the inductive, sensuous qualities given in the natural history stage of scientific inquiry which Goethe emphasized, is not the art of Goethe's poetry or Goethe's time, but, instead, the art of the French impressionists and America's Georgia O'Keeffe. Goethe's art falls within the camp of the classical artists rather than of the more recent modernists and impressionists. Only the latter come near giving us nature, as immediately apprehended, without any element of theoretically known, mathematical proportion added. Goethe's morphology and his art referred to the form of external public objects, geometrically, and, hence, mathematically, proportioned. Thus, for all his objection to Newton's mathematical concept of nature, Goethe's own art, often, at least, had the mathematical concept within it.

Bishop Berkeley makes it inescapably clear that the external object, conceived as an entity with a persisting, three-dimensional proportion the same for all observers, notwithstanding their differing sensuous images of it, if it exists at all, is known by thought and is not a purely empirical datum within felt, qualitative, aesthetic immediacy. It is by restricting itself to the qualitative datum and by letting go of the postulated, public, external object, with its constant geometrical proportion, that recent impressionistic art arises, and abstractionism is made possible. Furthermore, it is only by bringing the mathematical concept, with its ratios and proportions, into the fuzzy images and impressions of aesthetic immediacy, and by foreshortening and sharpening the images according to the laws of geometrical optics of mathematical physics, that the classical art of the West, of which Goethe's own art is a specific instance, comes into being. Thus, Goethe's natural history, morphological science, with its reference to plants and animals conceived as three-dimensional external objects, and his own poetry give the lie to his theory that the mathematical physicist's science is an evil so far as the artist and the humanist are concerned. Goethe's own science of morphology and his own art embodied the mathematical factor as well as the aesthetically immediate factor. Thus, while Goethe's theory of both art and science was one-sided and attendantly partial, his actual art was an illustration of the richer and more complete understanding of both art and science in our own time.

But it is merely an illustration. This is the case because his actual art took its theoretically designated factor from the rather simple-minded, geometrical mathematics of Euclid and applied it to common-sense objects, thereby restricting itself and losing the generality and the greater deductive fertility and wider range of applicability of a morphology identified with the relatedness of nature of contemporary experimentally verified, mathematical physics.

Contemporary art, like contemporary thought, is with Goethe in the insistence upon finding inspiration for the arts, the humanities, and human values generally in nature —and in a nature in which sensuously immediate and formal or morphological factors are combined. But it is moving away from the conception of the morphological in terms of the common-sense, three-dimensional Euclidian regular solid objects to which Goethe's art and Goethe's science, for the most part, restricted themselves. This movement away has taken two directions. The first is a withdrawal from the external common-sense object of classical art to the pure datum of the immediately apprehended, aesthetic continuum which induction, unsupplemented with theory, gives one. This movement shows itself in impressionism in painting, music, and literature, and in the subsequent abstractionism which the release of images from common-sense, Euclidian, three-dimensional objects made possible.

The second movement away from Goethe's common-sense, intuitive morphology is in the direction of scientific objects and relatedness with more subtlety, greater generality, and an attendantly greater range of applicability. This movement shows itself in the physical chemistry of Willard Gibbs, the relational mechanics and electromagnetics of Mach and Einstein, and the quantum mechanics of Planck, Heisenberg, Schrödinger, and Dirac. Gibbs' physical chemistry, in which the second law of thermodynamics is basic, reveals nature as the irreversible process in time which Goethe's genetic morphology envisaged. Mach's and Einstein's relational theory replaced Newton's analytic particle physics with field physics, thereby revealing relatedness or form to be the scientifically basic thing which Goethe's emphasis upon morphology sought to establish. Quantum mechanics, with its *exclusion principle* of Pauli, establishes the conclusion that even though atomicity and particle physics may be required, the atomic parts have formal or morphological restrictions placed by nature upon what they can do. Thus, although modern science in the last one hundred and fifty years has moved away from Goethe's natural history common-sense morphology, this movement in all three of its major parts has been toward Goethe's emphasis upon the relationally morphological as scientifically significant and basic.

Two of the most spectacular and refreshingly creative achievements of our time are in art on the one hand and in mathematical physics on the other. It is by uniting the products of these two creations of the contemporary human spirit—the existential, aesthetic component of the art of impressionism or the art of a Georgia O'Keeffe and the formal theoretic component designated by the mathematical physicists—that Goethe's vision of human values, rooted in a science of nature at once both qualitatively vivid and essentially morphological, is being achieved. In this achievement, a scientific basis is being laid for a truly universal ideology for our world, which may bring into harmony those Oriental and Latin cultures rooted in the intuitive values of aesthetic immediacy, and those Western cultures whose values stem from the more abstract, imageless, theoretically known *logos* of a logically or mathematically formulated doctrine. More than any other thinker of the traditional modern world, Goethe foresaw, often vaguely and in a restricted form, to be sure, the riches of contemporary creative artistic, scientific, and philosophical thought in which a purer intuition of existential aesthetic immediacy and a more universal and fertile conception of the formal or the morphological are being combined.

11

WHITEHEAD'S PROSE AND
CONCRETE EXPERIENCE *

WHITEHEAD's prose is paradoxical. Upon
a first reading it seems to be unnecessarily artificial. With
later readings, however, one awakes of a sudden with the
startling realization that for almost the first time one is
observing the facts of experience freshly, directly, and in
the concrete.

To read Whitehead with understanding is to realize
why. We suppose that we observe directly the data of our
experience. In one sense this is true. Obviously, we sense
what we sense. But human beings are more than their
sense organs. Each one of us has an association area in
his brain. This area, or more exactly one's introspected
imagination which is its correlate, acts upon the aesthetically impressionistic images given by our senses to infer
the common-sense and scientific objects or persons which
the sensory images signify. What we believe we see is,
therefore, always the product of the presented, impres-

* Originally published as the Foreword to Donald W. Sherburne's
A Whiteheadian Aesthetic, Yale University Press, New Haven,
1961, pp. xiii–xxix.

sionistic images and our habitually conditioned or conscious inferences from them.

To confuse the latter with the former is obviously to commit an error. Kant called this error "dogmatic slumbering." Whitehead calls it "the fallacy of misplaced concreteness" or "the confusion of an entity of thought with a concrete factor of fact."

That this is an error, the reader can check for himself. Who has not had the experience of seeing the image of a person in the near distance which one believes to be that of one's friend Tom, only to find, on closer scrutiny of subsequent images, that one has inferred the wrong person, and that the successive impressions signify a complete stranger, instead. Nor is this a rare occurrence. Any courtroom contains it as a prevalent phenomenon. Whenever several direct witnesses of even a recent event try honestly to describe what they saw, rare indeed is it the case that they do not contradict one another on, at least, some points about what they "saw." Of course, in some cases there may be deliberate liars. But the real difficulty in determining what the law calls "the facts of the case" does not arise solely from the perjurers. Its source, also, is the failure of the average, well-intentioned witness to distinguish with sufficient precision between what he infers from the impressionistic images he senses and the images themselves. Such dogmatic slumbering, which produces the fallacy of misplaced concreteness, the legal profession calls the error of mistaken identity.

In any proper courtroom, precisely because this error is so frequent, cross-examination of each witness is required before his testimony is allowed to stand. What a competent cross-examiner does is to shift the attention of the witness, the court, and the jury from what the witness says he saw—let us say the defendant Tom Smith—to a more precise description of the images which led him to infer that the person he saw was Tom Smith. If the witness' description of the images is such that they are compatible with its being someone else, then doubt is thrown on the witness' statement of what he "saw." If, on the other hand, the witness describes certain details of the images which are peculiar to the images of Tom Smith, then the effect of the cross-examination is to substantiate, rather than to shake, his testimony.

Unfortunately, most people in arriving at their home-made, amateurish, common-sense, scientific and philosophical beliefs are not subject to such cross-examination. The consequence is that they frequently go through life not merely believing that the entities of thought which they have inferred from the concrete events and impressionistic images of their sensuous experience are the concrete facts themselves but, even worse, the inferred entities of thought, which they think they see, are the result of errors of mistaken identity. Then, under the delusion that they are describing the concrete facts of their experience which the senses give them directly, they have identified both themselves and their universe with nonexistent entities and objects.

In committing this prevalent error, we do more than slander the erroneously identified person and the erroneously interpreted concrete facts of our experience. We also harm ourselves. This self-harm does not arise solely from having made erroneous inferences from the sensed images to the signified entity of thought, thereby quite unintentionally affirming a falsehood while supposing one is merely describing a fact. There is also the harm to oneself which follows inevitably from having cut oneself off, aesthetically and emotively, from the living water that the human spirit requires for its own refreshment. Robbed, thus, of the aesthetic, emotive materials of one's own and nature's concrete aesthetic immediacy, one becomes a dull stuffed shirt, prattling bromidic, pseudomoral, common-sense platitudes about dead entities of thought that refer to nothing concrete nor to anything verifiably inferable from the concrete. To read Whitehead with care, looking to one's concrete experience rather than to the dull, dead commonplaces of conventional thought, to learn what his words mean, is to give oneself the chance of escaping from this prevalent and unfortunate condition.

Even so, the escape is not easy. For the trouble is in oneself rather than in Whitehead's prose. The confusion of erroneously inferred entities of thought with the concrete colorful events and aesthetically moving, impressionistic qualities and continuum of one's immediate experience would not be so prevalent were there not some unconscious, previously conditioned habit of thought in us which has been corrupting both our thinking and our conduct. By going behind the countless abstract nouns in our ordinary language, Whitehead, and other competent contemporary students of the relations between words and the sources of their meaning, have located one major source of this trouble. It is the subject-predicate grammar of English prose or any other Aryan language, such as Sanskrit, Spanish, Greek, Latin, French, or German, with which, quite unconsciously and habitually, we think about and describe the concrete facts of our experience. Once this is realized, it becomes evident that it is not Whitehead's prose but ordinary language that is the artificial mode of discourse. Or, to say the same thing positively, it becomes evident that a fresh return to concrete experience will require an unfamiliar terminology to describe what one finds there.

But unless one is to be left with a purely private language which no one else understands, the only language we have for doing this is our ordinary one. At this point the paradox shifts from Whitehead's prose to our own. The very grammar of the sentences we use to give a more correct description of the aesthetically vivid, emotively moving qualities and events of our concrete experience is, itself, the product of old, erroneously inferred entities of thought. Hence, in attempting to correct our corrupted thinking and conduct by writing supposedly clear English sentences, which any conventional nitwit who runs can read, we unconsciously and inevitably recorrupt it.

What has to be realized is that this omnipresent corruption is imbedded in our common-sense beliefs, most of our traditional scientific, philosophical, religious, and aesthetic theories and in the discourse and conduct of our literary humanists and of our moralizing and nonmoralizing politicians. It will help us to see how our ordinary language can be modified so as to correct this situation, if we use a particular concrete experience to show how English grammar has caused us to describe it falsely and to commit several errors of mistaken identity in designating what it signifies.

To be concrete about one's experience, one must, at least in the initial stage of its description, be autobiographical. My summers are usually spent in a cottage on a hilltop in New Hampshire, which commands a remarkable view. Frequently, I look up to find myself immersed in a panoramic continuum of diversified colors and sensuous forms, never twice the same, which is breath-taking in its immediately experienced natural beauty. If this is not concrete experience, what is? Upon some occasions one portion of this concrete, aesthetic, panoramic continuum is to be distinguished from the remainder by an indescribable aesthetic quality to which the English language gives the name "blue."

Were someone who had never experienced this particular concrete object of my senses to ask me what the word "blue" means, neither I nor anyone else could tell him. If he did, however, have in his mind the idea of a material thing or a conscious person, one could say negatively that "blue" denotes neither a material thing nor a person. In other words, it is not the kind of factor of knowledge with which either the physicist or the psychologist is primarily concerned. If, however, our inquirer were acquainted with the contemporary impressionistic or abstract art in which concrete factors of fact, such as "yel-

low," are presented in and for themselves without any
reference to material objects or persons which they may
or may not signify, then we could say to our questioner
that "blue" is like this impressionistic painter's "yellow."
But this means that the concrete factors of fact which one
immediately experiences are essentially and inescapably
aesthetic in the sense of the impressionistic artist. Art in
this pristine sense of sensuous images, bereft of human
inferences beyond them, whether presented breath-takingly
upon occasion by nature or created artificially by the impressionistic artist, the writer elsewhere has called "art in
its first function." [1] Words referring for their entire meaning to such indescribable, immediately sensed images and
experienced items he has called "concepts by intuition," [2]
meaning thereby a word and idea which gets its entire
meaning from something which is directly sensed, introspected, or experienced, and not referring to something
such as a table, a chair, or Tom Smith who may be correctly or incorrectly inferred from what I immediately
sense and experience.

So far in describing my concrete New Hampshirian experience, my English language has not led me astray. But
the concrete blues and sensuous shapes which differentiate
my breath-taking panoramic continuum of immediacy, signify entities of thought beyond themselves, exactly as the
aforementioned impressionistic images signified in fact the
presence of a total stranger, when one had initially and
erroneously inferred that they signified the presence of
one's friend Tom.

It is precisely at this point, when I move in thought
beyond the bare, concrete impressionistic qualities and
images of the concrete panoramic continuum that is immediate experience to what they signify, that the subject-
predicate grammar of my English prose, or of any other
Aryan language, can lead me, as it has led countless scientists, philosophers, and people of common sense, into the
most serious errors. For unless I am aware of what the

grammar of this language may do to me if I do not watch it most suspiciously, I am likely to describe the "blue" part of my breath-taking, panoramic, New Hampshire experience by thinking and saying, "The water in Squam Lake is blue." Note what has happened. I have torn the blue portion of the all-embracing, breath-taking, panoramic continuum of concrete aesthetic immediacy away from this continuum, to fasten it to an entity of thought, "The water of Squam Lake," which I infer the "blue" signifies. But similar blues also signify the sky or an oasis in the desert that is not there.

The latter possibility of error is not, however, the most serious danger. By a further experience of images, I can determine whether or not the "blue" truly signifies "The water of Squam Lake" in this particular occasion. The more serious danger arises when I then walk down through the woods to the lake for a swim and, before plunging in, cup up a handful of its water to observe that it is not blue but clear and colorless. Then, if I do not watch most suspiciously the substance-property strait jacket that is my English grammatical habit of thought, it is likely to do the following to me, as it has done to Aristotle, St. Thomas, Locke, Descartes, Hobbes, Marx, and many modern scientists and philosophers and countless people of common sense: I run the risk, since the blue must be the property of some substance, if the subject-predicate grammar of any Aryan language is to have its way, of saying, "The water of Squam Lake only *appeared* to be blue when I was in my cottage on the hilltop; it is *really* clear and colorless." Forthwith, all the concrete, colorful, breath-taking, aesthetic qualities of my concrete experience are torn away from supposedly real things to be assigned to the phantasmic limbo of appearances. Even worse, the entity of thought called a material substance, bereft of consciousness and all emotive or aesthetic qualities, arises in one's mind to be taken not merely as the only real thing in my experience, but also as the initial datum of my experience before I made any inferences from it. In short, one becomes a common-sense materialist with one's feet supposedly on the ground but with one's capacity to either see or make correct inferences from the concrete facts of oneself and nature utterly corrupted and confused. Forthwith, artists are regarded as effeminate dilettantes, dealing with ephemeral rather than with real things, and the materialistically-minded, contemporary Hobbesian lawyers and statesmen in the free world and the similarly materialistic Marxist Communists who believe that a realistic foreign policy for their own nation in this atomic age can be built on little more than bigger and better hardware, become regarded by the populace as statesmen who are "facing the facts."

But the errors of this patently false description of the concrete facts of experience, into which the subject-predicate grammar has led these common-sense materialists, do not end at this point. For a question immediately arises, If the concretely real is a collection of unconscious, unaesthetic, material substances, why does the blue which I saw from the top of the hill exist at all, even as an appearance? Again subject-predicate grammar is likely to take over, thereby leading me to infer still another nonexistent entity. This second error of mistaken identity usually takes on the following form: Since every quality must be attached to some substance and since the blue is not a property of the unaesthetic, material substances that are "The water of Squam Lake," there must be a different nonmaterial substance to which the blue is attached as its property. Forthwith, the additional entity of thought, known supposedly introspectively with direct concreteness and called a conscious or mental substance, is what I "really" saw when I sensed the blue. But, immediately, even such naïveté notes something to be fishy in one's English prose when one is thus forced to say, "My conscious substantial self is blue." The usual way to get out of this nonsensical predicament in which I have placed myself by using English prose to describe a concrete, breath-taking, panoramic, aesthetic experience, is to retain both the material and the mental substances that this prose has led me erroneously to infer and to then affirm that the blue is the phantasmically projected effect of the action of the material substances upon my private mental substance.

Now the conscious self is stripped of all aesthetic qualities also. Little remains for a person, who thinks of himself in this way, to do but to contemplate his own dull, unaesthetic, blank tabletish, conscious interior and then utter vacuous, moral, and religious platitudes about its equally empty spiritual nature. Need one wonder that the power politicians believe that hardware is more trustworthy than such a spirituality and morality?

Nor are the so-called humanists, who prattle today about the preciousness and importance of art and the humanities, better. For what is the discipline that gives them any competence to speak on anything? Clearly it is literature, or, more specifically, the literature of the English or some other Aryan language. Hence, this subject-predicate mentality is in them also and in everything that they write. Consequently, all they can possibly do is either to talk romantically in an empty way about art as the creative act of such a blank tabletish, essentially unaesthetic human spirit or else to indulge in discourse about the equally unaesthetic gadgets and techniques of the artist or the media of communication. What there is of significance in any concretely-known human being or experience for the artist to say or show, they rarely know or say.

To escape from these errors and confusion by removing the erroneously inferred entities of thought which the subject-predicate grammar of our ordinary language has caused us to foist on ourselves and nature, as if they were the concrete and real facts of our immediate experience, is not easy. More than an expert cross-examiner of what experience witnesses is required. To state what stands up under such cross-examination in our ordinary language without its subject-predicate grammar falsifying the facts of the case in the very statement of them—this is our most difficult problem. Whitehead's method of solving it determined the character of his prose.

When one becomes aware of the fact that one's ordinary language has corrupted the concrete facts of our experience in the very act of stating them, only two available procedures are possible: Either (a) one throws away ordinary language to seek in symbolic logic and pure mathematics a symbolism which will not distort the concrete facts of experience and what they correctly signify, or else (b) one keeps ordinary language but introduces technical terms and unconventional usages which minimize its danger of distorting what we see in the very act of stating it. The theoretical mathematical physicist uses the first of these two procedures, often supplementing it with the second. Every competent contemporary philosopher uses the second procedure, checking it by appeal to the first. Whitehead's competence as a mathematician, symbolic logician, and philosophical analyst of concrete experience was such that in his different articles and books he used both methods. It is likely that one of the mathematical possibles listed in his earlier 1905 paper, "On Mathematical Concepts of the Material World," [3] is the metaphysical system which was stated in his technically modified English prose in *Process and Reality*.

Each procedure has its advantages and disadvantages. Hence, both must be used. Because symbolic logic and mathematics deal with the possible imageless relational structures of all possible conceivable worlds, their language, if properly chosen, can fit itself to any concrete experience and what it correctly signifies as tested empirically without risk of distortion. The danger is thereby escaped of forcing the particular facts of concrete aesthetic immediacy into the Procrustean bed of the subject-predicate grammar of Aryan linguistic prose. The disadvantages of a complete symbolic logical and mathematical language are, however, twofold. First, as is obvious, it does not have the wide popular appeal and reach of ordinary prose. Second, its entity terms are always variables. This means that one must go outside the mathematical symbolism to the material constants which are the values of its variables and to some, but not all, of the nonmathematical concepts of ordinary prose, those, namely, which the writer, just above, called "concepts by intuition." This appeal to the concepts by intuition of ordinary prose, e.g., to words such as "blue" in the sense used earlier, is necessary in order to correlate the unobservable entity variables and their many-termed relations, designated by the mathematically expressed postulates or axioms, with the concrete data of concrete experience. Otherwise, the mathematically expressed statement of the concrete facts of our experience and what they signify could not be verified as being the correct one.

Since the concrete data denoted by concepts by intuiton require the symbols of ordinary language for their statement, the problem becomes that of preserving the latter words in ordinary language, such as "blue," while eliminating the distortions of concrete experience and the erroneously inferred entities of thought entailed by its two-termed, subject-predicate grammar.

The reason why mathematics, and, particularly, its symbolic logic of relations, are required to show us how to do this is easy to understand and applies as much to the reader's ordinary facts of his immediate experience as to the more technical, experimentally determined facts of mathematical physics. Expressed mathematically in terms of the logic of relations, the reason is that any concrete sensed property, such as "blue" or "hot," is a function of many variables and not, as subject-predicate grammar supposes, of merely one, namely, the substance of which it is supposed to be a predicate. Once this is realized, the need to find either an unaesthetic material substance or an unaesthetic mental substance to which to fasten the "blue" which is sensed vanishes; also, the necessity of throwing aesthetic immediacy out of oneself and nature vanishes along with it.

But since ordinary prose requires one to fasten every property to some subject term, how can one express in this prose the concrete fact that the "blue" which I directly sense is a function of many variables, i.e., whether the sun is shining, whether there are clouds in the sky, where I am located when I sense it, and many other factors? The answer, and this is the answer which Whitehead gives, is by making the subject of the English sentence not a substance, but a many-termed relation of which the blue is but one of the terms. This has the effect of stating in English prose that the blue is not the property of a substance, i.e., it is not a function of but one variable but is, instead, a function of many variables designating several other facts of concrete experience and what they signify. This is the point of the thesis of Chapter VII in *The Concept of Nature* which, more than any other, is, in this writer's judgment, the key to Whitehead's entire philosophy. This key thesis is that sense objects, such as blue, "ingress" into nature in many-termed relations. An example of such ingression, similar to my concrete, New Hampshirian example, he describes as follows: "The sense-awareness of the blue as situated in a certain event which I call the situation, is . . . exhibited as the sense-awareness of a relation between the blue, the percipient event of the observer, the situation, and intervening events."[4]

When he commented to me on his use of the somewhat unfamiliar word "ingression" to describe this many-termed relation between the concretely sensed blue and other concrete entities and events of our experience, soon after he had written it in the early 1920's, he said that he chose this word for two reasons: First, in the hope that its unfamiliarity would shock the reader out of his habit of supposing that the qualities we directly sense are related to other facts of concrete experience by the two-termed relation of predicate of a substance. Second, because the ambiguity of the word "ingression" leaves open, exactly as does any concrete experience, the precise many-termed relation and its many terms upon which the existence of the "blue" as a concrete fact of nature depends for its existence in a particular occasion and situation. This is for future images and occasions to determine. Forthwith, the real world is the aesthetically breath-taking, colorful world and it is no longer necessary to infer nonexistent, unaesthetic material, and mental substances whose interaction has the effect of throwing our emotive, aesthetic selves and the other directly sensed concrete facts of experience out of nature as unreal phantasms. The aesthetic implications are obvious. In *Process and Reality* a noun is selected to denote this many-termed relational ingression of any concrete factor of fact into the totality of concrete facts and what they signify. This noun is Nexus.

The procedure should now be clear for solving the linguistic paradox of using ordinary language to correct its distortions of what it tries to say. This procedure consists in retaining its concepts by intuition, such as "blue" or "painful" in their ordinary meaning, while also using other words in a technical way, which is, in part, their ordinary meaning and, in part, a novel meaning. This is what Kant did. It is what Whitehead has done. It is what the writer attempted to do with his expressions "the differentiated aesthetic continuum" and "the undifferentiated aesthetic continuum."[5] These are all attempts to direct attention back from the old, erroneously inferred entities of thought to the concrete inescapably aesthetic and moral data of our immediate experience.

It may be noted, parenthetically, that the contemporary European existentialists' attempt to shift attention from what they call the *Sein* to the here-now-*Da*-ness of this *Sein* in concrete human experiences and concerns is a linguistically confused and romantically irresponsible attempt in the same direction. It is confused because, neglectful of the logic of many-termed relations, it is dominated still by the subject-predicate thing-language. It is romantically irresponsible because, surreptitiously, it is still under the obsession of the pseudocreativity of self-sufficient mental substances or voluntaristic spirits, a creativity which is pseudo precisely because the spiritual consciousness from which it proceeds is either a vacuous blank tablet or an arbitrary and romantic Fichtean will with no relational norms whatever to guide it.

There are also the contemporary Oxfordian, ordinary language philosophers and legal analysts. Reasons, to be noted in the final chapter, exist for believing that they have been misled by a too literal interpretation of the two mysticisms of the "perfect language" and the ordinary linguistic paradigms of Wittgenstein. The result is a confusion of the paradigmatic examples of their own, all too ordinary, English prose, with the nature of things. More specifically, when ordinary English prose is taken paradigmatically, as not further analyzable into nominalistic, radically empirical concepts by intuition, which cannot say but point, and into logically realistic concepts by intellection, which neither say nor point but show, the consequence is the bastard and self-contradictory corruption of both pointing and showing, which is naïve realism.

Metaphorically speaking, the consequence in the case of a too literal interpretation of the later Wittgenstein is that the dull, wonderless distortions of the looking glass itself have been confused with what any glass is for. One would have done better to have followed the purely English and more wonderlandish, but less linguistically naïve, Alice.

At this point, the great Hume did not help matters. No one in modern times makes us aware, as does this notable Scot, of what we would be left with by way of factually warrantable beliefs if all that is directly and indirectly warrantable is restricted, radically empirically, to what is given either introspectively or through the so-called outer senses. This is why anyone who has not been wakened from his naïve "dogmatic slumbers," as were both Kant and Einstein by their reading and studying of Hume, is likely to keep his mind in the narcotic and dogmatic stupor which is naïve realistic slumberland. More specifically, one will suppose that a persisting, determinate self and external objects in public space-time are given as facts by naïve, or direct, introspection and observation. Unfortunately, however, Hume never distinguished naïve realism from concept by intellection logical realism.

Also, being a Scot, the Scottish (naïve) Realism, which is incompatible with his radical empiricism, was present in him as an inherited cultural artifact, as it was in G. E. Moore later. Consequently, as Hume himself wrote, he believed "in practice" in the naïve realism which he knew to be false in fact. This practice of oscillating back and forth between a theoretically nonsensical and factually false naïve realism in which one believes "in practice" and the nominalistic, radical empiricism, which, so far as it goes, is true in fact, we have in *Philosophical Anthropology and Practical Politics* called "the fallacy of the Humean oscillator." Most, if not all, contemporary Anglo-American ordinary language philosophers are guilty of this error and inconsistency.

Nevertheless, in his appeal to what he did "in practice," Hume was correct on one point. He saw that meaningful knowledge of a personal self, which is, in some sense, the same person today that it was yesterday, and of external objects in public space and time, is not given by direct introspection or observation radically empirically through the "inner or outer" senses and can be known only by means of indirectly confirmed theory. What he overlooked is that if his appeal to what happens pragmatically "in practice" is not to contradict his correct description of what is radically empirically the case in fact, he must add to his nominalistic semantic premise, inherited, via Bishop Berkeley, from Locke's *Essay Concerning Human Understanding,* the additional epistemological thesis that there are also logically realistic, indirectly and pragmatically confirmed concepts by postulation that, in whole or part, are concepts by intellection. In other words, he must affirm, with the Democritean, Platonic, Stoic, and modern mathematical natural scientists and philosophers, that, in addition to the nominalistic and relativistic ideas that get their meaning entirely from the senses, there are also concepts in the intellect, the form and content of which are not first in the senses. The precise contemporary content of such ideas in Einstein's physics and Quantum Mechanics will concern us in the final chapters. We shall also give what we believe to be the more correct interpretation of Wittgenstein in Chapter 17.

Having, after the manner of Whitehead, in a linguistically clear and empirically responsible way, in part at least, rid ourselves of the old, naïve realistic, erroneously inferred entities of thought and having returned to concrete immediacy to find its aesthetically vivid and breathtaking events, the many-termed relational concrete facts, rather than the phantasmic ephemeral projections, of ourselves and our world, we are in a position to pass to the more correctly inferred entities of thought which these concrete facts signify. These signified entities, in their lawful, many-termed relations to the concrete, provide their novel criterion of the beautiful. The significance of recent impressionistic and abstract art is that, like Whitehead in his earlier *Principles of Natural Knowledge* and *The Concept of Nature,* it has, in its return to the impressionistic images and continuum of concrete immediacy, broken us and art free from the old Euclidian proportions and perspectives and other old entities of thought and theology which, in major part, defined the traditional classical Western concept of the beautiful.

But, as Whitehead also realized, these inescapably aesthetic concrete particulars signify objects and meanings beyond themselves, even though these objects and meanings are not the traditional, erroneously inferred entities of thought, which, in such major part, made the classical concept of the beautiful what it was. Moreover, as he noted, the persisting objects and meanings project themselves back into the particular aesthetic occasions of concrete immediacy. It is this concept of the beautiful, identified not with concrete aesthetic immediacy *per se* but with what it signifies, which the writer had in mind when he spoke of "art in its second function." [6] Whitehead's specification of the categories that define the beautiful in this second, fuller, and novel sense of what the concrete signifies was implicit in his earlier works on the philosophy of natural knowledge and mathematical physics. It was partially articulated in the two chapters on "Abstraction" and "God" in *Science and the Modern World* and further articulated in *Religion in the Making*. The first systematic summary and statement occurred, however, in his major work, *Process and Reality*. Some of the aesthetic implications of the latter work have been indicated, recently, by Mary A. Wyman in her book, *The Lure for Feeling,*[7] the title of which is a phrase of Whitehead's.

Notwithstanding the indubitably aesthetic character of Whitehead's account of both concrete experience and what it signifies, he never wrote a book on aesthetics. Perhaps the reason was that he believed that he had already done so in the books that he did write.

Whether this be the explanation, I do not know. I do know, however, that in the early 1920's when he took me page by page and chapter by chapter through *The Principles of Natural Knowledge* and *The Concept of Nature,* he often stopped to point out the aesthetic character of the concrete facts from which all science, philosophy, and reflection take their inception. Upon one occasion he added that, unless one finds something aesthetic in the concrete facts from which anyone starts his knowledge, be he philosopher, scientist, or man of common sense, he will never come out at the end of his reflections with an adequate theory of art.

Whatever may be the reason why Whitehead did not write a book in which art was his major concern, we are in a position now to interpret the importance of the recent book, *A Whiteheadian Aesthetic,* by Professor Donald W. Sherburne.[8] It is an attempt to answer one question: If Whitehead had written the book on aesthetics, which is implicit in the books that he did write, what would this book be?

The conclusions speak for themselves. We may, perhaps, best describe the result in the way in which Plato described his own cosmological theory in his *Timaeus.* If this is not Whitehead's book on aesthetics, then it is, at least, very much like it. Some of us, however, who have spent decades in the study of and reflection upon Whitehead's work, believe that Professor Sherburne has done even more than give a documented and reasonable answer to the foregoing important question. For, by illuminating certain of Whitehead's abstract distinctions and categories by means of particular aesthetic materials he has given us not merely a richer and Whiteheadian kind of understanding of art, but also a deeper insight into Whitehead's very concrete, most original, subtle, and systematic philosophy.

12

TAGORE: AN ASIAN POETIC AND POLITICAL GENIUS *

TAGORE was a beautiful harmony of the provincial and the cosmopolitan. He belongs, unequivocally, to India. No other place than the source of Hinduism and Buddhism could have produced him or the images of his poetry. Speaking thus, provincially, from the heart of his native land he says something, however, that expresses the deepest and best in human hearts everywhere. Hence all humanity, equally rightfully with Indians, claim him today as their own.

His language was Bengali. His theme also bespoke the culture of his native province. An Indian of Tagore's genius from another Indian state would have behaved and written differently, as did Gandhi of Gujarat and Iqbal of Lahore. Nevertheless, Tagore's Bengali poetry and prose had, in essential part, a different style and spirit from the Bengali which he learned in his youth. India's cultural historian and able diplomat, Dr. K. M. Panikkar, tells us why in his interesting and important book, *Asia and West-*

---

* The first part of this chapter is a revised section of a chapter to be published in the D. M. Datta Festschrift volume edited by Charles A. Moore of the University of Hawaii.

ern Dominance. The reasons were that (1) India in Tagore's time was dominated by the British; (2) he mastered English and the classics of the English-speaking world. He could hardly, therefore, have missed the influence of Locke's *Letter Concerning Toleration* and his *Of Civil Government* which Jefferson embodied in the American Declaration of Independence and the Bill of Rights of the Constitution of the United States.

These Anglo-American philosophical and political classics may well have reminded Tagore of his native India. For over the ages, rather than for a mere couple of recent centuries, India has been notable for the manner in which her sons and daughters of countless different races, religious faiths, and social customs have lived together without the faith, race, zeal, or customs of one corrupting or destroying that of the other. Thus, notwithstanding the provincial differences between his India, Locke's London, Jefferson's and Lincoln's America, Bengali-speaking Hindus, Buddhists, Jains, and Muslims and modern, English-speaking Judaic-Christians, Tagore, by seeking out the deepest and best in the provincialism of each, found something harmonious between them.

But he also learned from the English-speaking West, while confirming his own in that culture and its philosophy. Otherwise, the Bengali language which he inherited would not have been transformed in both its style and its modern spirit into the Anglicized Bengali which Dr. Panikkar tells us it became in Tagore's hands. To understand, therefore, what one is honoring when one honors Tagore is to realize that, in both the form and the substance of what he did, the soul and linguistic syntax of the modern English-speaking nations at their religiously tolerant and multiparty political best went, by way of the spirit and language of Bengal, into the soul of India to harmonize there beautifully with the best in her own pluralistic religious and political tradition.

Even so, Tagore gave predominant expression, as his

poetic images show, to but one part of India's religious, political, and cultural heritage—namely, its Hindu-Buddhist component. Yet Bengal is as Muslim as Hindu, as is much of the rest of India. Again his provincialism shows. Just as Iqbal of Lahore gave poetic, religious, and political form, in his native Urdu, equally Anglicized, beautiful, and profound, to Islamic India, so Tagore in Bengali voiced the ancient spirit and modern vision of Buddhist-Hindu India. The major themes and images of Iqbal's *The Tulip of Sinai, The Secret of the Self, Persian Psalms,* and *Question and Answer* are (1) *the tulip* that is an Indian Muslim examining his own deepest self to rededicate himself to Allah and (2) *the caravan* symbolizing the spirit of Islam that is thereby set on the march again, not into a Holy War, but towards that Divine self which was implicit in one's own self before the caravan set off. Tagore's images in "The Gardener," "The Crescent Moon," "Gitanjali," and his other poems and plays are (1) *the carefree lovely girl in the swing* who says: "In this playhouse of infinite forms I have had my play and here have caught sight of him that is formless" and (2) *"the dewdrop upon a lotus leaf"* afloat on the pool, persisting with calm equanimity through the transitorily whipped-up waves that, from time to time, would disturb its placidity.

It is upon this lotus that the Buddha is seated in most of the paintings and statues that portray him. The present official seal of Free India is Buddhist. Note, also, in any painting or statue of the Blessed One, the blissful equanimity of the timeless pool's placidity that is reflected from within his face. Contrast this with the religion of Islam, which regards such religious imagery as infamous and idolatrous, or with Christianity, which portrays the face of its Saviour in agony on the cross. Contrast it even with much Hindu Indian religious art that pictures the creator, his mouth drooling blood and gore, as he devours his human creatures. Clearly, Tagore has picked and eliminated even within his Buddhist-Hindu Bengal and India.

Nevertheless, he regarded himself to be as deeply Hindu as he is Buddhist. Nor is this difficult to understand. For the Buddha was the first-born son of a second (ruling) caste Hindu maharaja, destined by this Aryan-Hindu, racial patriarchal primogeniture to be king when his royal father retired; and, although the Hindu Buddha repudiated, as did the Hindu Gandhi and Ambedkar in our century, the Hindu codes of law of Status caste, he did so because he was convinced that Aryan racialism and its castes were incompatible with the very earliest Vedic, and the persisting Hindu teaching that the true self in all persons, like the timeless pool in all its transitory waves, is not merely equal, but identical in all human beings and even with the Divine consciousness. With this concept of the person, only egalitarian free democracy is politically and culturally compatible, as Tagore makes evident in the characters of Supriya and Malini in his play of the latter name.

It is such a Buddhistically reformed Hindu Indian soul that Tagore put, poetically, before his fellow countrymen as both the oldest and deepest part of their own past and present selves and the most trustworthy guide to their future. It was, moreover, by mastering and incorporating the English and American contractual common law, after the manner in which Tagore mastered and incorporated in his Bengali the style and modern liberal spirit of the English language and its classics, that Free India's Constitutional Committee, chaired by the Buddhist-Hindu-minded, British and American educated Ambedkar, contractually constructed the present government of Free India with its written constitution containing its Fundamental Freedoms, the equivalent of the American Bill of Rights. In this legal and political system, Aryan-Hindu racialism with its caste is repudiated; also, all of India's sons and daughters are treated under a common law which they themselves freely and contractually create as if their truest real selves are identical. Clearly, the Buddhist official seal of this government is of more than antiquarian import; also, Tagore's contribution to India's nationalism is not negligible.

But Tagore's nationalism transcended all national boundaries, as did the spirit of his Buddhist Hinduism. Because his religious philosophy taught him that the deepest and real self in all persons, whether Buddhist Hindus or not, is, like the timeless pool or ocean in its relation to its transitorily different waves, the same in all mankind and even all cosmic creatures, Tagore envisaged the different religions and religious nations of the world as diverse, wave-like differentiations of the Divine self in all of us.

This led him to seek out the deepest and best in all religions and religiously rooted peoples. Like India's present Vice President, Professor Radhakrishnan, he realized that God is one, though the ways to Him be many. Conversely, the revelations of God to men are many. For clearly the Divine, which is timeless, indeterminate, and infinite, cannot be revealed in determinate, transitory, finite terms without being exhibited as but one manifestation of its infinite nature. Any nation or religion, consequently, which is to be true to the deepest nature of its own adherents, must behave similarly, in the same cosmopolitan and tolerant spirit, enriching its deepest understanding of its own self and provincial nation by seeing God's different, religiously political manifestations in other religious faiths and nations. This Tagore did for Islam as well as Buddhist-Hindu India, and for all the other religious civilizations and nations of the world as well.

At this point, he struck a note in concord with the Stoic Roman cosmopolitans when, repudiating the religious racialism of what Sir Henry Maine called "law of Status" tribal nations, they created contractual legal science to give the *jus civile* of any other tribal religion and nation the same status under Roman law that was enjoyed by the *jus civile* of their own tribal Roman nation and its religion. This note echoes still in the doctrine of religious and political toleration of England's Locke and Jefferson's and Lincoln's America. The manner in which it has been reinforced by Gandhi, Ambedkar and Nehru's India, to re-echo throughout Africa and the rest of the world, is today a commonplace.

Judging, however, by the number of contemporary nations that permit only a one-party political system, it is easier for many contemporary politicians to hear this note in its anti-imperialistic, than in its domestic, political overtones. Conversely, in the writer's own nation, at least, it is easier for many to voice this note in its implications for the domestic and foreign policy of other nations than it is to apply it, consistently domestically, themselves. The old religions and customs, all of which, originally, and many of which still, are rooted in race and in caste, do not make easy, what Sir Henry Maine called, the "shift from Status to Contract."

In any event, the cultural content of Tagore's genius is clear. He looked at the beliefs and practices of his own religion and nation and at those of the English-speaking, modern liberal democratic nations, not solely in terms of the patent facts indicating where each falls short of its ideals, but also in terms of the deepest beliefs and most consistent behavior of each at its best. Because the beliefs concerning the part of any person's self that is not man-made, of both (1) his provincial Buddhist Hinduism and (2) the modern, tolerative, multiparty, democratic English-speaking nations taught that all human beings were normatively either (a) first-order, factually identical or (b) contractually and, hence, legally and politically, equal with respect to their obligations and their privileges, he found, as we can find, the universal and the cosmopolitan in the provincial. Also, having thus discovered and then existentially committed himself to these two basic philosophical conceptions of both the religious and the secular moral person which, if not identical, were harmonious, the one reinforcing and adding something to the insights of the other, Tagore's poetic spirit expressed this philosophical synthesis in a beautiful harmony.

This experience and rich conception of life's meaning, Tagore then generalized, as we have noted above, for all mankind. Was this generalization warranted?

To answer this question, the ambiguity of the word "warranted" needs to be watched. There is its second-order artifactual cultural reference and its first-order factual naturalistic meaning.

In the former of these two senses, Tagore's bipolar cultural philosophy is not warrantably generalizable for all other artifactual cultural nations and their man-made cultural personalities. Obviously, the political and personal cultural philosophy of Marx and the present Communist nations is not merely different from the Buddhist-Hindu religious and the Anglo-American liberal democratic philosophies of the person and his cultural artifacts, but also incompatible with them. As a recent reviewer in *Pravda* said of books by the writer and by Professor Crane Brinton, cosmopolitanism is "a bourgeois morality" and, therefore, by definition for Communists, not merely outmoded, but evil. (The confusion upon which the latter judgment rests will become evident in later chapters when we examine what the word "bourgeois" means.) Nor is religious toleration compatible with any Communist culture, since, for Marx and his followers, religion in any form is "an opium of the people" and, hence, an evil that is to be eradicated if life's true moral and political meaning is to be found.

There are, however, other people than the Communists whose personal and cultural philosophy and its customs are incompatible with Tagore's cultural philosophy, were it generalized for all mankind. The white, patriarchal, Filmerian Protestant Christians in the Old American South today, with their belief that only racially white, Aryan folk are fit to vote freely, govern, and have the best

government-supported education, are one example. Similar
are the Aryan Mimamsa dualistic, right-wing Fundamentalist Hindus, still persisting in Free India, with their customs of caste and belief that a Free India that represents
the majority of Indians must have lighter skinned Hindu-
Aryans in the positions of topmost religious and political
leadership. Another example is to be found in the non-
modern-minded sultans and sheiks and their countless
Islamic Fundamentalist followers, who believe that the
source of religious and political authority, with its sumptu-
ous privileges, derives from their racially pure, Arabic,
patrilineal breeding and descent from a relative of the
Prophet. Another example appears with many political
leaders in contemporary Africa who (1) profess the cosmopolitan contractual liberal democratic principles of
Locke, Jefferson, and Lincoln in order to eliminate "the
Western imperialists" from whom, incidentally, they
learned these principles, and then (2) revert to the religion and politics of local tribal authority and race to
produce the present political anarchy. In its purely cultural second-order factual, humanistic reference, therefore, Tagore's cultural philosophy is not warrantably universal for all mankind.

Nevertheless, there is another, the most important, sense
in which his generalization may be warranted. For, as
noted just above, the word "warranted" has two meanings—namely, its second-order artifactual cultural, and its
first-order factual, naturalistic reference. Consequently, although it is not at present warrantably generalizable in
the former of these two senses, it may be in the latter.
Is this the case?

It has been noted that Tagore's cultural philosophy has
two philosophical parts. They are: (1) Its Buddhist reformed Hindu concept of the first-order factual person
and (2) its modern Western free democratic concept of
the moral, legal, and political person. At the end of Chapter 2, and in greater detail in the writer's *The Complexity*

of Legal and Ethical Experience, we gave the syntactical and first-order factual empirical grounds, determinable by anyone anywhere, for the universal validity of (2). It remains to determine whether this is the case also for Tagore's Buddhist-Hindu concept of the person.

This first-order factual, descriptive thesis is that each and every human being in the nonman-made naturalistic portion of himself or herself is what the Buddhist intuition of Nirvana, or the unqualified nondualistic Vedantic Hinduism, affirms. Does first-order factual, empirical evidence, determinable again by anyone anywhere, indicate this to be the case? If so, what is this empirical evidence?

Such evidence is well-known to those who have been brought up in Indian culture where the psychological experimental operations of meditation, Yoga, etc., have been practiced. Their aim, experimentally, is to eliminate all the relativistic differentiations of sensing and introspecting from one's all-embracing, radically empirical, immediate experience, to be left with the undifferentiated Atman-that-is-Brahman, which, like the pool embracing its transitory waves, is identical not merely in all persons but also is the Divine consciousness.

Because Western scientists, philosophers, and religious people are accustomed to think only about radically empirical, first-order facts of experience and knowledge, which are differentiated and, hence, determinate—factors that are this rather than that—it is, in the writer's judgment, very difficult to convey in English to Westerners the empirical evidence for this Buddhist-Hindu concept of any person's self in terms of Buddhist and Hindu language, whether Westerners read this in the original Sanskrit and Pali or in a translation, or whether they listen to expert Asian scholars' statements about what it means. When this method is used, the following thing happens again and again: Because it does not occur to Westerners to think that anything undifferentiated exists or is real, they unconsciously read into Nirvana, or the undifferentiated

Atman-that-is-Brahman, Western and Semitic religious determinate concepts of reality, conscious personality, and the Divine consciousness. Once this is done, the sentences of the Hindu and Buddhist texts, whether read in the original or expert translations, become either meaningless nonsense or without any empirical justification whatever.

At this point it may well be asked: But you are a Westerner; how then can you have your apparent confidence that you understand the Buddhist and Hindu concept of the self? The answer is: I wouldn't if I depended on any of the latter methods to determine what it means. The fact is, that in analyzing the theories of recent mathematical physics, I found myself wrestling with the problem of relating (a) its imageless, theoretically known, unobservable, mathematically constructed scientific objects and their laws to (b) the concrete differentiated data of radically empirical, immediate conscious experience, so that both were accounted for with the minimum number of elementary assumptions. For reasons which are to be found in greater detail in the last chapter of my first book, *Science and First Principles,* it became evident that if one is not to be left with as many elementary concepts in one's philosophical analysis of recent mathematical physics as there are different sense qualities relative to different people over the whole of human history, thereby creating a philosophical beard so prodigious that even an Occam's razor powered by atomic energy could not shave it, it is necessary to assume something immediately experienced, all-embracing, psychical, and *undifferentiated.* With such an elemental, purely existentially experienced factor taken as primitive, together with one imageless mathematically constructed concept by postulation that is the physicist's field equation taken also as primitive, the countless sensed, introspected differentiations relative to particular percipients and occasions can be derived as defined concepts. With but these two primitives, the elemental assumptions are not multiplied beyond necessity and Occam's principle is not violated.

The problem then became that of finding a way to express this primitive, radically empirical factor. Note again its characteristics. It is conscious, immediately experienced, *undifferentiated,* embracing both the transitory relative, differentiated knower and the differentiated objects of knowledge, identical in both subject and object and yet the spontaneously creative source of all the differentiated *esse est percipi* qualities that come and go as transitory particulars within it. Little did the writer realize at the time that ancient Asian philosophers had attempted to use determinate words referring to differentiated factors of experience to express the undifferentiated and had given up trying to do so, realizing it to be, strictly speaking, impossible.

There is a linguistic reason for the conclusion. The Sanskrit and Pali texts themselves tell us they are useless to this end. When asked by his pupil what the word "Brahman" means, the guru who knows, bats the question back to the pupil, asking him to state what he thinks it means, knowing full well that, whatever the reply, it will be wrong and will have to be answered with the words "Neti! Neti!," i.e., it isn't this, nor any other determinate this. Paradoxically, in such a reply the guru has answered the pupil's original question, the point being that Brahman is undifferentiated and, hence, cannot be described positively in any determinate language.

Not knowing in the 1920's of these experiences of my ancient Asian Buddhist and Hindu predecessors, the writer proceeded to try to solve the problem of describing the indescribable. The first result, which appears in the final chapter of *Science and First Principles,* attempted to describe this primitive factor as "bare indeterminate experienced quality." When Whitehead read this with much interest, he said that the word *"quale"* would be better, since quality is a determinate thing. Then it became evident that the expression "bare indeterminate experienced quality" was self-contradictory, since to predicate indeterminateness of a determinate quality is to affirm a contradiction. Clearly this expression would not do. Nor did *"quale"* seem satisfactory, since even it suggested too much the atomic and locally provincial.

During this same period, the following question occurred of a sudden to the writer: Isn't the factor in concrete experience and human consciousness, which I am trying futilely to describe, precisely what the Buddhist philosophers mean by "Nirvana" and the Hindus by the "Atman-that-is-Brahman without differences"? It was with this question in mind and with the hope of getting an answer to it that the writer went to the first East-West Philosopher's Conference in Honolulu in 1939 and presented there what appears now in the conference volume, *Philosophy—East and West* (1944), edited by Professor Charles A. Moore.

By then it had become evident that an expression had to be found which would not *describe* this fact in anybody's conscious experience, but *point to* where it is to be found, since only immediately experiencing it can give it. Reacting from the localized atomicity of the word "quality" and even its less determinate form *"quale,"* the writer selected the word "continuum." This gave expression to the all-embracing character, the Brahmanic cosmical nature of this elemental factor, in anyone's experience. But the word "continuum" in mathematical physics has a determinate, imageless, axiomatically constructed concept by postulation that is wholly a concept by intellection meaning. Hence, the word "continuum" by itself will not do, if it is not to mislead Westerners, since the Brahman without differences is not a mathematically constructed, theoretically known, determinately relational entity. Instead, it is radically immediate experience with all differentiations of sensing and sensa removed, signifying nothing beyond itself.

What adjective best distinguishes the all-embracing, radically empirical continuum of immediacy with all sensing and sensed differentia eliminated? At this point the word "aesthetic" suggested itself, since art does not talk about its subject matter but shows it denotatively and existentially as immediately experienced. Even so, this use of the adjective "aesthetic" is misleading unless it is taken, as the writer specified in *The Meeting of East and West,* in the sense of impressionistic art rather than of art which signifies some doctrinally known or mathematically conceived and proportioned entity beyond itself. But the continuum of impressionistic, immediately experienced aesthetic immediacy is, except at its periphery, usually differentiated; whereas the primitive factor necessary to clarify the distinction between the mathematical constructs of mathematical physics and the concrete data of experience, without growing a prodigious philosophical beard, is this aesthetic continuum of immediacy without the differentiations which sensing and sensa exhibit. The adjective "undifferentiated" when added to the words "aesthetic continuum" seemed, therefore, to suffice to point the Western reader to the factor in question in his immediate experience, and to prevent anyone from supposing that it is an object of sense awareness, since both sensing and the objects of the senses are differentiated.

These autobiographical experiences have been given here to one end. They indicate the truth of Tagore's Buddhist-Hindu concept of the person to be empirically verifiable as a first-order fact by anyone anywhere in, at least, the following three ways: (1) By the Asian operational techniques of meditation and Yoga, in which all differentiations are removed from radically empirical experience as far as this is possible. (2) By William James' observation that radically empirical experience is an all-embracing continuum which is undifferentiated at its periphery and transitorily differentiated only at what he called "the focus of attention." Bakewell (who had known James personally), after reading my *Meeting of East and West,* said: "James in his description of radically empirical experience noted what you call 'the undifferentiated continuum.' " (3) It may well be the case, also, that the *existential import* of the unobservable, indirectly confirmed, differentiated, and imageless many-termed relational scientific objects (for which the writer used the words "concepts by postulation" to distinguish from naïve realistic entities) finds its denotative empirical meaning in what the Buddha named Nirvana, the nondualistic Vedantic Hindu refers to as the cosmic Brahman without differences, and the writer called "the undifferentiated aesthetic continuum." Concretely, this means that the latter factor gives any unobservable scientific object, such as an electron, its empirical existence, apart from which it would be a mere intellectually conceived mathematical possible; whereas the scientific object's concept by intellection many-termed relational universal laws give it its specific scientific properties, after the manner shown in Chapter 4.

In any event, Tagore was a genius. Clearly, also, his genius was fed by the two provincialisms of (1) his own Buddhist-Hindu India and (2) the influence of the modern, English-speaking world upon it. By probing these two major materials of his experience to their deepest and most elementary best, his poetry gave expression to a beautiful, cosmopolitan harmony which he generalized for all mankind. Both parts of this philosophy, when examined with respect to their first-order factual references, we have found to be empirically confirmable by anyone anywhere, and hence warrantably generalizable for all mankind.

13

LIFE'S CONTEMPORARY
RELIGIOUS MEANING

THE MERE FACT that contemporary knowl-
edge is human knowledge has religious import. For human knowledge means the possibility of error, and error
is the precondition for any human behavior that is the
causal effect of human knowledge being meaningfully sinful or virtuous. Clearly, sin and virtue are of religious significance.

Moreover, without knowledge that is human, man is
not responsible for any part of his conduct. Otherwise,
the religious problem of evil, concerning how a perfectly
good God can create a sinful human world, becomes insoluble. This is evident when one recalls from previous
chapters that facts *qua* facts merely are; hence, it is meaningless to talk about them being or not being in error.
Only descriptive human beliefs, concerning what facts
are, can be or not be in error. According to religion, God
is both perfectly good and the Creator of the first-order
facts of nature and nonman-made human nature. Consequently, unless there is human knowledge, which alone
is capable of being in error, and for which man is responsible, the sin and evil of man's doings are God's re-

sponsibility rather than man's. In other words, God would then be a sinner and the religious idea of God as both a perfectly good Being and the Creator of both nature and naturalistic human nature would be a self-contradictory and, hence, a nonsensical combination of words, analogous to "a round square."

The crucial importance of human knowledge for religion should not come as a surprise to people in the Semitic religious cultural tradition of Judaism, Christianity, or Islam. From where did those of us (secularists and religious alike) in Western and Middle Eastern civilization first get a poetic, metaphorical statement of the religious significance of human knowledge? Clearly, it was neither in Euclid's elements, nor Quantum Mechanics (as some today seem to suppose), nor in any one of the countless incompatible, purportedly self-warranting philosophies of our contemporary secular moral or religious humanists who, treating second-order, metaphorical, cultural artifacts autonomously, as if they were first-order facts, leave human error meaningless. Instead, as previous chapters have again and again emphasized, it was in the story of Adam and Eve, as handed down to us from the ancient Jews in one of the Semitic religious world's oldest classics.

But some contemporary humanists may say: This proves that it is in the humanities and their autonomous moral and religious philosophy, rather than in natural science and its naturalistic philosophy, that life's moral and religious meaning is to be found. The thoughtlessness of this pronouncement becomes evident when one attends to the substantive content of the story of Adam and Eve. As merely a humanistic cultural artifact it is poetry rather than religion, and not the most subtle or refined poetry at that; being, perhaps, more appropriate in the Folies Bergère or a Minsky Burlesque than in a Jewish synagogue, a Christian church, or an Islamic mosque.

Only the substance of this poetry makes this second-order, culturally relativistic artifact something not merely of religious, but also of world-wide secular moral, import. In fact, so far as the moral meaning of the story is concerned, its substantive content is as valid in its first-order factual, naturalistic meaning and reference for agnostics and atheists as it is for religious folk. This substantive content we now know very well. It is that sin or virtue, goodness or badness, and justice or injustice are meaningfully predicable of human behavior, only if that behavior is (1) the causal effect of human beliefs for which (2) man is responsible and which may be descriptively in error or not in error, (3) as determinable by human beings, with respect to the first-order facts of naturalistically caused or God-made nature and natural man. Otherwise, in the Garden of Eden story, Adam and Eve would not have been innocent, in the morally neutral meaning of this word, before they initially ate of the tree of human knowledge and then produced the first second-order cultural artifact.

It is to be noted, also, that all three items specified in the lengthy sentence just above are essential: (1) Being the causal effects of human beliefs is necessary because, let it be repeated, facts *qua* facts merely are, and are, therefore, incapable of error. Items (2) and (3) are also essential, for, unless man is responsible for the beliefs which he obtains by entering into human knowledge and is able by human means to determine whether or not they are in error, the responsibility for conduct, that is the causal effect of assenting to and existentially and voluntaristically committing oneself to any human belief, would not be man's responsibility.

This, in all likelihood, is why the ancient Hebrew religious poet and naturalistic sage had God warn Adam and Eve not to eat of the fruit of the tree of human knowledge. God had to make it unequivocally clear that the responsibility was man's and not nature's or that of nature's God.

Also, as emphasized in previous chapters, the reference

of this humanly and empirically testable knowledge has to be to the first-order facts of nature and of naturalistic nonman-made human nature. It cannot be to the cultural artifacts of the religious or secular humanists. For, before the first human being made his or her first descriptive judgment, thereby producing the first apple on the tree of human knowledge, there were no such cultural humanistic artifacts for the knowledge to refer to. Hence, any humanistic, second-order, cultural artifact, be it religious or secular, is meaningless apart from not merely a historically, but also a logically antecedent cognitive belief with respect to naturalistic first-order facts.

It is to be noted, also, that man's responsibility for his knowledge and its testing (3) by human means applies as much to his belief in the existence of God as the Creator of nature and naturalistic human nature, as it does to any other cognitive naturalistic belief. Consequently, to test whether man's belief in religion is meaningful and first-order factually warranted, it will not do to ground this warrant solely in an appeal to the second-order religious artifacts of the world's cultures as the modern religious and secular humanists, since the time of Kant, have tried to do. This is to beg the question concerning whether God as the Creator of first-order factual nature and human nature exists.

That such is the case becomes evident when one notes that there are atheistic and agnostic, as well as religious, humanists. Also there are cultures in the world and cultural philosophies, such as those of the Marxists and other atheists and agnostics, in which religion and its second-order cultural artifacts are regarded as the causal effect of a belief concerning first-order factual nature and natural man, which is not warranted. Certainly the religious humanist would not take the second-order anti-religious artifactual behavior of thoroughgoing Marxist Communists and other materialists and atheists or agnostics as empirical evidence that the belief in a Divine being is erroneous. But the consistent modern post-Kantian religious humanist cannot have his cake on this point and eat it also. If it is question-begging for the atheist or religious agnostic to present his cultural artifacts as empirical proof that the belief in religion is erroneous, it is similarly question-begging for the religious humanist to present his religious cultural artifacts as evidence for the theists' belief being meaningful and correct.

In point of fact, so far as first-order factual warrants for religious beliefs are concerned, the post-Kantian, modern religious humanists are in agreement with the atheists and religious agnostics. Such is the case because all three groups affirm that there is no meaning for religion in naturalistic first-order factual knowledge. The atheists and religious agnostics differ from the post-Kantian modern religious humanists merely in the reasons they give for this common conclusion. The atheists' and religious skeptics' reason is that an examination of first-order factual, empirically verified naturalistic knowledge provides no meaning for the beliefs of religion. The recent religious humanists' reason is that religion and ethics, including law and normative politics, are autonomous subjects and, hence, do not have to go, and would be misguided if they tried to go, to first-order factual natural knowledge for their cognitive meaning and warrant.

The reason for the error in the latter conclusion has been given in this and previous chapters. The humanistic conception of religion forces one to treat second-order cultural human artifacts as not further reducible, and, hence, as mere fact *qua* fact. This leaves error meaningless and the normative words good, bad, just, unjust, virtuous, or sinful in the humanists' autonomous language and philosophy equally so.

Moreover, if religion is an autonomous subject, with its personally and culturally relative cultural artifacts the sole empirical ground for its meaningfulness, then even for those of religious faith, who are persuaded by the cultural artifacts of their own particular faith and culture, another question has to be faced. Moreover, the presence of humanists in their own midst or culture who are atheists or agnostics makes the facing of this question inescapable. The question is whether or not the particular religious cultural artifacts of one's own particular religious denomination and faith, or any other, are not mere religious poetry, as Santayana affirmed, or mere escape-hatch expressions of wishful thinking, as the Marxists, in their description of religion as "the opium of the people," maintain. In other words: Is religion something that arises not from having faced, but from having failed to face, what the able and sensitive religious philosopher Professor Paul Tillich has called *The Courage To Be* in the first-order factual sense of the word "be"?

The culturally artifactual example from the Semitic religious tradition, which we have so frequently used, will serve to make this inescapable question more concrete. Taken merely autonomously, the Garden of Eden story is, so far as the question of the existence of God is concerned, mere religious poetry in which a being in apparently human form, with the proper name God, is portrayed as issuing commands in an orchard to a nude male and female sitting under an apple tree with nothing but a solitary, stray, wind-blown fig leaf available as the very partial clothing for one of them. Certainly this is not sufficient ground for warranting the belief in a Divine being. Moreover, if on warrantable grounds one did believe in such a being, one could hardly believe that He is quite so anthropomorphic in his first-order factual nature as this metaphorical story of God in an apple orchard makes Him out to be.

This does not mean that the Hebrew religious poet's anthropomorphic way of bringing the object of warrantable religious knowledge into his story is not something more than dramatically methaphorical second-order artifactual poetry, and something other than escape-hatch poisonous wishful thinking. It may also be a metaphorically poetic way of trying to say something that is cognitively knowable, humanly testable, and not sophomorically anthropomorphic or nudely sexual. In other words, it may be the result of the courage to face the first-order facts of nature and human nature that be.

But if such be the case, neither this nor any other religious cultural artifact, or its purportedly self-warranting humanistic religious philosophy, tells us what this less anthropomorphic and nonescape-hatch "something more" is. Only an empirically scientific facing of the first-order facts of nature, including nonman-made human nature and its naturalistic philosophy, can do so.

Nor does a religion of revelation alter the situation. If anything, it makes matters more difficult. First, the Prophets or Revealers usually speak in parables. They require some kind of interpretation, after the manner of God in the Garden of Eden, before the parables become meaningful or clear. Second, man's commitment to accept or not accept this revelation must be his, rather than God's, responsibility. Otherwise, without the error which man's cognitive beliefs and man's responsibility for those beliefs alone makes possible, man's virtue or vice in either accepting or not accepting the revelation is left meaningless. This entails that man himself must pass judgment on whether or not the revealed pronouncements are, as determined by him, first-order factually confirmed or not. He cannot, after the manner of experienced professionals in an army camp and most politicians, "pass the buck" to someone else or to God. As the Vicar of Lostock, Boston in England has recently said on a British broadcast, published afterward in *The Listener* of December 21, 1961: "To whom am I ultimately responsible? . . . God knows. He has left the decision to me. And this still holds true even if He should not be there at all."

Even though the good Vicar leaves it a bit unclear how a God, who may not be, "knows" anything, the point of his entire statement stands. This point, I take it, is that the question of what the culturally relative artifacts of his particular religion's revelation mean, or even whether their God "be there" in the sense of first-order factual there-ness, are questions which man, in the light of the first-order factual evidence available to him, must take the responsibility for answering, with all the possibilities of error that this involves. Neither revelation nor God can do it for him. Otherwise it would be meaningless for God, the good Vicar, or anyone else to evaluate the artifactual behavior of anyone with respect to religion as virtuous or sinful. For, let it be repeated, where the possibility of error is absent, human sin or virtue are also.

Furthermore, the error has to be with respect to human descriptive statements about first-order naturalistic facts. It cannot be error in one's descriptive judgment of second-order cultural artifacts, for the question dividing the person of religious faith and the atheist or the agnostic is precisely whether religious cultural artifacts ought to be.

We conclude, therefore, that if the normative words in the cultural artifacts of religious believers have a meaning other than that of mere poetry or an escape-hatch from "the courage to be," this meaning must be found in the first-order facts of nature and nonman-made human nature.

14

RELIGION AND NATURAL KNOWLEDGE

Two aspects of natural knowledge are relevant. One is the generic method by which it is known; the other, its specific content. Historically, in both the Orient and Occident, man's conception of God has been determined as much by the way of knowing as by what is known. We shall start with the generic method, bringing in part of the specific content of Einstein's mathematical physics by way of example. The natural knowledge of early man everywhere, and, especially, Buddhist and Hindu Asian man, will also be considered.

Appropriately, we begin with contemporary mathematical natural knowledge, since today its technology, at least, is wanted by the entire world, and its theory is being advanced as much by Asian as by European and American scientists. Also, apart from Western contractual legal and political thinking, it is the major thing the rest of the world wants from the modern West.

Chapter 3 has shown that contemporary mathematical physics is the most practical knowledge the world has ever possessed. It is also the most speculatively discovered, theoretical, and imagelessly intellectual. Other chapters have made it evident that our common-sense beliefs (a) in our own selves as determinate persisting persons and (b) in external objects in a public spatio-temporal world are theoretically meaningful and empirically confirmable only by means of such speculatively discovered, imageless, intellectually conceived theory with its indirect method of empirical verification in crucial experiments. The supposedly meaningful, naïve realistic notions of conscious mental substances and material substances, whether the latter be Aristotelianly teleological or not, have been found to be nonexistent empirically and self-contradictory theoretically. In summary, both common-sense and natural science require many-termed relational concepts by intellection that are confirmed indirectly by the epistemic correlation of (1) their more relativistic logically deduced theorems with (2) completely relative imageful empirical data denoted by nominalistic concepts by intuition.

Reasons, referred to in a previous chapter, have also been given in Part I of the writer's *Philosophical Anthropology and Practical Politics,* for believing that the epistemic correlations are one-many or many-one in the case of objects that are other than the knower and are one-one when the object known is the knower himself. The latter one-oneness has the consequences of making the relatedness of one's introspectively known self, with its concept by intuition and concept by intellection ideas, isomorphic with the relatedness of the epistemically correlated and indirectly confirmed trapped impulses in one's neurophysiological cortical self that were described in Chapter 1. This isomorphism insures that the two relatednesses are an identity. In other words, one's completely known self is a single person.

It was shown in the chapter on Korzybski's semantics that, in the case of concepts by intellection, relations determine the properties of the entities they relate according to universally quantified laws. The identity, or isomorphism, of the relatedness of one's introspected ideational and of part of one's cortical neurophysiological self has two exceedingly important consequences for moral man. First, it means that relationally conceived, invariant, conscious man is, in part, causally self-initiating man so far as some of the scientific events of his brain and the motor behavior of his body are concerned. This self-initiation gives, in naturalistic terms, what Kant's analysis of normative language showed to be a necessary precondition for meaningful personal moral freedom and responsibility. Second, as shown in Chapter 1, it enables us to understand how evaluatively and descriptively believing man can causally effect his own second-order artifactual human behavior. The unbridgable gulf between natural man and moral man and between the *Naturwissenschaften* and the humanistic *Geistenwissenschaften* is removed. Moreover, it is done in such a way that human error and, therefore, normative words are made cognitively, as well as persuasively and emotively, meaningful.

The fact that the epistemic correlations are not one-one, when the object known is other than the knower, explains two things: first, why the relatedness of sensed objects, events, and qualities is not isomorphic with the relatedness of external common-sense and scientific objects and events in public, logically realistic space-time; second, why, therefore, any abstractive theory of objective knowledge, such as that of either Aristotle or Whitehead, does not work. For the detailed empirical and epistemological grounds for this conclusion, see the writer's chapters, "Whitehead's Philosophy of Science" and "Einstein's Conception of Science," in the respective Whitehead and Einstein volumes of the Library of Living Philosophers, together with Einstein's comments in the latter volume on my description of his conception of science.

So much for the method and the theory of knowledge of contemporary mathematical natural knowledge. What is its content?

Let us answer this question in terms of Einstein's Special and General Theories of Relativity. For Quantum Mechanics, see Professor Werner Heisenberg's *Philosophy and Physics* and its Introductory Preface, in which the present writer analyzes and compares the strong, deterministic concept of mechanical causality of Newton's and Einstein's Theories with its less strong meaning in Quantum Mechanics; also, Chapters 15 and 18 of the present book. The weaker meaning, which Quantum Mechanics finds it necessary to assume in its definition of the state of any naturalistic system, is also relevant to the problem of human freedom and causal determinism.

In considering the content of the Special and General Theories of Relativity, the reader must not allow himself to be misled, as Hitler was, and countless humanists and social scientists have been, by the word "Relativity" in the names of these two theories. This word is in their names because the most elemental principle and assumption of Einstein's two theories is the Principle of Relativity. To get at the content of either theory, we must, therefore, first determine what this principle means and then go on to the other assumptions of each theory.

The Principle of Relativity has two epistemically correlated meanings. One is its concept by intellection, logically realistic meaning. The other is its nominalistic concept by intuition, radically empirical, and operational meaning. Empirically and operationally the Principle of Relativity faces, accepts, and fits natural knowledge to all the relativity of radically empirically known facts as described in previous chapters. Moreover, it predicts even greater relativity of all directly sensed or operationally measured objects, events, space, and time to where one stands when one looks at nature, than was found to be the case by even (1) the ancient Asian Confucians, Hindus, and Buddhists, (2) the ancient Greek Sophists, Democriteans, Platonists, and Stoics and (3) by Galilei, Newton, Berkeley, Hume, and William James. Hence, in the concept by intuition and operational portion of its meaning,

the Principle of Relativity affirms that all objects, properties, and events given by mere observation are not external
objects or events in public space and time but are, instead, relative to the perceiver, his various sense organs,
and when and where he stands when he looks at natural
phenomena. This is the first part of what Einstein meant
when he wrote that physics (like common sense) rests on
the belief in an external world, and we only know such
a world by speculative means; we do not observe it naïvely
or directly. This also is why naïve realism is an empirically
false theory.

But there is a second part of what he meant. Otherwise,
we would not know an external world at all. This second
part arises from the fact that the Principle of Relativity,
also, has its concept by intellection logically realistic meaning. This meaning is that the imageless, many-termed
relational, postulationally constructed laws of natural
knowledge remain constant, or, in other words, invariant,
through all the relativity to the perceiver, his sense organs,
and the place where he stands or to which he refers his
empirical observations. Consequently, any scientific theory
resting on the Principle of Relativity affirms, without contradiction, that (1) in the observational, imageful, nominalistic, and operational part of natural knowledge all is
relative and (2), in its concept by intellection logically
realistic part, there is nevertheless an invariant, and in this
very specific sense, an objective space-time and its events
and objects the same for all knowers.

Mathematically, this bipolar theme, which the Principle
of Relativity affirms, is expressed by saying that the speculatively discovered, indirectly confirmed, many-termed relational universal laws of nature must remain constant or
invariant for any transformation of co-ordinates. The epistemically correlated empirical values of the variables will
be different when the observations are made from one
place in nature rather than another, but the laws relating
the variables will be identical.

It might be thought, at first, that such objectivity would be empty. Two considerations show, however, that such is far from being the case. First, it will be recalled from Chapter 4 that, in concept by intellection language, the formal properties of the relations are everything. They define the scientific objects and events that are the relata in the many-termed relations. Second, the formal properties of these relations, in any theory for which the Principle of Relativity holds, are such that the invariant theory itself prescribes what, in the concept by intellection sense of "what," will be observed in one frame by one perceiver or one sense organ rather than another. In short, the formal properties of the invariant relations are such that they themselves specify what is mathematically invariant and objective and what is relative in the theory.

This will become evident in the sequel, when we (1) pass from one theory to another in modern physics in which the Principle of Relativity holds and (2) find that the concept by intellection specification of what is absolute and what is relative changes from one theory to the next. It shows, also, in the mathematical fact that, in any theory for which the Principle of Relativity holds, there are transformation equations taking one from the relativistic epistemically correlated images and operationally determined empirical values of the variables as determined in one frame of reference to their quite different empirical values as determined in a different frame. Without the invariant objective, formal laws of the scientific theory, the mathematical relational content of these transformation equations could not be specified. We shall illustrate this also in a moment by the difference between the transformation equations and the invariant laws in Newton's Mechanics and in Einstein's Special Theory of Relativity.

So much for the meaning of the word "relativity" in the name of Einstein's theories. It expresses the fact that the elemental postulate of both theories is the Principle of Relativity with its relativistic concepts by intuition and its objective and relative concepts by intellection, the relativistic concepts by intellection being in epistemic correlation with the relativistic directly sensed data denoted by concepts by intuition.

One must not suppose that the Principle of Relativity originated with Einstein. It applies to geometry in the case of the Pythagorean theorem of the ancient Greeks. In fact, the evolution of Western scientific knowledge, apart from the naïve realism of the Aristotelian era, may be described as little more than successive generalizations of the Pythagorean theorem. Galilei discovered that the Principle of Relativity applies to the uniform motions of natural objects and, following him, Newton made the principle basic in his dynamical Mechanics.

But how, then, can Einstein's theory differ so markedly from Newton's as we have found in previous chapters that it does? The answer is twofold:

(1) The Principle of Relativity did not hold in Maxwell's Electromagnetics. The Michelson-Morley experiment was performed precisely in order to confirm this implication of Maxwell's theory. Its failure to do so was what made its findings so disturbing. What Einstein's Special Theory of Relativity did was to extend Galilei's and Newton's Principle of Relativity from mechanics to electromagnetics, thereby giving the latter science objective knowledge, which escapes relativity to where one happens to be standing in nature when one looks at its phenomena, just as Newton's theory had done. It was this extension which reconciled the Michelson-Morley experiment with Newton's theory so far as the Principle of Relativity in that theory is concerned.

(2) However, when the Principle of Relativity was extended to electromagnetics, an even more shocking thing occurred. As Einstein's distinguished later colleague, the theoretical mathematical physicist, Weyl, first expressed it to the writer in Zurich in 1927, "It was the genius of Einstein to have discovered that light has a unique meta-

physical status in the universe." Expressed in less purple prose, this means that light propagation is not like mule propagation, automobile propagation, rocket propagation, or even the motion of a baseball. In the case of all the latter propagations, the motion is defined relationally in terms of space and time; whereas in the unique case of light propagation, space and time are relationally defined in terms of it. Expressed in theological language, Eddington's dramatic crucial experiment, which showed Newton's and Maxwell's theory of the relation between space, time, and light propagation to be false and Einstein's to be correct, means that when God created the universe, He said "Let there be light" and, after that, added, "Now there can be space-time and the motion of other things."

God said "space-time." How do we know? Because the many different, crucial experiments confirming Einstein's Special Theory, and disconfirming Maxwell's and Newton's, entail two things: First, both (a) sensed and operationally measured "public" space and (b) sensed and operationally determined time are one thing when "publicly" observed from one physical object in nature and a different thing when observed from any other object moving relative to the first with a constant velocity. Concretely, this means that events which occur "publicly" at the same time in one frame will not happen simultaneously as seen or measured from another frame. Also, the spatial distance between two events will be different in one frame from what it is when observed or measured from a different frame. Second, the Principle of Relativity, in its logically realistic concept by intellection meaning, requires, however, that something else be objectively absolute or invariant for any transformation of coördinates which the shift of the observer from one frame to another entails. In the Special Theory of Relativity, this "something" is the four-dimensional chronogeometrical distance between any two events, called for short "space-time." Consequently, after God had said, "Let there be light," He then said, "ds^2 = dx^2 + dy^2 + dz^2 — c^{2}t^2, meaning thereby "Now there can be objective four-dimensional space-time." Then other things than light were able to move.

The latter result means that there are two postulates in Einstein's Special Theory of Relativity. They are: I. The Principle of Relativity for Galilean frames of reference. II. The Principle of the Absolute Velocity of Light *in vacuo*. It is the latter principle which warrants Weyl's description of Einstein's genius. Nothing in the universe but light satisfies Postulate II.

This is why the transformation equations of Einstein's Special Theory of the Principle of Relativity contain *c* as a constant, thereby expressing the objectivity and absoluteness of the velocity of light through the relativity that space, independently, and time, independently, exhibit, when one looks at the four-dimensional local events of nature from different external objects in nature. It is also why the transformation equations required by the Principle of Relativity in Galilei's and Newton's physics did not contain the constant *c* and, as a consequence, left both (1) independent three-dimensional Euclidian metrical space and (2) one-dimensional noncyclical independent serially ordered time, invariant and, therefore, objective. We now see how, as the Principle of Relativity is extended from one branch of natural knowledge to another, in this case from mechanics to electromagnetics, one's concepts of what is objective and what is relative in human first-ordered factual knowledge alter accordingly.

In Postulate I, above, of Einstein's Special Theory of Relativity, it is to be noted that the Principle of Relativity is qualified by the additional phrase "for Galilean frames of reference." It was precisely this qualification which drove Einstein on to the discovery of his General Theory of Relativity.

Newton was very well aware, with respect to his Mathematical Mechanics, as Einstein was with respect to his mechanical and electromagnetic Special Theory of Relativity, that a theory, which thus restricts the Principle of Relativity on which it rests, has one very obvious weakness. This weakness is that if Eddington or anyone else had stood on a non-Galilean frame of reference, or referred his observations to such a frame, the laws of nature of both Newton's Mechanics and Einstein's Special Theory of Relativity would be found to be empirically false in the precise empirical sense that Eddington found Newton's theory to be false for even a Galilean frame of reference when he (Eddington) looked at his aforementioned photographic plate.

Clearly, as Einstein noted, any such theory is unsatisfactory. The laws of nature ought to be independent of where the man of common sense or science stands when he looks at nature. Moreover, "objectivity" is not objective unless this is the case.

Einstein achieved this unrestricted kind of objectivity for the science of mechanics (but not for electromagnetics) in his General Theory of Relativity. Its basic assumption is the Principle of Relativity without any restriction whatever. This is why it is called the General Theory of Relativity. Quantum Mechanics also requires the same principle-of-relativity invariance.

The results in the case of Einstein's General Theory are striking: (1) The Pythagorean theorem had to be generalized to contain ten variables instead of merely the four $x, y, z,$ and t variables and the constant c of the Special Theory of Relativity. (2) The invariant tensor equation for gravitation of the General Theory, containing these ten g_{ik}'s, included the one g_{ik}, or field potential, of Newton's Gravitational Theory and combined Newton's three laws of motion into one law. Modern natural knowledge is shaved by Occam's razor with a vengeance. (3) The objective invariant chronogeometry of the universe is found not to be metrically homogeneous and Euclidian everywhere and always, but is, instead, differentially Riemannian with Euclidian geometry present only in the infinitely small and where the localized concentrations of mass-energy are negligible. Hence, just as Newton's Mechanics and Maxwell's Electromagnetics came out of Einstein's mechanical and electromagnetic Special Theory of Relativity as special cases of the latter, so Einstein's Special Theory of absolute space-time comes out of the quite differentially Riemannian space-time of the General Theory of Relativity as a special case. This is the remarkable thing about logically realistic, speculatively discovered, and indirectly confirmed natural knowledge. The more facts it encompasses, the less is assumed theoretically. One's entities are not multiplied beyond necessity. Thus, the medieval Father Occam is kept busy in Heaven sharpening his razor.

We should now understand also what Einstein meant when he frequently said: "God does not wear His heart on His sleeve." It was quite usual for him to use religious language to describe contemporary mathematical physics. God would probably have returned the compliment by saying, "Let there be the Einsteinian tensor equation for gravitation." What Einstein meant, in all likelihood, was that the objective in nature is not on its naïvely observed surface. Instead, to use our own language, it is approached only asymptotically, by trial and error, with speculatively discovered, imageless, many-termed relational theory which (i) satisfies the Principle of Relativity and (ii) is exceedingly difficult for finite human erring minds to find with the concept by intellection content that gets confirmed, concept-by-intuitionwise, in epistemically correlated crucial experiments. Einstein's delightful and brief way of saying this is much to be preferred—*provided* one knows, from his mathematical language, what his anthropomorphic theological language means.

It was noted in Chapter 3 that any theory in natural science gives knowledge of mind and its meaningful ideas as well as empirically verified knowledge of nature. Such is the case because mind has to be the kind of thing which can entertain the different semantic, or epistemological, species of ideas that the verified theories of natural science contain. Both the Theories of Relativity and Quantum Mechanics leave no doubt concerning what these epistemological species of ideas are. They are nominalistic concepts by radically empirical intuition in epistemic correlation with logically realistic concepts by intellection.

They are realistic because they do give meaning to an objective space-time and its events and objects, which remain invariant through all the relativity of sensed events, properties, objects, and sensed space and time. They are logically (rather than naïvely) realistic, not merely because imageful substance-poverty naïve realism is a self-contradictory and, hence, meaningless notion, but also because, as given in successively generalized "Pythagorean theorems," they are not defined, in either their form or their content, by imageful ideas or properties given first to the senses. It is impossible to sense or even imagine a four-dimensional metrical continuum, to say nothing about sensing whether it has homogeneous or heterogeneous metrical properties everywhere and always.

That no one senses a public space embracing the whole of the physical universe through all of time is evident to anyone, quite apart from mathematical physics, who stops to think for even a moment. The writer's sense of sight reaches only to the local horizon. A Britisher in a London fog hardly senses a space reaching farther than the end of his nose.

The same is even more obvious for public time. Consider what we know about time as given merely to our senses. To have knowledge of public time through the senses we must first sense which of all the events, not merely on the other side of the earth in Australia, but also throughout the entire cosmos, happen at the same time and which do not. Sensing, when one is located in New Haven, which events are happening at the same moment in Melbourne, certainly takes a bit of doing. As the British would say, "This is a pretty big cup of tea." To be able to sense such events over the entire universe is a cup of tea so big that one is justified in doubting whether Aristotle, St. Thomas, Maritain, Mortimer Adler, Whitehead, or even my beloved friend and colleague, Professor Paul Weiss, are about to drink it. It is precisely at this point that the writer, in his article, "Whitehead's Philosophy of Science," in the Whitehead volume of the Library of Living Philosophers, left Whitehead's epistemological philosophy of both common sense and physics for that of Einstein.

It is easy to show that we do not know with our senses the public now-ness of even two spatially separated events which are within the local horizon and no farther apart than a relatively few miles. Consider the following example:

Imagine two loud and very sharp explosions which occur eight miles apart. Suppose, also, that a level, straight road, upon which we and others are standing, connects the places of the two explosions and that a person, A, is at a point near the easternmost explosion, a person, B, is midway between the two explosions, and a person, C, is at a point near the westernmost explosion. Suppose, also, that the three people are from the bush of some un-Westernized, isolated spot in Africa and, therefore, know nothing about the Western mathematical physics of acoustics with its concept by intellection theories and their technological gadgets, such as telescopes and Greenwich-time-set watches. Let us then ask these three persons, A, B, and C, the following question: Did the two explosions heard by you occur at the same time, or not? Let it be noted that unless these three persons give the same answer to this question, then no one senses a public time even over the short distance of eight miles, to say nothing about over the spatial extension of the entire cosmos.

Let us suppose also that beside the person, A, Aristotle is located, beside B there stands St. Thomas, and beside C

Professor Mortimer Adler, each to confirm for us that what A, B, and C report is respectively correct. The plain fact is that if B and St. Thomas standing beside him report that they heard the two explosions as occurring at the same time, A and Aristotle to the east will report that the explosions did not happen at the same time and will add that the explosion nearest them occurred first. C and Professor Adler will report the exact reverse, insisting quite correctly that the westernmost explosion occurred first and the easternmost afterward. In short, even within the local horizon, sensed now-ness, i.e., sensed temporal simultaneity, is not public now-ness. Hence, we no more know a public time through the senses as given in naïve observation than we know a public space. But for any object to be an external object, i.e., a public object the same for all knowers, it must be in public space and time. It follows that even if, as is not the case, any object given to our senses were, qualitatively and imagefully, the same object for all observers, that object would not be an external public object.

The reader can confirm this conclusion quite independently of the aforementioned observations of the two explosions by trying to keep precise social engagements without his mathematically astronomical, Greenwich-time-set watch continuously at hand or similar public clocks in sight. He can confirm it, also, by traveling to the villages of Mexico or to even the Westernized portion of Northern Rhodesia, where the natives, possessing no watches or not understanding why they have to wind them even if they do, are unable to keep, because they do not know, a precise simultaneous social engagement.

Comparative anthropology shows another thing. For most people the world over, including the naïve realistic Aristotle, time is thought of as cyclical. To anyone whose intellect contains no ideas but those whose content is given first through the senses, this is obvious. Clearly, our senses give us, not a linear time extending from an infinite past toward an infinite future, but the cyclical time that is darkness and light (day and night) and the sequence of the seasons. This shows that only if we follow Newton by taking linear serially ordered events, in the sense of Chapter 4, as the public temporal events of nature, does the modern Western man of "common sense" possess his naturalistic noncyclical linear way of thinking about time. In short, modern Western common sense is neither radically empirical nor naïvely realistic.

This does not mean that we do not know external objects in a public spatio-temporal world. The fact that the indirectly verified, concept by postulation theories of modern physics satisfy the Principle of Relativity proves that we do. What it does mean, however, is that such is the case only for a theory of knowledge which epistemically correlates (1) nominalistic concepts by intuition denoting sensed objects and events that are not public, with (2) concept by intellection invariant objects and events as verified indirectly in crucial experiments.

An Aristotelian or Thomistic kind of "intellect," therefore, which has no content in its ideas, except as given first through the senses, simply will not do. This is to confuse the intellect with one's private, subjective imagination. For the same reason, a mind containing *only* the nominalistic concepts by intuition prescribed by Locke's *Essay Concerning Human Understanding* won't do either.

Locke gave no evidence for his conclusion that these are *the only* meaningful ideas, as Leibniz noted. We know Locke's *non sequitur* to be false. Locke arrived at it from his early naïve realistic notion of the mind as a naïvely introspected mental substance which initially is a blank tablet upon which the senses write perishing particular imageful impressions. Being blank, there can be no ideas in it that are not first in the senses. Neither concept by intuition introspective knowledge nor concept by intellection, indirectly confirmed theory, as Chapter 1 has shown, warrants this blank-tabletish theory of mind.

In any event, the following scientists and philosophers, to name but a few, agree that mathematics and mathematical physics contain ideas in the intellect which are not first in the senses: Poincaré, Einstein, Duhem, Cassirer, Reichenbach, Professors Henry Margenau, Rudolf Carnap, Ernest Nagel, Carl Hempel, Adolf Grünbaum, and the writer. They agree, also, that contemporary mathematical natural science requires and exemplifies the theory of knowledge which the writer calls (1) radical empiricism with its nominalistic concepts by intuition in (2) epistemic correlation with (3) formally or postulationally constructed concepts by intellection. Some call (1) protocol sentences or P plane words, (2) coördination definitions or rules of correspondence and (3) constructs or axiomatically constructed concepts.

Such verbal differences are normal in science, as Newton's and Leibniz' different nomenclatures for the calculus show. Only by trial and error, upon the part of several people who mean the same thing, can the best terminology for saying it be found. As Shakespeare wrote in *Romeo and Juliet*:

> What's in a name? That which we call a rose
> By any other name would smell as sweet.

Notwithstanding the agreement of all the aforementioned people and many others on the existence of concepts by intellection, these physicists and philosophers fall into two different groups in their interpretation of what these concepts refer to. Since anyone's conception of the relation of religion to natural knowledge depends on the answer one gives to the question in the philosophy of science that divides these two groups, it is necessary for us to turn aside, momentarily, from religion in order to face this important scientific and philosophical issue. First, we must clearly and concretely state the two different interpretations of scientific constructs, or concepts by intellection, which these two groups represent. Second, after thoroughly comprehending each interpretation, we must attempt to give a decisive resolution of the point at issue. Only then will we be able to specify the relation between religion and natural knowledge.

15

TO WHAT DOES
MATHEMATICAL PHYSICS REFER?

AT THE END of the previous chapter we
found that recent mathematical physicists and philosophers
agree that there are concepts in the intellect which are
not first in the senses, but differ about what it is to which
they refer. These two groups we shall call: (1) Logical
Nonrealists and (2) Logical Realists.

Group (1) makes physics look more like man-made
poetry than sober, realistic prose. These nonrealists com-
plicate matters further because they fall into two groups
who agree only on their negative thesis that irreducible
concepts by intellection do not have a realistic meaning
and, hence, have no ontological reference. In this, they
follow Kant. They differ, however, in their nonrealistic positive thesis. Thus (a) Poincaré, at least as frequently interpreted, and Duhem affirm that such concepts are mere
subjective linguistic conventions upon which people of
common sense and science must agree if they are to
communicate. (b) Cassirer and Professor Margenau hold
that although concepts by intellection are not realistic
and ontological, they have a much more important and
even necessary function than the linguistic conventionalists

216

suppose. This additional function is that the concepts by intellection enjoy a neo-Kantian *als ob* (as if) regulative status.

Since the neo-Kantian version (b) is the richer and more scientifically specific of these two nonrealistic theories, we shall concentrate on it. If (b) fails, we can be sure (a) will also. Even so, our final logical analysis and empirical findings will apply to both.

In his book, *An Essay on Man,* Cassirer both (a) specifies the two points upon which (1) logical nonrealists and (2) logical realists agree and (b) the distinguishing mark of human beings which he brings forward as evidence for his neo-Kantian nonrealism. The two factors of agreement appear near the end of the book where he accepts the writer's distinction between (i) natural history concepts by inspection and (ii) concepts by postulation, interpreting the latter correctly as "a system of well-ordered symbols," and also shows that (ii) does not derive from or reduce to (i). The point of disagreement appears in Chapters 2 and 3 where he defines man as "an *animal symbolicum.*"

Unfortunately, the latter expression is ambiguous. If one emphasizes the word "animal" in the expression, Cassirer can easily be made to appear to be a naïve, natural history realist. In fact, when he seeks confirmation for his symbolic theory of man in the empirical conclusions of the natural history biologist, Uexküll, and the natural history psychologist, Köhler, this is precisely what Cassirer is. Yet his Kantinism and neo-Kantinism tells him that this is dogmatic, slumberland nonsense if taken as a serious theory of man's nature.

If, on the other hand, one emphasizes the word "symbolicum" in Cassirer's ambiguous definition of man, then one comes out of dogmatic, naïve realistic slumberland to become the neo-Kantian, nonrealistic Cassirer. In short, one becomes an *als ob* (as if) symbol-projecting subjectivist.

That this is the serious Cassirer, when the ambiguities of his language are made evident, is shown by other statements in his *Essay on Man,* the most important of which is that "mathematics is not a theory of things but a theory of symbols (p. 60)." From this it follows, since the concept by postulation language of mathematical physics is mathematical, that (1) the concept by postulation portion of mathematical physics is not about the object of knowledge, but solely about the scientists' symbols and (2) the only "things" that exist are the chaotic concept by perishing particulars which Berkeley, Hume, Kant, and the neo-Kantians have shown quite conclusively to be relative to the perceiver. In short, for Cassirer or any other consistent neo-Kantian, there are no *things,* in the sense of external objects in public space-time, the same for all knowers. This is the case, moreover, for any language, be it that of nominalistic concepts by inspection or neo-Kantian concepts by postulation.

When, therefore, Cassirer's neo-Kantian concept of man as a symbolic animal is combined with his monumental *Philosophy of Symbolic Forms,* the result is that the different departments of human knowledge, such as natural science, fantasies, painting, poetry, law, morals, and religion, are regarded as man's various species of "as if" symbol-projections. Consequently, as with Kant, symbols do not have a realistic epistemological and ontological reference. Religion then becomes, as with Santayana, mere poetry. Mathematical physics comes very close to being this also, since what it is talking about mathematically is nothing but the animal's own symbols.

The latter interpretation occurred, in fact, when Kant's Forms of Sensibility, space and time, and the Categories of the Understanding of Kant were found by the Marburg Cohens, Natorp, Cassirer, and Professor Margenau later to be merely hypothetical "as if" ways of thinking rather than categorical necessities of everyone's thinking. Thus, neo-Kantinism arose and nature, morals, law, religion, as well as fanciful poetry, and purposeful teleological judgments became, so far as any realistic objective reference is concerned, a mere symbol-projective *als ob,* as the post-Kantian Vaihinger saw.

Even so, there is a difference between the *als ob* poetry (1) that is mathematical physics and (2) that which is a fanciful novel, religion, morals, law, or a painting. Cassirer states this difference clearly on page 30 of his *Essay* where he distinguishes "between *propositional language* and *emotional language.*" Mathematical natural science is talking about the symbols of the former in their epistemic correlation with the chaotic, buzzing confusion of relativistically perishing particulars; morals, law, religion, and all normative subjects, about the symbols of the latter. The differences, therefore, are negligible, however much Cassirer's reference to Socrates' dialectic may attempt to disguise the fact, between any consistent neo-Kantian theory of the secular humanities or religion and the theory of Santayana and the contemporary emotivists, Professors C. L. Stevenson, A. J. Ayer, and the lawyer Alf Ross.

Cassirer noted, quite correctly, that whereas the *second-order artifactual* "as if" poetry of the humanities is *per se* relative to the evaluator, the symbol projection that is mathematical physics contains a concept which, when confirmed indirectly via its epistemic correlations with nominalistic concept by intuition data, gives mathematical physical language the same meaning for all physicists. This concept, we have already come upon independently in Chapter 14. It is *invariance* as specified by the Principle of Relativity.

Nevertheless, this did not, in Cassirer's mind, nor does it with Professor Margenau, warrant the thesis that concepts by intellection are to be interpreted logically realistically as designating external events and objects in ontologically existing nature. Instead, for both of these neo-Kantians, the latter idea is merely the neo-Kantian synthesis of (i) the concept by intuition data of what Professor Margenau calls the P plane, denoted by what I call concepts by intuition, and (ii) the layman's or scientific knower's concept by intellection "as if" symbolic projections.

There is another difference between these symbols of mathematical physics and those of morals, painting, law, or religion. Here Professor Margenau's principles governing the unique handling of concepts by intellection, or what he calls "constructs," in physics is most specific and illuminating. Such is the case because he is a working theoretical and experimental physicist in the Department of Physics as well as an official member of the Department of Philosophy at Yale University. What he notes is that the physicist's method imposes specific restrictions on the kind of constructs one symbolically projects. One of these is logical consistency; another is causality, in the restricted sense of the present state of the system entailing its future states, but leaving open how the state function is defined, etc. Since these regulative principles are not given by the senses, yet are the necessary presuppositions for making the constructs of any theory consistent and fertile, Professor Margenau calls them, in Chapter 5 of his *The Nature of Physical Reality,* "Metaphysical Requirements." This is a correct Kantian use of the word "metaphysical."

It is important to note, however, that, because he and Cassirer give the physicists' "constructs" a neo-Kantian *als ob* regulative status, rather than a logically realistic interpretation, both the concepts by postulation and the principles regulating them are metaphysical in a merely symbolic and epistemological, not in a logically realistic or ontological, metaphysical sense. This shows quite explicitly on page 102 of Professor Margenau's aforementioned book where he identifies the word "Nature" with solely the radically empirical concept by intuition data of the P plane, or what the writer calls "the differentiated aesthetic continuum," and not with what the epistemically correlated, speculatively discovered, indirectly verified constructs, or "concepts by intellection," designate. Since, as shown just above in the case of Cassirer, there are in Margenau's radically empirical *P* plane (i.e., the differentiated aesthetic continuum) no determinate "real" things in the sense of an object of knowledge the same for all knowers, it follows for my good friend and colleague, Professor Margenau, that his word "reality," like his word "Nature," becomes a bit Pickwickian in its meaning.

The word "reality" does, however, have a concept by postulation meaning also for him. This meaning he defines in his Chapter 15. Its definition makes reality something that is continuously changing as the subjective *als ob* constructs change. He correctly infers on page 295 that "this [definition] deals eternal reality . . . a crushing blow." It certainly does.

We are now able to understand in concrete terms, by way of contrast, the logical realists' interpretation of the words "real," "Nature," and "constructs" or "concepts by postulation." "Real" means any item of knowledge that is the same for all knowers. In Margenau's *P* plane of radically empirical immediacy, there is but one such factor. It is what I call "the undifferentiated aesthetic continuum." This, Margenau accepts, as his *Nature of Physical Reality* suggests on page 61. So far he, the logical nonrealist, and I, the logical realist, agree.

It is when we come to the concept by postulation component of common-sense and scientific language that the logical nonrealists and the logical realists part company. The former interpret concepts by postulation as referring to changing linguistic conventions or "as if" symbolic projections that are in rules of correspondence, or epistemic correlations, with Nature conceived as nothing but what Professor Margenau calls the "*P* plane" and I, "the differentiated aesthetic continuum." The logical realists, on the other hand, interpret them as referring, with specifications to be noted in a moment, to both (a) an external object of knowledge that exists independently of linguistic conventions or construct projectors and (b) an ontologically real knower.

Linguistically expressed, this means that Cassirer's thesis to the effect that man is a symbol-projecting animal is not merely an ambiguous, but also an elliptical sentence. Implicit in it is the additional clause, "whose symbols refer to more than both (i) their epistemic correlation with sensed perishing particulars and (ii) the subjective fact that man discovers, projects, and changes them."

This "more than" is what Einstein has in mind when, on page 37 of *The World As I See It,* he says: "I hold it true that pure thought can grasp reality, as the ancients dreamed." It is well known that the ancient Democritean, Platonic, and Stoic mathematical physicists, moral philosophers, lawyers, and natural theologians were logical realists. Also, Aristotle was a naïve realist; not an epistemologically idealistic neo-Kantian. Recently, Professor S. Sambursky, in his *Physics of the Stoics,* has given reasons for believing that the remarkable Stoic physicist, Chrysippus, was not merely a logical realist, but also one who anticipated the dynamic concept of the limit and of the infinite in 19th century mathematics and its physics. Einstein is even more explicit in his logically realistic interpretation of axiomatic constructs on page 60 of his book, where he identifies "the axiomatic sub-structure of physics" with "our conception of the structure of reality"; the changing concepts by postulation are not identified, as in the case of Margenau, with reality itself.

Even more noteworthy, because he is a pure mathematician, is the following statement by the late Professor G. H. Hardy in his Credo,

A Mathematician's Apology.

I believe that mathematical reality lies outside us, that our function is to discover or *observe* it [with the imageless intellectual eye], and that the theorems which we prove, and which we describe grandiloquently as our "creations," are simply our notes of our observations. (pp. 63–64.)

Nor does he leave us in doubt about why he believes this or what the mathematical physicist, as distinct from the pure mathematician, is doing. A few pages later he adds that, although,

neither physicists nor philosophers have ever given any convincing account . . . of how the physicist passes, from the confused mass of fact or sensation with which he starts, to the construction of the objects which he calls "real" . . . this need not prevent us from understanding roughly what a physicist is trying to do. It is plain that he is trying to *correlate* the incoherent body of crude fact confronting him with some definite and orderly scheme of abstract relations, the kind of scheme which he can borrow only from mathematics. (p. 69.)

The *italics* for the word "correlate" is mine. It points up the fact that Hardy was aware of what I call epistemic correlations. It shows, also, why I prefer to call the epistemological relation (which translates the knowledge given by the senses and denoted by concepts by intuition over into the knowledge of the ontologically real world shown by mathematically relational language) "epistemic correlations" rather than coördination definitions, since neither term in the relation can be defined in terms of its other term.

Hardy continues:

A mathematician, on the other hand, is working with his own mathematical reality. Of this reality . . . I take a "realistic" and not an "idealistic" [Kantian or neo-Kantian] view. (pp. 69–70.)

A few sentences later he tells us why:

> . . . "2" or "317" [in the sense of concept by intellection mathematics] has nothing to do with sensation, and its properties stand out the more clearly the more closely we scrutinize it. . . . Pure mathematics . . . seems to me a rock on which all [epistemological] idealism founders: 317 is a prime, not because we think so, or because our minds are shaped in one way rather than another, but *because it is so,* because mathematical reality is built that way. (p. 70.)

Professor Adolf Grünbaum, in his important articles on "Conventionalism in Geometry" in *The Axiomatic Method* (Amsterdam, 1959) and "The Duhemian Argument" in *Philosophy of Science* (January, 1960), reaches the same logical realistic position with respect to geometry and physics, being even more of a logical realist than was Einstein. I agree and go further, affirming that the concepts by intellection refer not merely to a logically realistic ontological object of knowledge, the same for all knowers and, hence, appropriately called reality, but also that such concepts implicitly presuppose a logically realistic and, therefore, ontological construct-discoverer and -maker. This is why Chapter 1 had to provide a logically realistic self with the logical syntax necessary and sufficient to be both a knowing and an erring self. Cassirer, Uexküll, and Köhler's naïve realistic *animal symbolicum,* while suggestive as an "as if," will not do.

Is there any decisive way of determining whether the logical nonrealists or the logical realists are correct on this crucial contemporary issue? The answer is Yes. Two considerations suffice to make it evident.

The first is that the logical realistic thesis has to be stated with great care. The word necessary to provide this care is "asymptotic." Just as in the case of the real (i.e., the same for all knowers) nominalistic factor in radically empirical immediacy (which we have pointed at with the words "the undifferentiated aesthetic continuum," and the Buddhists use the word "Nirvana" to denote) is known by any determinate human being, only to a higher and higher degree of approximation as he, operationally, eliminates one after another of the differentiations within the continuum of his existential immediate experience, so erring human mortals, with their partial factual knowledge, know the logically real, in the sense of Principle of Relativity invariance for all facts and for everyone, only by *asymptotic* approximation. It is the contribution of the conventionalists and the neo-Kantian epistemological idealists to never let us forget this.

It does not follow, however, that there is not, even so, a logically realistic, ontological reality which the neo-Kantian symbolic projections approach asymptotically, nearer and nearer, but never reach as their limit in the sense of Chapter 4. In fact, without the concept of the limit, the concept of asymptotic is meaningless. It is the merit of the logical realists to have made it clear to the conventionalists and the neo-Kantians that they have never shown that is not the case and that, therefore, there is no reason why it may not be the case.

When so stated with care in terms of asymptotically approximating toward but never perfectly achieving its logically realistic limit, the logically realistic interpretation of concepts by intellection has the two following merits: (1) It accounts for the subject-to-change-with-further-empirical-information character of such theories. (2) With an additional empirically verified assumption about the existential import of scientific objects, it makes it meaningful to say that the rocks were here on this earth, geological ages in the past, when there were no Poincarés present to specify a linguistic convention and keep it constant or any Cassirers to project symbols. Since it is difficult to doubt that Poincaré, Cassirer, and Professor

Margenau regard the latter belief to be meaningful, we conclude that concepts by intellection have to be interpreted logically realistically.

There is, however, a more decisive reason for this conclusion. As the writer has proved in Chapter 11 of the Festschrift in honor of Professor Paul Weiss entitled *Experience, Existence, and the Good,* the nonrealistic interpretation of concepts by intellection is self-contradictory. This becomes evident when one asks what one means by the person or animal that sets the linguistic convention and keeps it constant or projects the *als ob* regulative symbols. On either the conventionalist or the neo-Kantian theory, this convention-maker and symbol-projector must be (i) mere concept by intuition, radically empirical sensed or introspective data, or (ii) a mere subjective convention or subjectively projected *als ob* construct. In previous chapters, it was shown, as the ancient Hindus and Buddhists and the modern Hume have made evident, that a persisting determinate person (the kind necessary to keep a convention or construct constant) is not given either introspectively or through the outer senses. In fact, both the conventionalists and the neo-Kantians admit this. No alternative remains but for the convention-maker or the neo-Kantian construct-projector to be a mere *als ob* projective construct. But a construct which is constructed by a construct is an infinitely regressive contradiction in terms. Only a logically realistic convention-maker or symbol-projector will do.

Moreover, when one turns to the object of knowledge, the situation is even worse. There, the nonrealistic interpretation of concepts by intellection entails that both the conventionalist and the neo-Kantian must believe that his wife, or anyone else who is dear to him, has no ontologically realistic objective meaning, but is, instead, merely (1) some private, successive, perpetually perishing sense impression for which *to be* means merely *to be perceived* by him, together with (2) some of his own epistemically correlated private linguistic conventions or neo-Kantian *als ob* symbol-projections.

We conclude, therefore, that concepts by intellection have to be interpreted logically realistically. This means that Kant's dismissal of ontology from physics, psychology, religion, and philosophy generally, though seemingly justified at the time he did it, is an error. It means, also, that the naturalistic person, described in Chapter 1, is the real person and that when a scientist says something about nature, he means it.

This applies to Quantum Mechanics also. Consequently, when its logically realistic theory puts chance and its probability into the definition of the state of any naturalistic object or set of such objects, chance and its restriction on strong causal determination is ontologically in nature also. For a careful philosophical analysis of the difference between the strong deterministic concept of mechanical causality and the weaker mechanical causality of Quantum Mechanics, see my aforementioned Introductory Preface to Professor Werner Heisenberg's *Physics and Philosophy*. At this point, I have to differ with both Einstein and my very good friend and respected colleague, Professor Brand Blanshard. With respect to the position of the latter and my comments thereon, see *Determinism and Freedom in the Age of Modern Science* edited by Sidney Hook, New York University Press.

Quantum Mechanics has also imagefully disposed of imageful naïve realistic scientific objects. It did this when it showed that imageless many-termed relationally defined scientific objects behave in certain experiments *as if* they were imageful little local billiard balls and *as if* they were imageful little waves. In other words, if one naïve realistically insists on confusing Aryan imageful substance-property ordinary language syntax with the objective nature of things, the nature of things has incompatible imageful predicates at one and the same time. Nevertheless, in the imageless logically realistic concept by intellection mathematical postulates of Quantum Mechanics, there is no contradiction whatever. It apparently takes a long time for people to learn from Mach that even the scientific objects of Newton's so-called "particle physics" are not local, naïve realistic little billiard balls with the observer's subjective little images fastened to them, but are, instead, imageless many-termed relationally defined scientific objects.

As Socrates noted in his exposition of the divided line in Book VI of Plato's *Republic,* to get ideas that give objective naturalistic scientific knowledge and provide the common meanings necessary to define a common law or justice and goodness, the same for all knowers, we have to drop all images. Contemporary, experimentally confirmed, modern mathematical physics agrees with the Democritean, Platonic, and Stoic natural and moral philosophers and lawyers' thesis that there are logically realistic ideas in the intellect, the content, as well as the form, of which is not given first in the senses. The consequences are twofold. The first one is negative. The second one is positive.

Negatively, this means that the imageful billiard ball materialism of the Hobbesians of the early 17th century and the Haeckels of the mid-19th century when Marx constructed his dialectical materialism, is the product of bourgeois Aryan linguistic two-termed substance-property thinking and its very poverty-stricken fancy. With either scientific or common-sense realism, it has nothing to do. The same is true of the disembodied minds, spirits, mental substances, and windowless monads believed in by these traditional, bourgeois materialists' half-brothers, the personalistic pluralists and spiritualists. The causally interacting mental and material substances of Descartes and Locke are equally poverty-stricken and fanciful, as were the telelogical substances of Aristotle.

Positively, the logically realistic many-termed relational theory of one's personal identity through time and of external public common-sense or scientific events and objects (whether they be in the dimension of the small in Quantum Mechanics or in the dimension of the large in the cosmological Theory of Relativity) means that first-order factual nature and human nature is a many-termed imageless intellectually and systematically organic kind of thing. Nature is a universally lawful organism. It is a cosmos, not a chaos of colliding little billiard balls or heavy hardware.

Hence, although the intellectual content is different from what it was in the days of the ancient Democritean, Platonic, and Stoic physicists, natural philosophers, and natural theologians, logical realistically known nature is what they call *ratio* or *logos*. It is with this *Logos,* let it be recalled, that both Philo and the Stoic natural theologians and the Stoic-minded author of the first verse of the Fourth Judaic-Christian Gospel identified the *Word* (the Greek is λόγος that is God. We are not departing, therefore, from a traditional usage of very ancient standing when we identify the intellectual component of God's nature with the logically realistic Limit, in the sense of Chapter 4, that is approached asymptotically by the changing constructs of traditional and recent logically realistic mathematical physics. This conclusion has most interesting and important religious implications.

16

SOME LOGICAL REALISM
ABOUT RELIGION

It was shown in the previous chapter that both (1) an ancient traditional religious usage and (2) the only nonself-contradictory interpretation of the irreducible concepts by postulation in contemporary mathematical physics make it both meaningful and empirically necessary to identify the intellectual component of God's nature with the Limit, or organically related lawful *Logos,* that is approached asymptotically by the changing, logically realistic constructs of Western mathematical physics. One interesting religious implication becomes evident when we recall two things which were established in Chapter 14.

First, this asymptotic approach to its Limit, by the logically realistic theory of natural science, is methodologically implemented by wider empirical applications and further theoretical generalizations of the Principle of Relativity. Second, it is the unique merit of modern physics to have achieved a theoretical dynamics which satisfies the Principle of Relativity. Stated more concretely, this means that the invariant laws of contemporary natural science relate the state of an entity, or a system of entities, at one time, to their states at past and future times. Hence, for those empirical subject matters, in which logically realistic theory satisfying the Principle of Relativity has been discovered and verified in crucial experiments, we already possess eternally-now, invariant, organically related laws, or, in other words, a single, many-termed relational *Logos* that embraces the transitory events of the whole of space and the whole of time. This follows, as Chapter 14 showed, from the concept by intellection as distinct from the concept by intuition relativistic and operational definition of the Principle of Relativity.

The Limit that is such an invariant, eternally-now *Logos,* extended to all subjects, would be tautologically omniscient. Hence, the Word that is this *Logos* and is God is Omniscient also.

We shall find in a later chapter that Quantum Mechanics, even when it satisfies the Principle of Relativity, places a qualification on this Omniscience and Omnipotence of God. For reasons which will become evident in the final chapter, this qualified Omniscience and Omnipotence may be Self-imposed.

Another implication of this logically realistic meaning of the intellectual component of the word God is that His creation of nature is a many-termed relational *logical* creation *within which first-order factual man, able to commit error as he eats from the tree of natural knowledge,* is one of the relationally specified terms. The phrase in italics is what distinguishes theism from pantheism. God's creativity is, therefore, not a temporal act committed long ago in the infinite past. The latter type of creator is the product of the misleading poetry of either an anthropomorphic carpenter or a long-bearded, snooping old man in an apple orchard whom Occam should have shaved with his razor and disposed of long ago.

This substitution of logical realism and its ontology for the naïve realism of Aristotle and St. Thomas need, in no way, seriously disturb nonnaïve Roman Catholic thinkers.

It merely means that they were misled in not staying with William of Champeaux with his Stoic logically realistic concept of God and His logically relational creativity. It was a pity, therefore, when they allowed the romantic Abélard and Heloïse and that later naïve realistic layman, named Thomas Aquinas, to persuade them to move through nominalism to that mistaken fashion of the moment, as it turned out to be, which is medieval Aristotelianism and its cast-iron, dogmatic scholasticism. The latter's cognitive cocksureness encouraged intolerant inquisitorial activities in Europe and Latin America, as now with some Roman Catholics and others in the United States. This Aristotelian and Thomistic, naïve realism put Roman Catholic orthodoxy and its leadership at odds with the modern world from the moment it was born when Galilei, Descartes, and Newton rejected naïve realism for mathematically functional logical realism.

It was equally unfortunate that the Aryan, subject-predicate grammar of the modern Western world's ordinary languages led the followers of the founders of modern, logically realistic epistemology and natural science to fall back into the naïve realism of Hobbesian, nonteleological, material substances and Marxist dialectical materialism with their respective determinisms that entail the impossibility of error and, therefore, leave meaningless all the normative moral, legal, and political words of those who profess these self-contradictory, naïve realistic theories. Thus, the bourgeois (i.e., naïve realistic) world of the Marxist and Hobbesian materialists was born. These bourgeois fellows wallowed about until Mach, with his relational theory of mass, put modern man back on his logically realistic feet, and Einstein and the contemporary Quantum theorists carried on from there.

It is appropriate to call the invariant logically creative *Logos* that is God the intellectual love of God. It is to God, in this sense, that my friend and colleague, the expert symbolic logician, Professor Frederic B. Fitch, refers in his paper, "On God and Immortality," published in Volume 8, No. 4 of *Philosophy and Phenomenological Research*.

Such Divine Love is by no means an artificial use of this word. As noted in Chapter 4, the concept by intellection relation R interconnects all its terms in the logically consistent and, in this sense, loving relation which is peace and its systematically lawful organic harmony. Consequently, any human term in this *Logos* who takes this intellectual love of God as his beloved object is not a schizophrenic at war with himself, due to the presence of logically incompatible trapped universals in his cortex, but is, instead, a nonaggressive and peaceful person. This is why to love this intellectual love of God is to love and be at peace with one's fellow men.

There is an even more important reason why this concept-by-intellection love of God is not artificial. This reason became evident when that most spiritual and clearheaded of modern philosophers of religion, McTaggart, revealed fatal weaknesses in (i) Hegel's monistic Absolute concept of God, on the one hand, and (ii) Berkeleyian, Leibnizian, and Lotzean theistic personalistic pluralism, on the other hand.

Because the Divine Absolute of Hegel came to selfconsciousness dialectically and deterministically in both first-order factual nature and second-order artifactual cultural history, all human persons were left its puppets, just as in the case in its eastern European successor, dialectically deterministic Marxist materialism, with its similar first-order-second-order factually confused Natur-Geisteswissenschaftlichen-Historismus. Were either of these 19th-century theories true, the fact of error would not exist and the following evaluative expressions of the Hegelian ethical idealists and the Soviet and Chinese Marxist materialists would be meaningless: "positive personal moral and political freedom," "the ideal as distinct from the actual *is* of history," "the evil imperialists," or "the betrayal of the Party," to say nothing about more simple evaluative words, such as "good," "bad," "just," "unjust," "guilty" or "innocent," not to mention "sin in history."

The naïve realistic spiritual substances, of which God is one, of the theistic personalistic pluralists and the spiritual substance-material substance deists, kept persons from being quite such obviously deterministic puppets of the Deity but had two other fatal weaknesses. First, these personalistic spirits left it a mystery how one human person, trapped claustrophobically in his own spiritual interior, ever contacted another person to know him, to say nothing about contacting and knowing God. Second, if Berkeley's version is assumed, in which God's substantial spirit causally acts on the many human spirits, then nonsense is the result, as the theistic personalistic pluralist Leibniz indicated. The reason is that since causality is a temporal relation between the spatially related states of any entity or system of entities at different times, and spiritual substances were by definition for Berkeley, Locke, and Descartes neither spatial nor temporal, it is a self-contradictory and, hence, nonsensical combination of words to speak of the causal action of the spirit that is God on the spirits that are men and women.

When this is realized, such naïve realistic thinking leaves two alternatives: Either (1) the early deistic position of Locke, who finds a meaning for religion only by having God create the spiritual and material substances at the beginning of time and then forever have nothing to do with them; or (2) the position of Leibniz, who has God similarly create the windowless, spiritual monads and then synchronize what they privately tick out, after the manner of an anthropomorphic clockmaker. Both alternatives generate absurdities. First, such a God could commit suicide immediately after His infinitely past deistic creative acts, with no difference whatever in any fact of human experience. This would leave one with no eternally present meaning for either one's emotive or one's intellectual intuition and love of God. Prayer certainly would be meaning-less. Second, Occam has just telepathed from Heaven to say that, on the theory of either Locke's deism or Leibniz' pre-established harmony, he (Father Occam) finds no need for the hypothesis of God at all. Occam adds, also, that long ago he shaved this naïve realistic anthropomorphic entity and, accidentally, with malice aforethought, cut his throat, with good and sufficient reason because the existence of such a religious hypothesis "multiplies entities beyond necessity."

The cause of these errors in such theories of God should now be evident to us. After the manner of several contemporary, naïve realistic. English astronomers, they turn God's creative activity, with respect to nature, into the causal action, in the temporally distant past, of either an anthropomorphic carpenter or an anthropomorphic clockmaker. In short, they confuse metaphorical religious poetry with realistic scientific prose. The result of such a naïve realistic love of God is an unshaved old man snooping in an apple orchard, some schizophrenically frustrated old maids gossiping on their back porches, and a recent English writer of popular science in *Horizon* who expects to find God sitting behind a star in outer space when some similarly naïve Foundation "Head" provides him with a rocket strong enough to take him there.

Instead, as the spiritually sensitive and intellectually clearheaded McTaggart realized, *love* is, by its very nature, a determinate relation between beloved persons. If God then be love, He must be such a relation. From this logically realistic, intellectual love of God, Jesus' second law of love, "Thou shalt love thy neighbor as thyself," as recorded in Luke X:27 and in Matthew XXII:37, 39, follows tautologically from His first law of love, "Thou shalt love the Lord thy God with all thy heart, with all thy soul, and with all thy mind." It is the concept by intellection determinate content of such invariantly relational intellectual love of God that makes love without mind and its imageless intellect a contradiction in terms. Mere mushy, introspected sentiment will not do; nor will that Black Forest, Germanic melancholy or the satiated Left Bank Parisian boredom, which the Existentialists call *Sorge*.

The realization that God is not a temporally acting, naïve realistic substance, but an eternally-now, logically realistic relation between beloved creatures is what McTaggart meant when he said that he believed in the immortality of the soul but was an atheist. This did not mean that he believed that the word "God" has no meaning. Quite the contrary. What he meant was that God is love, and love is neither a naïve realistic substance nor a causal relation between such substances but is a logically realistic relation.

It is interesting to note that the Buddhists say the same thing. This they do when they affirm that the Buddha was an atheist. They, too, were correct, even though the component of God's nature, to which they refer when they make this statement, is not the intellectual love of God of the logically realistic component of God's nature to which McTaggart referred and we now refer. What the Buddha and the Buddhists mean when they say this is not that they are irreligious and that there is no such thing as the Divine Blissfulness; instead, what they mean is that such Blissfulness is not a determinate naïve realistic entity.

This Buddhistic love of God, being undifferentiated rather than the logically realistic, differentiated *Logos,* is appropriately called the undifferentiatedly emotive love of God. These two loves, (1) the radically empirical undifferentiated emotive love and (2) the intellectual love, make up God's complete nature. They are also the two components of His creativity.

Two implications remain to be made explicit. The words "eternal" and "mystical" denote them. We shall regard the words "immortal" or "timeless in the sense of the eternally-now" as having the same meaning as the word "eternal."

Our previous analysis has shown that religion has to do with those two first-order factors in ourselves and in all things which are eternal. The part of God's nature which is radically empirically and existentially experienced, when its transitory and relativistic differentiations are approximately neglected or abstracted away, meets this condition. Only its differentiated particulars are temporary and transitory. The same eternally-now timelessness characterizes the Limit as approached asymptotically by man's imageless, intellectually known, theoretically dynamic, logically realistic theories of what It is. As shown just above, this Limit remains invariant through all the transitory events of all space-time that are its terms. Such would not be the case were the theories of modern mathematical physics merely statical, rather than dynamical theories whose laws relate the present state of any natural system to its past and future states, thereby timelessly embracing the whole of cosmic four-dimensional space-time.

Our semantic analysis of both ordinary and mathematical language has demonstrated that no word in its nominalistic, radically empirical meaning can be deduced from that same word in its logically realistic concept by intellection meaning. This is why epistemic correlations are necessary and present in the method of meaningful and verifiable realistic common-sense or scientific knowledge. For example, the ineffable and indescribable particular perishing quality that the word "yellow" nominalistically denotes, cannot be deduced from "yellow" in the logically realistic meaning of the relational number of an electromagnetic "wave length."

This has one very important implication concerning what language can and cannot say. This implication enables us to understand what the word "mystical" means, when it is something more than a meaningless noise or a mere set of marks on paper.

17

LANGUAGE, MYSTICISM AND GOD

Two things about language became evident at the end of the previous chapter. First, any elementary word or other symbol, in its nominalistic, radically empirical concept by intuition meaning, cannot be deduced from that same word or symbol in its logically realistic concept by intellection meaning. Nor is the converse deduction possible. This is why epistemic correlations are necessary to relate the one world of discourse and species of knowledge to the other. Second, elementary nominalistic concept by intuition words cannot say what they are talking about. They can merely point at it denotatively, and, even then, only for one who, quite independently, has immediately, and in this specific sense, intuitively, experienced what is being pointed at. For example, that, at which the elementary nominalistic word "yellow" points but cannot say, is one example of such intuitively immediate knowledge. Another example is the unsayable something in anyone's radically empirical immediacy of experience, which the writer, in the chapter on Tagore, tried very clumsily to point at by using the nominalistic words "the undifferentiated aesthetic continuum."

There is also a different species of elementary knowledge, which cannot be said by any language. Hence, it
has to be known by immediate intuition independently
of the language which tries to, but cannot, say it. This is
the imageless knowledge of the logically realistic, many-
termed relational intellectual intuition.

In the chapter on Whitehead's English prose, brief reference was made parenthetically to the mysticisms of
Wittgenstein. There is nothing noncommon-sensical, un-
scientific, or nonsensically esoteric about mysticism. In
fact, without its immediate knowledge of the two species
noted just above, there is neither common sense nor science, since, in the last analysis, no language is able to say
anything unless one knows what is referred to, apart
from the language.

Wittgenstein knew this. Moreover, in an age when laymen, scientists, and even most theologians had dismissed
mysticism as something, at best, having no meaning for
them and, at worst, merely esoteric, purple prose nonsense, it was his genius to have rediscovered that there is
no knowledge of any kind that is not, in its elements,
mystical. Furthermore, since the compound items of
knowledge, defined in terms of its elements, are meaningless, except as its elements are meaningful, this entails
that all knowledge is mystical.

In 1932–33 the writer spent his sabbatical year at the
University of Cambridge where, during most of two of its
three terms, he attended Wittgenstein's lectures and also
came to know him personally outside these lectures in an
unexpectedly intimate and self-revelatory way. The result
was that, although I learned nothing from listening to
Wittgenstein's lectures and trying, with others present, to
take them with linguistic literalness, I did learn, I venture
to believe, everything when Wittgenstein self-revealed to
me, between the lines so to speak, one or two of his personal past experiences. These experiences involved nothing
more esoteric than the emotively felt awareness of the

inner feeling illuminating the face of a person in a hospital on the Continent, where Wittgenstein was detained once, on his way from Austria to England. The experience was, undoubtedly, a mystical one; but it was mystical precisely in the sense in which the immediate intuition of a particular ineffable "yellow" is mystical—the precise sense, namely, that no words can describe it or even point at it, unless one knows with immediacy what is being pointed at, apart from the words.

I am well aware that I may be in error, since this remarkable and rare person usually spoke and frequently wrote "through a glass darkly." I cautiously venture to believe, however, that what Wittgenstein tried to say, but knew that he could not say, shows in two things: First, the foregoing self-revelatory experiences as conveyed to me; second, the immediate and lasting impression which he gave and left with me when one ignores his words and sensed or recalls with immediacy what he was doing in his lectures.

This impression was that of a caged animal walking, often impulsively, back and forth before his audience in his little, blank, square closet of a lecture room, trying, as it were, to escape from his cage but unable to do so. Frequently, he would break off his sentence in the middle, with a shrug of his shoulders and an expression on his face suggesting the futility of it all. In other words, he was trying to say what cannot be said, and his listeners were taking his words literally, thereby missing the point that saying can say nothing. His entire effort and everybody's presence there was ridiculous and futile because, with all his saying and all of everybody's intent listening, saying cannot say anything.

Whether this was the point of his lecturing habits and of his two or three rare and prized revelatory personal statements to me, I do not know with certainty, nor does it matter. The point is that if this is what he was trying to say and knew that he couldn't say, he was correct. The reason, let it be repeated, is that no words mean or can say anything, except as one knows, with inexpressible and unsayable immediacy, what the words are pointing at or showing, independently of the words themselves. Such knowledge is what the word "mystical" means.

If such be the case, he probably arrived at it, as his own books confirm, in the following way: This way, which appears first in his *Tractatus Logico-Philosophicus* and continues in his later works, was by the coming, like Whitehead, quite independently to a critical and conscious awareness of the limitations of language, while also realizing that one can only convey to others the knowledge of its limitations by means of language. These limitations are evident when one realizes what any particular language, be it ordinary or what Wittgenstein called "a perfect language," can and cannot do.

In this book, we have used a different way. It consists in distinguishing the different semantic or epistemological species of meaning any ordinary word or scientific symbol may have. This is why, if we are to avoid falling into nonsense, we have had to be so persistently pedantic in our prose, always indicating, when any word is written, whether it is to be understood in its concept by intuition, its concept by intellection, or some other meaning.

What any language cannot do, as Wittgenstein knew, is to say what it is trying to say. It can only point at it, in the case of nominalistic radically empirical concepts, by intuition. It can only show it, in the case of imageless logically realistic concepts, by intellection. In either case, what is pointed at or shown has to be known with immediacy apart from language and all such knowledge, let it be repeated, is what the word "mysticism" means.

As suggested at the beginning of this chapter, there are two species of mysticism. One is quite different from the other.

The one, exemplified above in the case of the word "yellow" and the words "the undifferentiated aesthetic continuum," is that of the radically empirical, existential immediacy of experience, at which elementary nominalistic concept by intuition words point, but cannot say, unless one has immediately, and, in this very precise sense, mystically experienced independently of them that at which they point. For this reason, the marks on paper, "green" in their nominalistic reference, are meaningless so far as I am concerned, even though I do have an idea of what they mean in their concept by intellection, electromagnetic reference. Such is the case because, being "color blind with respect to green," I have never had and, because of the epistemically correlated rods and cones in my eyeballs, never can have the mystically immediate experience of this indescribable and unsayable quality.

The other, and quite different, species of mysticism is that of the imageless intellectual immediacy or intuition, which concept by intellection sentences and their formal syntax self-show, but can neither point at nor say. "Serial order" in the sense of Chapter 4 is an example; as are also its concepts of "number" and "limit."

The timelessly invariant, eternally-now factors in these two species of mystical knowledge give, respectively, the two inseparable components of the first-order factual eternal nature of ourselves and all other natural creatures that is the complete mystical knowledge of God.

The later and the earlier Wittgenstein illustrate these two kinds of mysticism. The "perfect language" of the earlier Wittgenstein of the *Tractatus* is that of the concept by intellection language and its mysticism, which neither points nor says but self-shows. The ordinary language of the later Wittgenstein of *Philosophical Investigations* contains the existential and radically empirical kind of mysticism in which language cannot say or show but points purely denotatively.

We say "contains" because, unfortunately, ordinary language, especially when it is English or any other Aryan language, is paradigmatically ambiguous. This is why the professed clarity of the present English ordinary language professors and lawyers is spurious. Their paradigms do not point unambiguously outside themselves as is supposed. The reason is that any ordinary Aryan linguistic word has, at least, two semantic references belonging to two quite different worlds of discourse. Alice, when she went from narcotic naïve realistic slumberland through the looking glass into wonderland, was aware of this.

As noted repeatedly, any ordinary Aryan linguistic word has its nominalistic, radically empirical concept by intuition meaning. It is in the latter sense only that any ordinary word is paradigmatically clear and conveys its meaning unambiguously, provided one has independently experienced what it is pointing at but cannot say. This unambiguous, radically empirical reference of pointer words leaves meaningless, however, the ordinary man's, the scientist's, or the theistic theologian's belief in the constancy of his determinate personality through time or in external objects in a public spatio-temporal world. It also leaves meaningless the legal person who is obligated today by a contract he entered into yesterday. Consequently, in its radically empirical, nominalistic and unambiguous, paradigmatic meaning, ordinary language philosophy is not ordinary at all, but of a character that shocks the beliefs of ordinary folk. In this shocking sense it is none the less correct, as previous chapters have shown, since the direct empirical intuition of radically empirical immediate facts does not warrant the belief in either persisting determinate selves or external objects in public space-time.

The other notion of ordinary language—the only one that makes it ordinary—is its naïve realistic notion which, if taken seriously, leaves one in dogmatic slumberland, as Kant was the first modern scientist and humanist to realize. We say "notion" because, again as previous chapters have shown, naïve realism is not a meaning at all but a self-contradictory combination of words.

Consequently, to the extent that any Oxfordian ordinary language philosopher's or lawyer's paradigmatic English sentence is interpreted in the only notion it has that is ordinary, the sentence is nonsense; and to the extent it is interpreted in the nominalistic, radically empirical sense that makes it meaningful, its meaning is both shockingly extraordinary, yet, nevertheless, true, pointing at something that exists, provided it points at only radically empirical relativistic perishing particulars. Even then, however, such is the case only if, with mystical immediacy, one knows what is being pointed at independently of the language and its pointing.

The only way, therefore, in which most people can avoid being misled by misinterpreting the later Wittgenstein is by doing three things: (1) Always interpret all paradigmatic English sentences nominalistically and radically empirically. (2) Watch for the analogical influences upon ordinary language of the epistemically correlated language of concepts by intellection which reflexively show, but cannot point or say, (3) In both cases, throw out naïve realistic notions as the self-contradictory combinations of words that they are. When one then seeks out the timeless factor in the later Wittgenstein of (1) and in the earlier Wittgenstein of (2), one has the two species of mysticism by means of which the complete nature of God is known.

In this knowledge there is nothing more mysterious than what occurs when one knows a particular ineffable, indescribable, and unsayable "yellow" or when one knows the showable, but equally unsayable or unpoint-at-able, formal properties of the many-termed relation called "serial order," as *shown* in Chapter 4. The existential and intellectual knowledge of God is, however, just as mystical and mysterious as is our existentially empirical mystical intuition of a particular "yellow" or our intellectual mystical intuition of imageless serial order.

It may be said, however, that, whereas one knows a "yellow," the being of which does not exist apart from a particular person's perception of it, it is not so clear how a mathematical physicist's showing of the timeless *logos* of his invariant, theoretically dynamic equations, as intellectually understood in his particular mind, also shows the *logos* of nature and of the intellectual love of God. The answer is contained in the word "isomorphic," that characterizes what Wittgenstein called "a perfect language."

A pointing language is not isomorphic with that at which it points. This is why it has to point and can neither say nor show. "A perfect language," on the other hand, is one in which the imageless, intellectually known meaning of the many-termed relatedness of its symbols is isomorphic with, and, hence, formally identical with, the relatedness of that to which it purports to refer and can neither point at nor say. Consequently, when any intellect using concept by intellection language, arrives at the specific, imageless, many-termed relational linguistic syntax, i.e., the particular, speculatively discovered, logically realistic theory, which, when pressed to its deductive consequences, is then, via its epistemic correlations, confirmed in crucial experiments, thereby accounting for all the first-order facts of nature and human nature—something no human theory yet has done—to that extent, the intellectually mystical intuition of the meaning of the local theory's syntax is intellectually identical with the intellectual love of God.

At the end of the previous chapter, reference was made to the two components of God's self-initiating activity, when He creates first-order factual nature and human nature. Analysis of the character of His creativity reveals Him to be an incurably playful Fellow. It remains to show why, and, in the end, use some all-too human poetry to do so.

18

THE POETRY OF GOD'S PLAYFULNESS

THE HINDUS have always known that God is full of fun. They express this knowledge poetically in the symbol of the carefree child in a swing.

The reason has been given in our chapter on Tagore. It was theirs and their Buddha's genius to have found the unsayable Eternal factor in ourselves and all other natural creatures that is mystically immediate in the nominalistically existential and radically empirical meaning of immediacy. This radically empirical component of God's nature is (when all the transitory, relativistic differentia that Maya-mask it are abstracted away) immediately experienceable as approximately undifferentiated. Being thus undifferentiated, this Eternal Self contains nothing to differentiate one person from another and, hence, is not merely identical in all persons but also identical with the Divine Self.

Consequently, when God playfully creates the unsayable aesthetically imageful, differentiated transitory sensing selves and their relativistic objects that Maya-mask both Himself and His-Self-in-each-one-of-us, He has no determinate laws to guide Him. In this conclusion, also, the Hindus and the Buddhists are correct. For no one, not even God Himself, can deduce the unsayable, mystically experienced differentiation that is a perishing particular "yellow" from the eternally-now undifferentiatedly Blissful existential love of God. This is why God playfully creates, for the sheer fun of it, the latter, perpetually perishing, and relativistic world of our senses.

Some ten years ago, my wife and I had the following experience with Princess Poon in Bangkok. The Princess showed us the Buddhist temple in which the Hindu-named Buddhist King of Thailand is crowned. There she told us that Buddhist monks in their yellow robes carry the ceremony before the high bronze Buddha almost to its conclusion. Then Hindu priests in white robes take over, placing the Crown of a Hindu-named Raj on the royal head. After describing this ceremony, the Princess took us several blocks away to a large traffic circle in the heart of Bangkok to show us, in the middle of that circle, two tall, upright poles with a crosspole at the top to which, when not weathered away, the ropes of a carefree child's swing are attached. She then added that this object is the religious symbol of God's playful creativity and is in that particular traffic circle, rather than any other, because, adjacent to the circle, is the white-walled compound of three Hindu temples with their white-robed Hindu priests, whom we met a moment later. These priests are kept there, at the annual expense of the present "secular" democratic Thai government, with little else to do (the Thais being Buddhists rather than caste Hindus) but to await the crowning of the next Thai king.

The obvious question arises: Why do the Thai lovers of their beautiful and beloved Buddha who repudiated kingship and its caste to point the eightfold path to Nirvana, in which all persons are not merely equal but identical, nevertheless have a Buddha-worshiping, Hindu-crowned King with a Hindu Indian high-caste name? This question is as important as it is interesting. Its importance

derives from its bearing on the respective implications of
Hinduism and Buddhism for domestic Asian and international law and politics. The interested reader may find
some light thrown on this most practical contemporary,
legal and political question in two places. The first is the
writer's *Cornell Law Quarterly* article (Summer, 1960)
entitled "The Comparative Philosophy of Comparative
Law." The second appears in the chapters on Asia in his
book *Philosophical Anthropology and Practical Politics.*
In any event:

> The Hindus are right,
> Who can't say, but do see
> That a gay child in a swing
> Is like God's creativity.

The intellectual love of God, in His contemporary,
human-known, mathematically physical content, is masked
also by the imageful and relativistic sensing and sensa that
the playful Buddhist-Brahman creates for the fun of it.
This is why, as Einstein realized, God does not wear His
heart on His sleeve. Such is the case because the intellectually known *logos* is not in the sensuous sensing and
its relativistic sensa; their relatedness is not isomorphic
with its relatedness. Hence, the *logos* that is God's intellectual love cannot be obtained from the Maya images of
the so-called sense "objects" by abstraction à la Aristotle
or by "the method of extensive abstraction" of Whitehead.
This intellectual and law-loving Creator loves the playful
also. But He pursues it, as the Anglo-Americans are wont
to say, by "playing the game" according to its universally
lawful rules, or *logos,* and "being a good sport" while
doing so.

Without this component of God's playfulness, human
players, capable of committing errors in their play, could
not be. In fact, there would be no meaning to making an

error, nor would there be any meaning for a judge or a referee. It is to be noted, in the case of the carefree child playing in her swing, that no umpire is present with his rules of the game, watching eagle-eyed what she does.

Concretely, there could be no "moment of truth" which the passionate Spaniards and Spanish Mexicans spend every Sabbath afternoon mystically knowing at their bull-fight when the matador confronts the bull. Nor would there be that prayerful, after-stopping-the-play-for-tea, infinitely intent, Buddha-like, English silence of a cricket match in Kent when every eye is sharply focused, awaiting that praeternatural English mastery of understatement which occurs when the referee, with a slight, slow motion of his finger, shows that the ball has clipped the wicket and that everyone can then pick up their tea-baskets to go home, with a sense of religious, legal, and political security, for High Tea, knowing full well that God will always uphold England so long as what Englishmen do is cricket.

God's creation of human beings, who may and do err as they play the game within its lawful rules, is present, also, in the Americans' baseball. Otherwise, there would be no "booting of the ball" after the manner of a clumsy and aesthetically crude, Brooklyn bum. Hear his religious language: "Blankety-blank. This burns me up like Hell." Nor would one in the next inning have the unsayable experience of seeing that same sinful, very human soul, the vulgar crowd still trying to boo him out of Flatbush, scoot, Peeweelike, back to his right, deep into the hole between Short and Third, to come up with the ball in the smooth single motion over to First that has the Divinely Creative Omniscient Anticipation, Beauty, and Grace of a Rizzuto as he nips an Eddie Collins at First by an eye-lash when the Umpire there, his ear on the ping in the baseman's mitt, his nose in the dust, and his eye on the runner's foot by the sack, snaps up his right arm, its Englishlike thumb pointing outward, with a shout that

means "Out!" If this be not Heaven and its Judgment
Day, what is? God has Spoken! Yes, He has spoken, even
though the fleet runner's coach does not believe God, and
emphatically says so, not realizing—his acquaintance with
Wittgenstein being slight—that not even the language of
a Durocher can say anything.

The source materials, as critically examined by the late
Professor Hardy in his research laboratory at the University of Cambridge, and the findings of serious, painful,
annual trips (unfinanced by any foundation) into the field,
as the anthropologists are wont to say, warrants the tenta-
tive conclusion, subject, of course, to reconfirmation on
future annual field trips, that:

> The Yanks-too are right
> When they show and so-see
> That to be without baseball
> Is not to Be.

The foregoing analysis shows that God's complete nature
and creative sportsmanship has, at least, three components: (1) Pure playfulness, without any lawful reason,
for the sheer fun of it, which Tagore's poetry of the dewdrop on the lotus and the carefree girl in the swing point
at but cannot say; (2) God's lawfully regulated sportsmanship (expressing His intellectual love or *Logos*) within the
rules of the game, which cricket and baseball show but
can neither point at nor say; (3) Essential also is His
creation of some first-order factual natural creatures who
are capable of committing errors and the inclusion of them
in His game. With apologies to, and admiration of, the
Shropshire Lad, a Wisconsin lad finds that

> Sports do more than
> Malt and Milton can
> To point and show
> God's Ways to man.

It appears that God also indulges in a more disturbing game, in addition to that of playing like a carefree Girl in a swing, being the tea-drinking, unemotional, and silently patient Gentleman who is cricket, or the more passionately dramatic and boisterous One who is baseball. Recent scientific detectives, the trinity of whom are Planck, Schrödinger, and Heisenberg, have found that He has been running away from human eyes, into the Monte Carlo recesses of the atom, to gamble.

The clues, which led the detectives to raid His hideout and catch Him in the very act, have to do with experiments referring to what is called "black-body radiation." Like the interference images in the Michelson-Morley experiment, these unexpected "black-body" findings were not what they should be according to all previous strongly mechanically causal theories, such as Einstein's and Newton's, in which it was taken for granted that only sinfully erring men would ever play games of chance.

If the religious reader is shocked by this implication of Quantum Mechanics, he is not the first. Before him, Einstein was also. He expressed his shock at this sacrilegious slander of God's name, which Quantum Mechanics affirms to be warranted, by saying "God does not play dice."

A comparison of Quantum Mechanics with his own or Newton's theory of mechanics will show what Einstein meant. In Einstein's two theories and in Newton's, chance and its derivative concept of probability appear only on the concept by the intuitional, nominalistic, and operational side of modern physics. There it refers only to human error resulting from the imperfections of the human observations and man-made measuring instruments by means of which the speculatively discovered, logically realistic scientific theories are put indirectly to an experimental test. Consequently, although games of chance were played in the God-made physical universe of Einstein's, Newton's, and similar completely deterministic causal theories, they were played only by sinful erring human beings. Hence, in Newton's and Einstein's physics, logically realistic first-order factual nature was not created by a Divine gambler who played with dice.

In accounting, however, as Einstein's and Newton's theories did not, for the aforementioned black-body radiation and other experimental findings, Quantum Mechanical theorists found it necessary to introduce chance and its concept of probability into the logically realistic definition of the state of any naturalistic system at any moment of time. What this means, mathematically, is that, whereas, for example, in Newton's physics the state function of any natural system is made completely determinate when the epistemically correlated empirical values of its two independent variables, the momenta and the positions of the masses of the system, are determined at any present moment of time, these momenta and position variables in Quantum Mechanics are accompanied by probability aggregate numbers. This means that chance and its probability are in God-made and God-responsible first-order factual nature. Using Einstein's theological answer, this means that God, and not merely erring sinful man, is a gambler.

No wonder that Einstein was shocked and never persuaded by Quantum Mechanics. So shocked was he, that he would not allow himself to take the theory seriously, except as a temporary and misleading "as if" which a strongly deterministic causal theory would eventually explain away so that only erring sinful men, and not God, played dice.

There are several unfortunate consequences of such a scientific conclusion. The first is that any experimental data, which traditional theories do not account for, can be explained away in terms of any older theory, however ancient it may be, in this manner. If this type of reasoning be permissible in science, then Einstein's theories are not to be taken seriously, either. The second, very weighty consideration is that Quantum Mechanics is not incompatible with either Einstein's or Newton's theories. Instead, while having the unique merit of accounting for indubitable, correctly inspectable concept by intuition images and data, which Newton's and Einstein's theories do not predict or explain, Quantum Mechanics gives rise to Einstein's Special and General Theories and to Newton's Mechanics as special cases of itself, precisely in the manner in which Einstein's Special Theory comes out of his own General Theory and Newton's Mechanics is part of both. The third and decisive reason why Einstein's refusal to take Quantum Mechanics seriously is unfortunate, has been given by the writer in his aforementioned Introduction to Professor Heisenberg's *Physics and Philosophy*. It is that Einstein's conclusion, with respect to Quantum Mechanics, is incompatible with his own conception of scientific method. We conclude, therefore, with the overwhelming majority of contemporary physicists who do take Quantum Mechanics seriously, that God is a gambler who plays dice. It appears, consequently, that He does not allow Himself to become bored by playing merely one kind of game.

That this important, scientific conclusion need not be disturbing theologically is shown by the 1962 Terry Lectures at Yale University, delivered by the philosophically professional and expert mathematical physicist, Professor Norbert Wiener. Like Einstein, he, in those lectures, discussed Quantum Mechanics, when supplemented with communication engineering theory, in religious language.

What God's playing of games of chance means is that His intellectual love of lawful universalism is not absolute. Instead, it is exactly like that of the rules of the games of cricket and baseball in which the rules restrict the players within certain limits, but not so completely that everything they do is antecedently determined, thereby making error meaningless. This suggests that if God in His playful creation of nature and natural man did not play dice, human error and, therefore, moral, legal, and political man or even religious man, would be meaningless and impossible. In short, for God to create human beings who are not mere puppets, He has to play dice when He creates His universe. Hence, for moral man to be, the mechanical causality of nature cannot be the strong, completely deterministic causality of pre-Quantum Mechanics, but must, instead, be that prescribed by the state functions of Quantum Mechanics.

This has two implications. The first is that chance threatens the lawfulness of nature. The reason is that, so far as chance operates in nature, unrestrained by law, anarchy and chaos result, and the intellectual love of God is defeated. This means that to the extent there is irreducible chance, there is a naturalistic meaning for the Devil. Consequently, as Professor Wiener observed, God is playing the game with the Devil and giving him a real chance in the game. Nevertheless, the Devil cannot permanently defeat God in this game because, even in Quantum Mechanics, chance operates within the restrictions specified by its invariant universal laws.

The second implication is more important for ordinary human and religious experience. It means that, frequently, human beings, notwithstanding the most moral, devoutly religious, and self-responsible attempts to obey both the secular law and God's will, find their lot to be not the rewards they expect, but the destruction by natural events of everything they cherish on earth. This suggests that the Quantum Mechanical definition of the states of any natural system is the only theory that accounts for what theologians have called "natural evil," as distinct from man-responsible moral evil.

Between these two different kinds of evil, which every human being experiences at one time or another in his or her life, there is a prodigious difference. This difference is that which distinguishes tragically painful misfortune from personally responsible moral guilt.

Guilt reminds us that there is also a man-made Devil. This is the deposit of self-responsible, second-order artifactual human behavior, which is the mechanical effect, in the strong meaning of the word "cause," of false human beliefs concerning first-order factual man, nature, and Nature's God. The accumulation of these false beliefs and their artifacts, handed on by humanists not merely unto the third and fourth generations, but throughout the whole of human cultural history, provides meaning for "sin in history." Because historians by definition look to the past as the criterion of everything that is good, beautiful, true, and Divine, we need hardly be surprised that history is as full of sin as some contemporary historical theologians try to make us believe. Nevertheless, as the foregoing chapters, referring to ancient Asia, Greece, Rome, and Israel, show, there is also a considerable amount of virtue in history. It takes, as Chapters 2 and 13 have shown, naturalistic scientists and philosophers, however, to tell which artifacts of cultural history are sinful and which are not. This is done, let it be recalled, by testing the first-order factual beliefs, of which the historical cultural artifacts are the cultural effects, and, apart from which, their normative words are meaningless, against the first-order facts of the nonman-made part of man, nature, and Nature's God.

The findings of our halting and incomplete quest for life's meaning have put an emphasis upon human knowledge of what is empirically and humanly verifiable as true regarding the first-order facts of nature and the nonman-made part of human nature. This, we have found to be the meaning of personal moral goodness, legal and political justice, and religious virtue. Otherwise, error is meaningless and the words "good," "legally and politically just," and "religiously virtuous" are also. The French have a saying: To know all is to forgive all. If this be so, then empirical and intellectual truthfulness also mean mercy.

Know:
To err is human.
Not to, but mercifully
To allow others to,
Divine.

Life has one other meaning. It is that the quest for its meaning is never over. This is what keeps life from ever becoming boring for those who are aesthetically sensitive to the diversity of its imagefully impressionistic, perpetually perishing facts, the deceptive subtleties of its languages, and the problems raised by its mysteries. It is the quest that gives life its zest.

Perhaps everything might have been more perfect had God made that natural creature called man like a stone or planet, devoid of the capacity (1) to entertain and speculatively discover propositions or descriptive beliefs, which may be in error and (2) to take responsibility for those to which he gives his consent, thereby guiding his artifactual behavior accordingly. The result, however, without any perhaps, would have been as boring for Him as it would be for us.

At last we may gather the fruits of our eating of the tree of human knowledge:

That unshaved patriarch told a fib;
Such snooping silly rot, about a rib.
The gay Virgin is God, She aswinging
Beauty everywhere from the Beginning.

Man was a dead stone.
So God said:
"Let there be error."
Thus moral man was born.

A mortal man then said:
"Blessed be the merciful
For they asymptotically
Shall see God."

Later than Man shocks:
"My human asymptotic
Limit is errorless.
Hence, isomorphically
I am both man and God."
Here endeth our paradox.

NOTES

CHAPTER 1

1. Matthew VII:20.
2. Pitirim A. Sorokin, *Society, Culture, and Personality* (New York: Harper & Brothers, 1947), pp. 145–49; 333–35; and *Social and Cultural Dynamics* (New York: American Book Co., 1937).
3. Chiang Monlin, *Tides from the West* (New Haven: Yale University Press, 1947). See also F. S. C. Northrop, *The Taming of the Nations* (New York: The Macmillan Company, 1952), Chap. VII.
4. F. S. C. Northrop (ed.), *Ideological Differences and World Order* (New Haven: Yale University Press, 1949), Chap. XVII, "The Philosophy of the Navaho Indians."
5. F. S. C. Northrop, *The Meeting of East and West* (New York: The Macmillan Company, 1946).
6. For the relevant bibliography and the systematic summary of the work of these men, see writer's Chapter XIX in *Ideological Differences and World Order, op. cit.;* his *Philosophical Anthropology and Practical Politics* (New York: The Macmillan Company, 1960), Part I; and John von Neumann, *The Computer and the Brain* (New Haven: Yale University Press, 1958).
7. John von Neumann, *op. cit.,* especially pp. 33 ff.

259

CHAPTER 3

1. Alfred North Whitehead, *Science and the Modern World*
   (New York: The Macmillan Company, 1925), pp. 14–15.

CHAPTER 8

1. Available on request from the Embassy of Burma, Wash-
   ington, D.C.
2. Mohandas K. Gandhi, *Gandhi's Autobiography* (Washing-
   ton, D.C.: Public Affairs Press, 1948), pp. 4 and 90.
3. Esther Warner, *New Song in a Strange Land* (Boston:
   Houghton Mifflin Company, 1948), p. 36.
4. Marvin Bressler and Richard D. Lambert, *Indian Students
   on an American Campus* (Minneapolis: University of Min-
   nesota Press, 1956).
5. Sir Henry Maine, *Ancient Law* (London: Murray, 1908).
6. F. S. C. Northrop, *European Union and United States Foreign Policy* (New York: The Macmillan Company, 1954).
7. Stella Kramrisch, *The Hindu Temple* (University of Cal-
   cutta Press, 1946).
8. Jacques Masui (ed.), *Yoga: Science de l'homme intégral*
   (Paris: Les Cahiers du Sud, 1953). See also Pitirim A.
   Sorokin (ed.), *Forms and Techniques of Altruistic and
   Spiritual Growth* (Boston: Beacon Press, 1954).
9. E. Adamson Hoebel, *The Law of Primitive Man: A Study
   in Comparative Legal Dynamics* (Cambridge: Harvard
   University Press, 1954).

CHAPTER 10

1. Ernst Cassirer, *Rousseau—Kant—Goethe* (Princeton, N.J.:
   Princeton University Press, 1945), p. 62.
2. *Ibid.*

3. For a further detailed development of this point, see F. S. C. Northrop, *The Logic of the Sciences and the Humanities,* New York: The Macmillan Company, 1947.

4. See Isaac Newton, *Mathematical Principles of Natural Philosophy and His System of the World,* trans. Andrew Motte, rev. Florian Cajori (University of California Press, 1934), p. 6; and E. A. Burtt, *Metaphysical Foundations of Physics* (New York: Harcourt, Brace and Company, 1925), pp. 73–80 and 228–37.

5. For a further development of this fact and its significance for the humanities and the harmonious unification of the differing values of the world's cultures, see F. S. C. Northrop, *The Meeting of East and West, op. cit.,* Chapter XII; also H. Margenau, "Methodology of Modern Physics," *Philosophy of Science,* II, 1935, pp. 48–72 and 164–87, and *The Nature of Physical Reality* (New York: McGraw-Hill Book Company, 1950).

CHAPTER 12

1. F. S. C. Northrop, *The Logic of the Sciences and the Humanities, op. cit.,* Chapter 9.

2. *Ibid.,* Chapter 5.

3. F. S. C. Northrop and Mason W. Gross, *Alfred North Whitehead. An Anthology* (New York: The Macmillan Company, 1953), pp. 13–82. See also Ruth Nanda Anshen (ed.), *Alfred North Whitehead: His Reflections on Man and Nature* (New York: Harper & Brothers, 1961).

4. Alfred North Whitehead, *The Concept of Nature* (Cambridge University Press, 1920), p. 152.

5. F. S. C. Northrop, *The Meeting of East and West, op. cit.*, pp. 303–11 and 335 ff.

6. *Ibid., The Logic of the Sciences and the Humanities, op. cit.* Note 1, Chapter 9, previously printed in *Furioso*, Vol. I, No. 4, 1941.

7. Mary A. Wyman, *The Lure for Feeling* (New York: Philosophical Library, 1960).

8. Donald W. Sherburne, *A Whiteheadian Aesthetic* (New Haven: Yale University Press, 1961).